Balancing the Common Core Curriculum in Middle School Education

James H. Bunn

Balancing the Common Core Curriculum in Middle School Education

Composing Archimedes' Lever, the Equation, and the Sentence as an Interdisciplinary Unity

James H. Bunn
Professor Emeritus
Department of English
University at Buffalo
Williamsville, New York, USA

ISBN 978-3-319-83442-9   ISBN 978-3-319-46106-9 (eBook)
DOI 10.1007/978-3-319-46106-9

© The Editor(s) (if applicable) and The Author(s) 2017
Softcover reprint of the hardcover 1st edition 2017
This work is subject to copyright. All rights are solely and exclusively licensed by the Publisher, whether the whole or part of the material is concerned, specifically the rights of translation, reprinting, reuse of illustrations, recitation, broadcasting, reproduction on microfilms or in any other physical way, and transmission or information storage and retrieval, electronic adaptation, computer software, or by similar or dissimilar methodology now known or hereafter developed.
The use of general descriptive names, registered names, trademarks, service marks, etc. in this publication does not imply, even in the absence of a specific statement, that such names are exempt from the relevant protective laws and regulations and therefore free for general use.
The publisher, the authors and the editors are safe to assume that the advice and information in this book are believed to be true and accurate at the date of publication. Neither the publisher nor the authors or the editors give a warranty, express or implied, with respect to the material contained herein or for any errors or omissions that may have been made.

Cover Design by Fatima Jamadar

Printed on acid-free paper

This Palgrave Macmillan imprint is published by Springer Nature
The registered company is Springer International Publishing AG
The registered company address is: Gewerbestrasse 11, 6330 Cham, Switzerland

This project is dedicated to caring school teachers and librarians, mine and yours.

Preface

Balancing the Common Core Curriculum for Middle School Students: Composing Archimedes' Lever, the Equation, and the Sentence as An Interdisciplinary Unity.

A good education should include a scientific and technical component, a mathematical component, a writing component, plus an aesthetic and ethical component. These kinds of inquiry are often taught separately in schools and in the Common Core Curriculum. However, in everyday use, we often bring them together. So I feature here a new three-way intersection: the basic sciences and mechanics of levering on a seesaw, the basic formulations of patterning an algebraic equation, and the basic rules for writing a sentence in English. How do they intersect? In all three forms of inquiry, balance is the mainstay. The act of balancing is central to any construction, both in the real world and in more abstract models. So I show how "balancing up" is a basic method of problem solving in the sciences, in math, and in the English language.

Because this method of problem solving features information that balances as it combines, I use the idea of "balancing feedback." I draw a few simple communication diagrams for senders and receivers that show how feedback works in these compositions. In the sender-receiver diagrams I locate a common center of information transference located at a fulcrum on a balance beam or on a lever, at an equals sign, and at a verb. What exactly brings all three of these kinds of problem solving together at a center? The fulcrum's pivot "Δ", the equation's equals sign "=", and the word "is" in a sentence, all serve similar purposes as equalizers: they appear at the middle of a construction, where they combine and transfer information. Each sign is a "middle measure."

Balancing calls for a "middle measure." Aristotle's phrase lets me reorient these three forms of inquiry, in a final chapter, towards ethics and aesthetics.

Chapters: Introduction, Archimedes' Lever, The Equation, The Sentence, Conclusion: Seeking a Middle Measure. In each chapter I refer to pertinent sections of the Common Core Curriculum and/or Next Generation Science Standards.

Acknowledgments

Hans Christian von Baeyer, Judith Bunn, Ken Christianson, Arabella Lyon, Emily Wilson, Marlon Rice, and Anthony Rozak.

Special thanks go to Jim Waack who lent me his teaching manuals and lesson plans. And thanks to Mara Berkoff and Milana Vernikova, editors at Palgrave Publishers.

Special thanks to Tony Rozak who redrew my drawings and who provided special help with the manuscript early on.

Contents

1 Introduction: Balance at the Core — 1

2 Archimedes' Lever — 35

3 The Equation — 83

4 The Sentence — 119

5 Seeking a Middle Measure — 161

Bibliography — 209

Index — 219

List of Figures

Fig. 1.1   Sender-Receiver diagram for exchange of information—for a sentence, an equation, or a lever   8
Fig. 2.1   Plumb bob, pendulum, and tangency   41
Fig. 2.2   Hanging balance scales   45
Fig. 2.3   Hanging balance beam and lever are equivalent   47
Fig. 2.4   Body-based calipers   55
Fig. 2.5   Hinged gull wings   57
Fig. 2.6   Screw seen as an inclined plane in spiral form   66
Fig. 3.1   Squares drawn upon a Pythagorean triangle   92
Fig. 4.1   Reader-writer diagram for slots of syntax   125
Fig. 4.2   Sentence tree diagram with "is" at apex   136
Fig. 5.1   Bow and the Lyre   163

CHAPTER 1

Introduction: Balance at the Core

For more than a thousand years, the age-old methods of grammar, logic, and rhetoric were taught together as a *trivium*, where the Latin word did not mean "trivial," but instead meant a juncture of three ways, *trivia*.[1] Here we describe a new three-way intersection that brings together basic skills in science, mathematics, and language within a set of examples that are unified by the idea of balancing information. To that end, we feature three essential methods of problem-solving: the balancing lever, the balancing equation, and the balancing sentence. *The lever, the equation, and the sentence all feature methods of "balancing up" their parts into a combined equivalence.* Balancing then is a common core that mediates through the curriculum.

The lever, the equation, and the sentence are basic modes of inquiry that link one mind to another by way of their compositions. We reinforce the idea that the lever, the equation, and the sentence are fundamental ways of combining ideas and things into new discoveries. Each of these three modes of inquiry connects one thing with another into a composite. When they all work together, they intersect into a new three-way cloverleaf. These three modes of problem-solving are surely an essential core within a common core of learning, for they are fundamental skills upon which many kinds of computation, analysis, and creative discovery are later built. So our program may serve as a summary of middle-school standards, seen from the point of view of an eighth grader.

Although we begin with basic reviews of these skills, we consider them to be essential ways of solving larger real-life problems of balanced adjustment that students will discover along the way. Learning these skills amounts to what we think of as practical reasoning. We also feature a creative searching that amounts to a kind of playful combining of parts into new patterns of thought. We celebrate this kind of creative thinking as a balanced search for a "middle measure" in ethics and the arts (Chap. 5).

Any adequate education must include a writing component, a scientific and technical component, a mathematical component, and an aesthetic and ethical component. In each component balance is a first principle.

Why Is Balancing a First Principle?

Everybody knows how necessary balance is in the real world. What exactly is important about balance for us as teachers and learners? First of all, as a teaching premise it is not threatening because every child tacitly understands bodily balance. Keeping our balance is the basic aim of sensorimotor coordination. Think of a child's first halting steps as she coordinates the mind and the body in the world. Think of a toddler's delight as he or she steps away from the caring adult's holding hands. Recall a parent's joy when the child conquers a threatened imbalance and steps out to another parent's outstretched arms. For instance, here is a link to the painter David Hockney's discussion of a Rembrandt sketch of a child just learning to walk.[2] He thinks it is "the best drawing ever made." What an extraordinary claim about a commonplace happening. It seems such a simple sketch. He suggests that while the child stepping out from her mother's arms is learning how to walk, the whole composition is also about balance and imbalance. Studying this drawing would be a good introductory classroom exercise. What is so great about it? Along the way we shall suggest some sample classroom exercises, such as this one, for middle-school students.

As the child learning to walk suggests, everybody knows that good balance requires practice and care. Balancing may come naturally because of our arms and legs swinging together, but good balancing is a moving skill that depends on the actual exercise of motor and mental repetitions.[3] Good balancing acts are skills that come from the acts of taking things part and putting things back together, like a dancer practicing movements over and over. In Chap. 5, for instance, we describe Edgar Degas' painting, *The Rehearsal*, in which balancing ballerinas practice their moves and stances upon a grid of squares diagrammed on the floor. A training camp for baseball or soccer or tennis teaches fundamental skills by taking the movements apart and then by putting them back together again.

In the everyday world so much of our understanding about bodily and mental balancing is tacit. Balance is understood; we stand on it without thinking what it is we stand on. That is, we are only marginally aware that everyday problem-solving usually derives from our own feelings of muscular balance. Later on, we shall describe what some call "embodied learning." This tacit stance is what Michael Polanyi calls "from—to" thinking: We focus *from* our tacit knowledge of our use of a thing *to* (toward) a focal understanding of the problem to be solved.[4] For example, if we put on a blindfold, and we use a walking stick to tap, tap, tap the ground underneath us, we do not focus on our hand as we feel our way, but instead we focus toward the end of the stick to keep our balance. This is the way a hammer works as a lever, see Chap. 2. Or it is the way we use a probe in a lab or in the field. So in this project we are bringing our tacit uses of coordinating balance in the three modes of inquiry into focus. The definition of a coordinate, "equal in rank," lets us link our three methods of inquiry. Along the way, we widen the idea of coordination so that we may better understand how bodily coordination and cognitive coordination may be harmoniously united in a middle measure. We shall study this issue later on in Chap. 5 on "Middle Measure," for when we reason about practical problems in real life, the arts and sciences usually go together.

As we move around in the real world, maintaining balance is the first step. Then come the next steps of tryouts and rehearsals. Because keeping our balance is one of our very first skills of mental and motor coordination, it can be seen as the very base of our presumptions about *dynamic stability* in the real world of changing movements and actions. As we shall show, the presumption of dynamic stability is a point of departure for any theory of regular order and change in science and other disciplines of inquiry.

Then too, keeping our balance is a necessary step in any reasonable real action. So the skill of keeping our balance is not trivial. *As we continue through the world, we learn tacitly that the art of balancing is central to all walks of life*. How so? Here is our premise: In the real world a balancing skill requires the coming together, the coordination, of most of our mental and physical abilities. So this compositional cloverleaf seeks to make the understanding of balance an explicit method of problem-solving in a world of changes. A little later in this Introduction, we present some of the educational theory behind this method of balancing up.

To study balance is to study the movements of common life. Everyday our bodies are always compensating for change. Often these changes in balance are so commonplace that we hardly think about them. When we wake up in the morning from sleeping all night, we adjust from the extreme state of darkness to daylight. We get up; we dress; we go to the bathroom; and we eat breakfast. We walk to the school bus stop. Maybe we wish that we had dressed warmer because it is colder than it seemed from the doorstep as we walked out the door. Notice that these everyday activities let us adjust for the extreme oppositions we feel in nature and culture. We move from darkness to light, awakening from tiredness at night to recharged energy in the morning after a night's rest. At breakfast, we move from hunger to repletion of energy. Our bodies tacitly counterbalance for the extremes we feel in the changes of nature. All along the way, we shall demonstrate for students that *nature's forces run to opposite extremes*, but we adjust and correct as we seek a balance with all our faculties. In truth, the world of nature is never quite in balance, so we are always compensating for its changing dynamics.[5] Our cultures also run to extreme opposites and contradictions, as we shall also see. These are real-world compensations, and our prompt actions are reasonably realistic. This kind of attention to real-world, everyday, commonplace actions, like Rembrandt's quick sketch of a child learning to walk, is called "realism." Because we always self-correct for the oppositions and extremes of changing nature and culture, we tacitly measure our lives in terms of balance. Often we feel as if we are balancing on a seesaw that always tempts or threatens imbalance. Furthermore, as we show in Chap. 5, an essential part of play, teetering at the peak of a seesaw, is the risk of imbalance.

On top of motor skills, people seek mental balance in life in order to resolve imbalances in the real world of our own experiences. Here physical balance merges into larger metaphors that use balancing as governors. When we balance ourselves in daily life, we are correcting ourselves. In Chap. 4 on "The Sentence" we feature self-correction by way of language. Balancing is always a counterbalancing, sought in order to correct for imbalanced changes of opposition, confusion, disorder, and strife. We correct ourselves by understanding the chance imbalances in the oppositions of daily life. We seek balance in different ways: we build houses based on patterns of vertical and horizontal balance; we compose harmonious songs and music; we enact rhythmic rituals; we say prayers; and we invent laws of equity and fairness. We seek to make equitable judgments about balanced justice. We would do good for others just as we hope others would do for ourselves. We always seek to bring balance into our lives. If self-knowledge is the greatest of aims, at least for education, reasonable judgment is a balancing method. So this program also widens the model of teaching and learning from our three domains of instrumental combinations to larger principles of balanced design in real-world ethics, aesthetics, and play (Chap. 5).

As we proceed, we show students that people in different kinds of inquiry use the idea of balance as a guiding concept in slightly different ways. While dynamic balancing in the real world is a function of the sensory-motor system, cognitive balancing is widely used in other disciplines as model of mental self-regulation. Speaking in terms of student mental development, we define balancing as an act of self-correcting mind and body as the brain learns, develops itself, and moves on, ready to act, or not. The action of balancing is the mind's nature. Physically speaking, we begin to define balance as our awareness of a tense central point, as on a fulcrum, in an exchange between equal and opposite actions and reactions of forces. Although we use the word "balance" as if it were a static state, as if it were a noun, we show that balancing is an ongoing series of dynamic acts that achieve temporary adjustments in a spatiotemporal world of chance and change. As we shall show later, this idea of exchange features feedback of information back and forth between a sender and a receiver, an actor and a patient. Also we shall stress the importance of "balancing feedback" between a sender and a receiver as a crucial part of our educational theory.

Summary of the Compositional Cloverleaf

How do these general ideas about balancing apply to the lever, the equation, and the sentence? By the time they have reached the eighth grade, all middle-school students will have worked regularly with the compositions of mathematical numbers, algebraic equations, and the measurable actions of real things and energies. For example, in the English Language Arts section of the Common Core Curriculum under "Technological and Scientific Subjects," we find: "Determine the meaning of symbols, key terms, and other domain-specific words and phrases as they are used in a specific scientific or technical context relevant to grades 6–8 texts and topics."[6]

When these three forms of composition in science and math are united to solve a problem, the equals sign and the balancing pivot or fulcrum are seen as "the same." Equivalence is seen as a synonym for equilibrium. However, equivalence and equilibrium are not truly synonyms. Equivalence has as its roots the words *equi* (equal) and *valence* (strength), but through customary usage an equivalence is seen as a logical or grammatical connection (Here and there along the way we take apart and reassemble prefixes and suffixes, as per Common Core Standards).

A lever, an algebraic equation, and a sentence all interconnect different exchanges of things and actions into a combination by means of a balancing operation.

The verb "is," the fulcrum sign "Δ," and the equals sign "=," all serve a coupling or connecting function that brings together two parts of a composition into a combined balance. These coupling units mean that an act of bringing together, of synthesis, is taking place. Connecting their parts at the middle of a composition means that they are "middle measures." Learning these basic skills mean that we are organizing our experience of the world into balanced unities.

But as we shall see, they accomplish their tasks in slightly different ways. In our examples, we show how the three basic forms of inquiry—the lever, the equation, and the sentence—tend to confirm their reasonable judgments in different dimensions, even while balance remains the central aim. For instance, the lever and its related mechanics all confirm their inquiries by means of hands-on experiments with three-dimensional (3-D) modeling in real space and time. That is why labs and workshops and playgrounds are so important in all phases of learning. The algebraic equation and graphs depict their patterns primarily on a two-dimensional (2-D) plane that features visual thinking. The sentence tests and confirms with verbal communication, primarily in a one-dimensional (1-D) sequential string of words of noun, verb, and object. According to Common Core standards, students are introduced to 1-D, 2-D, and 3-D figures by the fifth grade.

So in Chap. 2 we feature 3-D thinking with leveraged tools. In Chap. 3 we feature 2-D visual thinking about equations on a plane. And in Chap. 4 we feature 1-D thinking in linear sentences. We stress that all three forms of inquiry, in their several dimensions, should go together to adequately test and confirm a discovery.[7] By itself, none of these forms can completely demonstrate a real-world assertion by itself.

Educational Theory: Embodied Learning

In Chap. 2, when we introduce levers with a child's experience on a seesaw, whether on a playground or in a controlled classroom exercise, we begin with the basic perceptual *feeling* of balanced leverage, and then we go on to describe the more abstract ratios of weights and measures. Here we employ the basic psychological and educational theory of "embodied knowledge." The concept of embodied knowledge presents the case that most thinking and learning proceeds from the perception of knowing from the body. The notion of an "embodied mind" means in part that much thinking and learning derives from sensorimotor experiences, and that reason itself is an embodied form of inference.[8] Our project examines the bodily based assumption that "balancing up" is a normal, everyday mental activity and that we do it almost all the time. So in Chap. 2, we begin with 3-D thinking with tools and machines. There we feature the basic law of reasoning in science and technology; it is the first conservation law of matter and energy: that in any energy exchange the sum must balance up (See below).

The theory of embodied knowledge has been usefully applied to teaching strategies that also incorporate interactive classroom experiences that involve computer learning as well.[9] For instance, many middle-school students, and some fifth graders, are given Chromebooks or iPads with which to do their exercises, and teachers can display Chromebook exercises on smart boards that feature interactive learning. As one teacher claims, "This kind of interactive learning is a 'game changer' in teaching and learning."[10]

How can we apply the concept of embodied learning to interactive computer instruction? To sketch out a basic communication model of interactive exchange, we use some simple diagrams from information and communication theory.

Information, Communication, and Embodied Learning

Most of us know that we are beset with masses of information much of the time, and many students know that ours has been called an Information Age. In order to emphasize its massive enormity, James Gleick called his recent book *The Information*.[11] He made the word seem like a massive noun to suggest its totally inclusive environment. Many people also know that Claude Shannon drew a now famous diagram of information exchange in order to standardize what happens as information is communicated in a code.[12] The advantage of Shannon's diagram is that it works for *any* communication. So we shall feature variations of this standard diagram for all three of our modes of inquiry. We shall draw similar Sender-Receiver diagrams for the fulcrum, the equation, and the sentence because the three modes are fundamental composites of information exchange. By way of these diagrams, we suggest that there is a simple balancing unity that underlies the complexities of information.

Figure 1.1 represents a basic Sender-Receiver model for the transfer and exchange of symbolic information. It is a variant of some standard models of communication, information theory, and linguistics. Let us look more closely at some of the elements of the diagram. The transfer of information depends on the **Code** we choose at the outset for our communication. We can choose a computer code or a Morse code or drum language (Gleick's opening example) or sign language or French or Chinese or DNA. Our **Code** means here the "inner" symbolic rules we have learned: those of

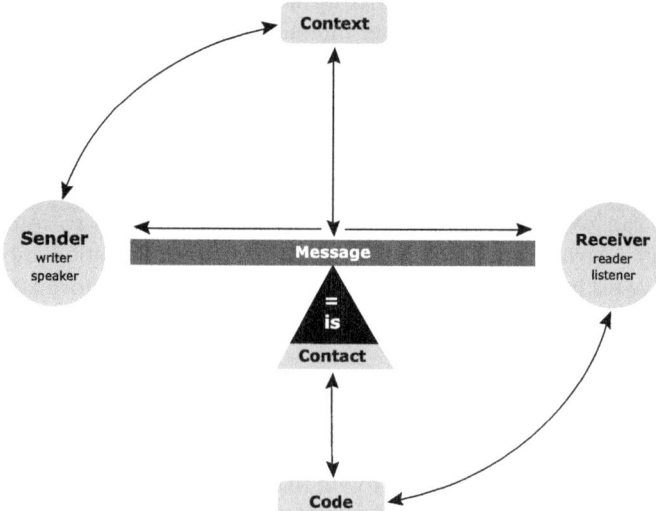

Fig. 1.1 Sender-Receiver diagram for exchange of information—for a sentence, an equation, or a lever
This diagram depicts a fulcrum underneath the horizontal bar, as the center of balance, but it could have an "=" sign or the verb "is," just as well

math, algebra, or grammar. But as warm-ups, teachers can review rules of card games, checkers, chess, or Morse code in order to understand how the choice of a given code predetermines the kind of information being exchanged, each according to its own rules. For instance, some middle-school students are also learning the codes of computer programming early on. Then they learn that a binary digit, a bit, is an elementary base of information theory, and it is composed of yes-no, either-or choices, which is the simplest modular code there can be. If you are ready and willing to exchange within the code, you enter into a kind of agreement or contract to take it on its own terms.

Context means the larger frames of reference, the playing fields, and the backgrounds of possible choices that are available for the selection of individual units of information within the code. For instance, there are rules for assembling phonemes into morphemes, morphemes into words, words into sentences (which we have stressed so far), and sentences into paragraphs (Chap. 4). Although each code prescribes the rules, the game is played within a larger context. The rules are not the game. The larger context includes the actual place where the message is sent: a playing field, a sheet of paper, and a video game on a computer screen. The code and the context go together, and they include the modular rules for assembling a communication into an exchange of information. The vertical line means that the code and the context are the rules being held in waiting, in the memory, awaiting possible use.[13] And the horizontal line represents the actual choices that are used to make a composition, where the act of communicating combines the composition into its larger context.

In each of the following chapters, in one format or another, we shall draw Sender-Receiver diagrams with vertical and horizontal axes that intersect at a center. This scrutiny at the crosshairs, so to speak, allows us to feature a common kind of orientation. For we can center a fulcrum sign, an equals sign, and the verb "is" at the middle point of a Sender-Receiver diagram, as in Fig. 1.1. *When we find the center of balance of a problem, we are on the way toward a fundamental orientation in space and time.*

Contact means the actual physical energies used to send and receive a message within a **channel** of communication. This contact involves some kind of energy flow that is really transporting information in a direction from a sender to a receiver. In any communication the physical contact of energy transmission is usually tacit, like a blindfolded person tap, tap, tapping a stick to seek her way. Because the contact is transmitted from a sender to a receiver, the energy moves in a necessary order from cause to effect. According to Next Generation Science Standards, we study cause and effect all through primary and middle school.[14] So we show here that a physical transmission of energy in a direction always underlies any communication as a contact. We deliver information by means of some kind of physical contact. *In this sense all information is truly based on the transfer and exchange of energies taken from the natural world.* For our purposes, these energy transmitters are sound waves for speech, light waves for writing and reading, and electronic transmissions for computers. Also, channeling information includes the physical senses of seeing, hearing, touching (for handling and weighing 3-D objects), even smelling! We can ask students how it is that smell works by touch. "Contact" is a good word because we can review with students that all the senses really transmit information by some kind of physical touching.[15] Information must be encoded and transmitted upon real physical objects: a sheet of paper, a computer screen, and an abacus. In short, information includes both the code and the context.

See Nex*t Generation Science Standards*: 1-PS4-4.

> Use tools and materials to design and build a device that uses light or sound to solve the problem of communicating over a distance. Clarification Statement: Examples of devices could include a light source to send signals, paper cup and string "telephones," and a pattern of drum beats. Assessment Boundary: Assessment does not include technological details for how communication devices work.]

The **message** is the actual communication that is sent. In the diagram it is set along the horizontal arrow to remind that the actual information being sent from a sender to a receiver is being strung along a line in a *following* sequence, in patterned intervals, in a direction, one unit after another, in time. The **message** is meant to be the actual act of writing or reading a formula, speaking or listening to a sentence, or balancing a lever with effort. The vertical arrow is meant to suggest that the code and the context are the rules held in our memories; they await possible use, ready to act. When you get ready to play a game of checkers, you remember the codes or rules of possible moves, and you also may remember possible moves that you made in the past as a larger context.

Any sent communication therefore combines the physical transmission, which is the contact, together with the meaning, which is the larger context. We have said that the main pivots of our methods of inquiry are the fulcrum (Δ), the equals sign (=), and the word "is." Each of these central symbols can be placed at the crossroads of the two axes of a Sender-Receiver diagram, for they symbolize the ways that a given code stipulates the *coming together* at the middle of a communication. We will show that at the center or crossroads of each Sender-Receiver diagram, where the vertical and horizontal axes come together, there is also a pointed issue of tense balance.

Feed forward and **feedback** are diagrammed as arched arrows between a sender and a receiver. They represent the exchange of information back and forth from memory to prediction. Feedback is now part of the everyday language of information theory, but it was first proposed by the founder of cybernetics, Norbert Wiener, as a way to describe a process of self-correction in the information sent back and forth (Gleick, 238–239). Wiener coined a new concept out of an old Greek word, *cybernos*, which meant a helmsman, as he moves a tiller back and forth as he aims forward. In Chap. 2, we describe a tiller as kind of lever that pivots on a fulcrum. Although less known than feedback, the idea of feeding forward is just as important. "Feedforward" highlights the skills and strategies of anticipating how the sender might predict the effect of the message being sent to a receiver. Feedback, however, involves the receiver checking back to the sender of the message, either with agreement or with criticism. All messages are in some sense forward-looking, prospective, anticipatory, which are at the same time based upon recollection backward. We remember backward as we live forward. Forward repetition is sometimes called redundancy, and yet it can build toward an unexpected prediction. As Gleick summarizes, "Information is surprise" (248). In each exchange of information a little future lies ahead. This is the whole realm of envisioning an idea and then re-visioning it. This is what we hope for students: that we are instilling kinds of inquiry that will serve them in their futures. See Chap. 4, "The Sentence," for the idea that language allows us to think backward and forward by thinking back upon its own compositional structures.

"Balancing Feedback"

In that phrase we can see how feedback and balance are often used together. The phrase is used to describe the main function of feedback, which corrects the speedup of a machine or any kind of organization that seems to run more or less by itself by a process of self-regulation. The most familiar example is a thermostat that can be set to govern automatically the temperature in a house. Or another common household example is a floating bulb in a toilet. Balancing feedback is often used as a substitute for "negative feedback." The thermostat keeps the temperature at a balanced level, and the toilet bulb keeps the water level balanced. If the thermostat breaks down, then the furnace just keeps on sending heat into a room, raising its temperature. If a toilet bulb breaks down or if some other part leaks, then the bulb might stay up continuously so that water keeps rushing into the tank. This kind of unbalanced out of control acceleration is called "positive feedback." The system is no longer self-correcting (See also Chaps. 2 and 5).

Understanding the principle of good feedback between students and teachers is a crucial part of good teaching and learning. As David N. Perkins shows, good feedback is not just corrective, for it can also be appreciative, but his main point is that different styles of feedback should occur often in order to be helpful for students.[16] In its section on motivation strategies, a Common Core overview suggests, "Offer non-judgmental feedback; praise sincere efforts on work tasks."[17] In the discipline sometimes called "Cognitive Learning," self-regulation is essential.[18]

This basic principle of balanced self-correction or self-regulation is also central to a larger method of inquiry called "systems thinking." We discuss systems thinking because much of its integrative principles have been used in Next Generation Science Standards, which features cross-cutting "systems" throughout (See Next Gen Science Standards). Beginning in kindergarten, students begin to work with "Cross-cutting Patterns and Cause/Effect." Note that in virtually all grades, cause and effect are featured in "Cross Cutting" or Core ideas. Our project is a cross-cutting exercise. A seesaw is a lever in which the learned experience of bodily balance is self-evident. An equation centers on a balance of information in which either side of an equals sign undergoes transformation. A sentence requires a balance of information governed by the rules for combining a subject and verb. These are three common cross-cutting patterns that center upon a balance of information between a sender and a receiver.

The main founder of systems theory expanded the principle of self-regulation from the study of organisms in biological inquiry to the study of large and small organizations in social sciences, business, and law.[19] Because all three of these methods of inquiry—the law of the lever, the equation, and the sentence—feature balanced forms of informational feedback, an interdisciplinary context for an understanding of balanced forms may be sought in systems thinking, where balance is not seen as a static concept but rather as a mobile instant within a dynamic flow, very like the snapshot of a waterfall. Concepts of balance and homeostasis are common to structural linguistics, economics, biology, and physics.[20] In these disciplines and elsewhere, "morphology," which is the study of patterned forms, features structures of balanced oppositions and interactions between marked and unmarked elements in a message.

Let us pause for a moment and consider the implications of this broader method of balance in terms of systems inquiry and our task. Beginning with our biological studies in middle-school labs, we can come to understand how balancing is any animal brain's old, old self-correcting system. In biology this principle is sometimes called "homeostasis." For example, a centipede's tiny motor system does a good job of coordinating the sequential movements of all those legs, which move in a rhythmic series. Its self-guidance depends on its balancing self-correction. But unlike a centipede, when humans intervene in the real world, we usually do not intervene directly. We intervene mostly by means of symbols that mediate our potential actions. Here is the origin of media studies. Our methods of balancing feedback are mediated by symbolic habits of thinking. A centipede does not know how it intervenes in the physical world. It does not even know much else about the world except for what its own little sensorimotor system of inquiry is organized for. But we can come to learn how our own symbolic systems depend on balancing feedback for our understanding. In later chapters we show how this basic balancing principle of self-regulation is common to the tracking of large-scale guidance systems like geosynchronous satellites, guided missile systems, and video games. Who can doubt that the essence of a balanced life, in most walks of life, is a ready self-correction that leads to self-knowledge?

Our very proposal anticipates a certain audience, which may or may not agree with the principle of balance, or with the practicality of its methods. So there is often a "tension" implied in the symbolic assertions exchanged in the feedback between a sender and a receiver. A mutual agreement is often lacking in a dialog, so it is "up in the air," held in abeyance, with judgment hovering in a tense balance. My assertions must "square" or balance up with what you know about teaching middle-school students what works and what does not.

In the background of our teaching is a tacit agreement with students that if they learn these methods of problem-solving, then these methods will serve them in a future, for we suppose that all teaching and learning are aimed toward preparing students for their possible future. Learning is preparation; its aim is all about anticipation. This is a teacher's implied promise: that these methods are going to be useful someday. And our agreement with students is that if you learn these models now, they will help you out eventually. If you learn our methods now, if you store them in your memories as how-to methods, then in the future you can come back and retrieve them in a different context.

We feature agreement and the exchange of information because each of these three models—the sentence, the equation, and the lever—is based upon an agreement about a set of rules or codes about how we exchange ideas within its own domain. *Each of these models of problem-solving in itself is a kind of contract about an exchange of information.* Along the way we examine the idea of contract as a basic kind of swap, which balances two different kinds of wishes or desires. There is therefore a larger issue of balanced exchange that we use implicitly when we use a fulcrum, an equation, and a sentence. We have said that a sentence is a basic assertion. Similarly a diagram of a lever or an equation is also implicitly a proposition within its framework. Each is an invitation to be tested by a specific audience, which is schooled in the symbolic system used. Hence every symbolic assertion is an invitation to search and to test, that is, to agree or to rejoin between a skilled sender and a receiver. No assertion really stands alone. Couched within a larger **context**, it is always part of an *exchange agreement*, which is an ongoing but implicit dialog between a writer and an audience in any communication system with its sets of premises about usage and belief. That is, in any communication, every symbolic assertion involves the *exchange* of information between a sender and a receiver, whose roles may reverse in a dialog. So every formula, every equation, and every sentence is to be seen as part of an implicit dialog or exchange of information.

Here is an overview of each chapter as it pertains to the balancing of compositions in their several dimensions.

Chapter 2 Archimedes' Lever

In the physical sciences, much analysis boils down to an understanding of the exchanging and balancing of certain amounts of mass and energy that are transported across distances of space and time. These demonstrations prove what are called, in the language of physics, "conservation laws." In

physics, for instance, the conservation laws of matter and energy are based on the ironclad law that energy exchanges must balance up.[21]
(Cross Ref: Next Generation Science "Energy", Grade 4)
Balancing-up is the main phenomenon of the energy-conservation principle.
What is changed on one side of a fulcrum, or an equation, or a formula of chemical reactions must balance up on the other side of a scale of measures. Albert Einstein's great discovery was that the conservation law of mass is basically the same as the conservation law of energy. *He also said the conservation laws are "balance" principles.*[22] The necessity of balancing up is an extremely important point, one that we shall follow throughout. Most principles of nature, and even of culture, are patterns composed of compounds seen as balanced unities. Further, as the physicist Richard Feynman says, all the different conservation laws are "secret ways of talking about energy" (*CPL*, 72). For instance, "Elastic energy and chemical energy both have the same origin, namely the forces between the atoms. When the atoms rearrange themselves in a new pattern some energy is changed, and if that quantity changes it means that some other quantity also has to change" (*CPL*, 71). We discuss atoms in Chap. 2. Another way to see this is to say that atoms of energy have been *transferred* or *exchanged*. The exchange of energies causes a new balanced pattern. As we shall see later, the conservation of matter and the conservation of energy are the basis for balancing a physical or a chemical equation. So in later chapters, we feature an exchange of energy back and forth across a diagrammatic scale of information, in which balancing and symmetry are used as measures.

Our beginning example is a playground seesaw, a balance beam that demonstrates *equal* and opposite forces on either side of a fulcrum. The teeter-tottering seesaw enacts Archimedes' law of the lever. Working with Archimedes' concept of a "center of gravity" at a fulcrum, as well as the association of a drawn vertical line picturing that center of pull up and down, we begin in Chap. 2 to demonstrate how a diagram of a balance scale, with its implicit vertical line at the fulcrum, can be our point of departure for the other intersections we are aiming for. We show how his work on balance can serve as the very foundation of mathematics, physics, mechanics, and geometry.

For the law of the lever, the basic diagram is a seesaw or balance beam, and its basic connecting sign, at the center of its gravity, is the fulcrum or "Δ". Exchanges of energy pivot or rotate around a fulcrum. Here, for instance, is a link called "Balancing Act" that demonstrates sample exercises on a balance beam.[23] In Chap. 2, we introduce the three classes of levers, how they move weights, and how they feature ratios in formulas. Then we describe how the three classes interconnect among the six basic machines, which are the essentials of mechanics and technics. We also show how levers combine into tongs and how tongs can become dividers, calipers, and other tools we use in schools.

Another discussion features the manipulation of a plumb line, used by carpenters and masons for finding verticals and horizontals in building. Also we introduce a pendulum that can make clear the diagrammatic relations between the balanced swing of arcs, rotational circles, and angles.

To sum up here, we show how the pendulum, the seesaw, and the lever are all variants of the same law of balancing. Since Archimedes extended his law of the lever to objects rotating around a pivot, we now understand that cycling and rotation symmetry are also parts of balancing. Throughout this book, we often use historical examples of compositions, such as Archimedes' discoveries, because we can learn how they evolved in the past and how they developed into modifications of the present day. In the Common Core Curriculum, the study of history is central to the Social Studies sections.

Chapter 3 The Equation

In Chap. 3, we begin with Neolithic interrelations among mathematics and weights and languages in order to show how they were first invented together in a real world of measuring and exchanging foodstuffs. Counting began as accounting. Then we discuss the early invention of the right angle as a fundamental unit of measure for building storehouses and temples. We also discuss the Pythagorean theorem as it derived from real-world measurements of areas. Then we move to Euclid's axioms of a more abstract geometry in order to show at the outset that the very idea of "equivalence" must be presumed when we begin to test a formulaic proposition. Here is his first given: "Things which are equal to the same thing are also equal to one another." We ask students about the presumption. Why is equivalence the first standard of measure?

The domains of math and algebra feature the balanced equation. At the outset of Chap. 3 we ask, what is elementary about an equation? An equation presumes that the equals sign ($=$) means that symbols on one side of the equation must balance up, or be equivalent, to those on the other side

INTRODUCTION: BALANCE AT THE CORE 17

of a scale. The basic equation looks like this: $a = b$. This equation is a bit puzzling, because the two symbols look different but they mean the same. Where is the underlying unity? The basic rule for finding equivalence in algebra is sometimes called The Golden Rule of Algebra: what you do on the left side of a formula you must also do on the right side. In Chap. 5 we review the Golden Rule of morality. Are these two rules equivalent?

We will show that algebra itself can be free of mathematical numbers, or that the letters in an equation may signify any two numbers, or even no numbers at all. We emphasize this very important fact about the above equation, and about algebraic equations at large: In algebra, the equation exists as a purely *grammatical* set of relations. By itself the algebraic symbol system has no reference whatsoever to an "outside" existence in a space and in time of a real world, whether of objects or persons or natures (See below). Algebra, by itself, is *not* about the real physical balancing of things and energies. It is all about grammatical patterns, without any content. This kind of equation abides in an "inner" domain of the pattern itself, that is, within the grammatical domain of pure symbols. So it can be helpful to teach the grammatical rules of assemblage without first confusing its grammar with those things that exist in the real world of space and time. Just as we learn and teach math as $1 + 2 = 3$, without necessarily applying the numbers to real blocks or weights in space and time, so we can separate the grammatical rules of combinations from the physical rules.

CHAPTER 4 THE SENTENCE

Cross reference: Common Core, Language Arts, Grade 1, "Foundations": Produce complete sentences when appropriate to task and situation.

"*The sentence is the basic unit of discourse.*"[24]

We explore this assertion throughout Chap. 4. Why is not a word more basic than a sentence? A sentence is the necessary foundation for speaking and writing meaningfully. What is it about a sentence that makes it the basic unit of speaking and writing? Is it like an equation? What is basic about it? Students learn that a sentence is not just a string; it is not just a linear list; it is not just a sequence. For in order to be defined as a sentence, there needs to be a noun combined with a verb. This idea is as old as Plato, who said that language (*logos*) is "the interlacing of noun and verb."[25] Well, why does there need to be a noun combined with a verb for meaningful discourse? How do the noun and the verb together balance information? In writing a sentence, how do we decide that the information is meaningful? The interweaving of noun, verb, and object creates a *balance of information* that is sent to a reader or listener. This idea of balanced information will be thoroughly tested in Chap. 4. Here is a beginning. By a balance of information in a sentence, we not only mean a type of rhetoric called "the balanced sentence." Instead, we suggest that any noun and verb combine or interweave into a balanced measure of information. The "subject" in a descriptive sentence is usually identified as a particular thing in the real world. A descriptive sentence usually involves a real particular thing identified as noun, but the predicate is usually a general or universal concept. "The dog is good." The subject with its identifying adjective points to a particular dog. Goodness is a universal concept. Consider also "The sun rises." The subject is "sun," and the predicate is "rises." We notice that the meaning of the sentence asserts a sort of balanced interval between subject and predicate. A sentence joins an object in space and an instant in time, and it involves a meaning that could be encased in any number of larger paragraphs. Usually the subject serves an identifying function in a spatial location, while the verb tense and its predicates often point to a time. Sentences often bring together existing things in space and time. Descriptive sentences are usually assertions whose meanings identify something that really exists as a combination of spatiotemporal unities. "Abraham Lincoln was a wise man." Lincoln once existed in the real world of space and time, but "wisdom" is a concept, not a thing. Most grammarians agree that the basic *composite* of subject and predicate, where the subject involves a real body in space–time, and where the predicate involves conceptual terms, amounts to the most important idea about sentence structure. The unifying of noun and verb makes for a connection that asserts something. By connecting noun and verb, the sentence implies a new transfer of meaning.

A sentence therefore has an extremely important role in all of our affairs. A sentence often asserts something; it is a predication. *There are no assertions without sentences.* We emphasize this idea in Chap. 4.

In English sentences, there is one basic unifier that balances information in an equivalence. *Often, the verb "is" is used as a synonym for the equals (=) sign.* A very important point in the composition of sentences is the very definition of "is." In English sentences, the verb "is" can serve two very different functions. As we shall see in Chap. 4, the verb "is" means both the "inner" grammatical form of logical connection (copula) and the "outer" essential statement about existence, about Being in the world:

"I am, s/he is, you are." "I am!" claims that "I exist." In grammar, a "copula" is a purely linking word that couples the subject and the object as a verb. "Is" is sometimes called a "dummy verb."[26] Yet in a sentence, the verb "is" may combine an assertion about the existence of something by way of its grammatical relation. "Lincoln is wise." Lincoln and wisdom are made equivalent in this sentence. This use of "is" in two combined ways can be a tricky action, for it also can lead to the invention of creative metaphor. "Tony is a beast." "You dog!" "Socrates is a centaur." Although not literally true as an assertion, for centaurs do not really exist, it may be metaphorically creative as an imaginative idea. Many sentences are amphibians, because they fuse together these two different domains, an existing subject and a non-existing predicate. So in our project, we work back and forth among various signs of *equivalence*: the verb, the equals sign, and the fulcrum.

CHAPTER 5: SEEKING A MIDDLE MEASURE

"The red sun seemed to tip one end of a pair of balance scales below the horizon, and simultaneously to lift an orange moon at the other."[27]

We shall see that balancing up is a basic measure of the natural world, and it is an equally important quality in ethics and aesthetics. While a middle measure is the central balancing point for our composition of a lever, an equation, or sentence, in the concluding Chap. 5 we widen the measure to include its role as we learn practical reason. So we widen the framework from the instrumental skills of composition in the first three chapters in order to discuss larger issues of balanced middle measure in other domains, namely ethics and the arts. Throughout this chapter, we celebrate a principle of creative discovery for students, and we describe it as a method of serious play that combines opposing forces.

Here is one example of how the sciences, the arts, and even ethics have been brought together. A distinguished scientist, Herman Weyl, wrote the first great book on symmetry involving *both* the arts and sciences, and he featured the balancing of bilateral symmetry both as a scientific and as an artistic concept. Weyl was one of the last century's great mathematicians of physics, so his description of balance and symmetry, in both the arts and the sciences, was a fundamental breakthrough in the study of grace and beauty from the point of view of general science. Arts and sciences come together in his descriptions. He introduced his brief history of symmetry in this way: "*Ebenmass* [even-mass] is a good German equivalent of the

Greek symmetry [which "means something like well-proportioned, well balanced"]; for like this it also carries the connotation of 'middle measure,' the mean towards which the virtuous should strive in their actions, according to Aristotle's *Nicomachean Ethics*...."[28] Here is an example of a family of related values, in which Weyl sees the science of well-balanced masses as a basic rationale for ethical action and aesthetic proportion. We shall explore contemporary ideas of middle measure and practical reason in Chap. 5.

Teachers may gradually widen the idea of a central balancing measure in order to address the great virtues of truth, beauty, and goodness, which Howard Gardner hopes to "reframe" for young people.[29] Here, for instance, is an example about justice, which we shall discuss in Chapter 5. Among the first cries about justice that children proclaim is: "That's not fair." Or for short, "No fair!" In this regard, Gardner quotes a character in Bernard Schlink's *Homecoming*: "Children hope against hope that what is good is true and beautiful and what is evil is false and ugly." Notice the balanced sentence. Gardner then notes that all through history the three qualities have been closely linked. As an instance he quotes the novelist Margaret Atwood's definition of perhaps the oldest articulation of their connection, all in one Egyptian word, *Ma-at*. In her first chapter, called "Ancient Balancing," she says,

> The term *Ma-at* meant truth, justice, balance, the governing principles of nature and the universe, the stately progression of time... the true, just, and moral standards of behavior, the way things are supposed to be—all those notions rolled up into one short word. Its opposite was physical chaos, selfishness, falsehood, evil behavior any sort of upset in the divinely ordained pattern of things.[30]

We take up the issues of justice and judgment in Chap. 5.

Perhaps the oldest visual image of a balance scale, an Egyptian wall painting, may be found online.[31] It visualizes justice and truth as icons on a balance scale. So it combines the mechanics of measurement with the idea of justice into a new unity. It shows Thoth measuring the ashes of a person on the arm of the scale, over and against the feather of truth, a symbol of Ma-at. Had the person lived a good life? Notice that Thoth has his fingers poised on a weight that can move along a sliding scale to get the right **ratio** of weight and distance.

INTRODUCTION: BALANCE AT THE CORE   21

Atwood says, "This concept –that there is an underlying balancing principle in the universe—, according to which we should act—appears to have been almost universal. In Chinese culture it's the Tao or Way, in Indian culture it's the wheel of karmic justice" (27). In Chapter 5, we review some of these principles from different cultures, all of which feature ethical and aesthetic balancing. In Buddhism the "Middle Way" is the central balancing principle of moderation. In Confucianism the term for the central pivot is *Chung Yung*. In Chap. 5, we show how this pivot of moral action also can be seen as a fundamental principle of aesthetics. In Islam, the term *Wasat* means middle and/or balance. Among the Romans, Aristotle's phrase became the philosophy of the *via media*. Balancing seems to be a basic way of the three media.

Finally, in Chapter 5 we feature works of discovery in both the arts and sciences in order to see how a middle measure serves as a guide for creative play that leads to discoveries, small and large.

Now we introduce some of the cross-cutting characteristics of these three forms of problem-solving, because it helps to see how they agree and how they differ in their rules of agreement, that is, their rules of assemblage into unities. Equalizing balance will be our point of departure.

"Inner" and "Outer" Rules

As a first step, we can ask students over and over about the ways that we know with our senses, our impressions of the outer world, as opposed to the ways that we know by reasoning with our learned symbols. We *contact* the outer world by means of our bodily sense impressions. This is the world of perceptions. We *correlate* the world with our own inner mental concepts, such as symbols of space and time, which make our impressions seem to be composed together into an intelligible world of signs that relate our senses with the world. We show that almost all thought with different kinds of languages involves the linking of our sensations of the "outer" world with our "inner" powers of using apt symbols. No matter what the sign—whether linguistic or pictorial or physical—this fundamental equivalent linkage guides our thinking and acting. Many of the problems of composition in any medium involve the real difficulty of making our conceptual symbols work in close correspondence with our impressions of the outer world. One of the very important first steps is understand how these three different methods of problem-solving must use a composite of inner and outer rules. We learn to accommodate ourselves to the combinations of these inner and outer rules.

We begin in Chapter 2 with the 3-D world of machines and machines because a child's first learning is "topological," as Jean Piaget taught.[32] A child's knowledge becomes "embodied" when she begins to connect with her surroundings in space by touch, by feeling. Consider the primary balancing act on the fulcrum of a seesaw. There is no grammar present at all in the action of a child's moving her body on the balancing arm. Here balancing is a tacit feeling of cause and effect, of pushing up and being pulled down. Her intuitive action is a balancing act in the real world, where she achieves dynamic equilibrium as she swivels up and down with her partner on the other side of the symmetrical board. As she rides up and down, she does not need to say, "I am seesawing." She needs no language; so she is not using a grammar. What is the "inner" grammar of a working fulcrum? There is none. It is all the sense perception of feeling. We diagnose this kind of balancing by physical and physiological contact. When I am hammering a nail, I am not saying, "I am hammering." Nor do I need to say over and over, "Hammer, hammer, hammer!" Nevertheless, a child can silently communicate with a partner on the other end of a seesaw by simply pushing down with her feet. This is in itself a purely physical signal based on a feeling of contact, of real connection. Charles Saunders Peirce, a late nineteenth-century polymath, called this sort of signal by real-world contact an "index."[33] A feeling of contact is a signal, purely physical. An "index" is a physical signal of touching and linking with something else, based on the mechanics of cause and effect. For Peirce, an index is a physical indicator, which communicates between a sender and a receiver in the present instant, right now, like a lightning bolt or a thunder clap, or a jolt from an electrical shock. A plumb bob, to be studied in Chapter 2, is an index, according to Peirce, a sign of "vertical direction." A spirit level is also an indexical sign (See also Chap. 2). When you are taking something apart and then putting it back together, you are thinking with your hands, so to speak, without talking to yourself, necessarily. In terms of our Sender-Receiver diagram, an index is a signal of **contact**. The energy channel is also the chief meaning of the message.

We also communicate with visual signs, with picture thinking, that connects inner and outer, like a child's drawings of her surroundings, or like Rembrandt's sketch of a child learning to walk, or like the Egyptian wall drawing of the balance scales. Just as some students are primarily topological thinkers, good with their hands, there are others who are primarily visual thinkers, good at drawing and geometrical figuring. Peirce called this kind of sign that connects inner and outer realms by picture thinking an "icon." Students can look up "icon" in a dictionary, as part of a glossary review. Maybe you have heard the word used with a special kind of Russian devotional painting called an icon. Some may have heard the old pun, "Great oafs from little icons grow." Peirce also said that because a picture becomes meaningful when we match the drawn representation with an inner image that we recall from our memory, then an icon primarily works primarily as a *past* recollection. If you try to draw a picture of a horse or a buffalo, you need to remember how it looks. Or if you show the picture to a classmate, she might say, "It's very like." Or maybe, "It's the spitting image!" For Peirce also as we shall see, an equation is primarily a picture sign because it represents its meaning in a visual pattern, such as $a/b = b/a$. In Chap. 3 we explore equations whose ratios and proportions are primarily iconic. Also, when you study Common Core math, you learn a system of place values, where you draw a pattern of bundles, like groups of tens. The numbers themselves are not icons; they are symbols, to be described next, but the layout into patterns is a visual arrangement. In Chap. 3 we shall notice that many icons are drawn on a 2-D plane, like the flat pages of a sheet of paper, or more graphically, in the **context** of plane geometry, not topological, but flat. Graphs with their x-y axes are planar icons. Our Sender-Receiver diagrams are primarily 2-D representations in their layout.

Peirce's third kind of sign is what he called a "symbol." A symbol is sign that only works once we have learned its **code**. A symbol is a verbal sign that we have learned by conventional grammars. When kids learn their "A-B-Cs," they are learning a conventional sign system. Letters in an alphabet are learned symbols, as are systems of numbers. A symbol does not point to one thing in particular. It points to a kind of thing. Algebra is as symbolic system that is purely grammar. In algebra, the "=" sign is a pure copula. So in algebra the idea of equivalence is strictly symbolic. But when algebra is applied to an existing object or objects in the "outside" world, as in most of its uses, as with weights and measures or with chemical elements, then equivalence takes on its double meaning. If $a + 2a = 3a$, where a is the symbol for sheep, as in 1 sheep + 2 sheep = 3 sheep, then the inner and the outer meaning of equivalence are combined as an amphibious composite. Throughout, then, we can heed different uses of the idea of symbolic equivalence, both in terms of grammar and in terms of existing things.

Peirce thought that a symbol points primarily toward a possible future. While an index is a connecting sign that connects in the present, like a shock or like a loving touch, and while an icon works by connecting the image with a past memory, a symbol points forward. A symbol is a learned grammatical sign that usually occurs in a following sequence, like words in a sentence. So the information in a following sequence of symbols is unfolding as we go along reading or listening or counting. In a sentence the meaning is impending. Usually part of a following sequence, placed in a string of words, a symbol's meaning aims toward what might be happening next, in a possible future. In Chapter 4 we shall call this kind of unfolding toward what is coming next a "hovering" effect. Because symbols occur in coded strings of meaning, like sentences or paragraphs, they occur primarily as 1-D signs. These three kinds of signs are oriented in time toward the present, the past, and the future. The three kinds of signs will become useful as we study, in Chap. 2, 3-D levers that balance in real space and time; when we study, in Chap. 3, 2-D equations that balance as transformations on a plane; and when we study, in Chap. 4, sentences that connect their information along a 1-D sequence.

Three Patterns of Connecting Ideas into a Balanced Likeness: Matching, Following, and Cause and Effect

In the previous section, we described three kinds of signs. An index seems to work mainly by cause and effect; a visual icon seems to relate by means of matching up a likeness; a symbol seems to connect with another symbol in a following sequence. What do we do when we balance up an assemblage? As we shall see along the way, in all three forms of inquiry, we match components into a likeness; we link them together into sequences; and we try to link components by way of a cause that leads to an effect. These are basic methods of combining ideas and symbols in our minds. These three kinds of associations are the ways we begin to make patterns into designs. Throughout the Core Curriculum, these methods of combination are used, either explicitly or tacitly.

See also Chapter 3 "The Equation" for definitions of "bundling" numbers, a matching exercise, and "skipping" numbers, a following exercise. The x-y axis of a Sender-Receiver diagram lets students see how we tacitly use the mental associations of matching and following. On the vertical axis of Code and Context, you get ready to match up elements of a code. On the horizontal axis, you assemble the components into a following sequence. Where the components of the two come together at the crisscross, whether fulcrum, or equation, or "is," you have a combination that makes for a dynamic balancing. The three forms of composition all use the same basic ways of *patterning* symbols into these three kinds of linkages based on our awareness of **likeness**. We **match** up one thing with another. We make or see things that **follow** one another in sequences. And we can see the relation between **cause and effect**. In other words, to find a likeness you must use these three basic patternings. They are the primary mental algorithms for connecting up an equivalence, a sentence, or an equilibrium.

Historical Background

Lots of people have worked on the ways that the mind connects or associates one idea with another. In the history of ideas, this definition of mental likeness has been called "the association of ideas."[34] John Locke and David Hume classified three ways of putting together likenesses or associations. We connect or associate ideas by (1) resemblance, by (2) contiguity, and by (3) cause and effect. Matching resemblances is the first kind of association. "This leaf looks like a willow." The second kind of association is to find ideas next to each other in an orderly linear series, a casual or causal sequence of things or actions divided into before and after. The objects in a sequence often touch one another. They are adjacent in a string. They abut one another within a common border. If they are next to each other, they are contiguous, that is, they are in contact; they rub shoulders with each other in a parade, like the railroad cars on a train, with their coupling links, or the concatenation of dominoes falling in a linear sequence. When you watch a three-year-old child assembling dining-room chairs into a train, you know that this is an act of creative play that is teaching about following sequences. Many middle-school students tend to be literalists of the imagination, so this kind of exercise with real 3-D things helps to make clear some of the vagaries of thinking with symbols.

As we work with these Sender-Receiver diagrams, we shall see that matching, following and cause/effect are necessary components of balancing feedback.

These three kinds of linkages seem to be the basic ways we connect our ideas into patterns, and they can help us to distinguish our three modes of inquiry one from another. Patterning is featured in both the Common Core curriculum and in Next Generation Science Standards.

So when we match and follow, we are seeking to reveal unapparent likenesses of things and actions, masses and energies. We are seeking unities amid varieties of chance and necessity. In manipulating things on a fulcrum, in expressing an equation, or in stringing words together linearly in a sentence, we are matching and following in basic combinations. In each of these symbolic forms of inquiry, we use matching and following as components that help to identify and describe what is being balanced. When we look for the center of balance in any composition, we are on the way to discovery.

In several contemporary disciplines, similar associations are used for matching and following patterns respectively. For instance, in mathematics, we speak of cardinal and ordinal numbers. The numbers "five" and "ten" are not the same concept as the idea that "sixth" follows "fifth" or that "ninth" precedes "tenth." In grammar, we speak of nouns and verbs. In linguistics and semiotics, we speak of paradigm and syntagm; in psychoanalysis: displacement and condensation; in psychology: correspondence and succession; and in anthropology: substitution magic and contiguity magic. Here are two examples of "contiguity" magic from children's stories that feature physical contact, the feeling of touch: A visual example is the chain of people who touch the golden goose in "The Golden Goose Girl." A similar nursery rhyme is: "This Is the House That Jack Built." In most disciplines, we see that the three ways of ordering symbols are matching, following, and cause and effect.

How is it that many disciplines recognize these three basic kinds of knowing by association? Matching, following, and cause and effect are the three essential ways that we compose and organize our thoughts into patterns in space and in time (See Next Generation Science Standards for the emphasis on "patterns in interdisciplinary work). Matching and following, sometimes called correspondence and succession, are two very fundamental methods of identifying patterns in space and intervals in time. All three of our methods of inquiry compose patterns in these ways.

How do students begin to compose into patterns? To learn how to set apart a problem in a different framework like a model of discovery and then to take its structure apart and then to recompose its parts is one of the basic and essential patterning skills.

In the sciences especially we may begin with an assumption of spatiotemporal unity of cause and effect, but then we take things apart and then put them back together, on a different plane, a diagram of an equation or grid, in patterns of space and time. The practice of taking things apart and then of putting them back together is a definition of a skill. In our program, the different plane is a group of three compositional diagrams.

But now we divide things up and then we synthesize them on a different plane of symbols, into models of matching, following, and cause and effect, in order to better understand what we see and what we do in our experiences. When we match and follow one idea with another, we *balance* together similar things and their following sequential chains into a balanced unity. For the association of cause and effect, we can explore examples that bring things that match, and things that follow one another in a serial order, into a summing up that might be called a law of inertia, for instance. "To sum up" combines the two other kinds of likeness into conformity. When we associate cause with effect, we are evaluating the connections. You can test this idea with balanced expressions like "Where there is smoke, there is fire." This is a kind of summing up, which at the same time allows us to remember that smoke is the antecedent *index* of an impending fire, but smoke is the not the cause of fire. Thinking in terms of number *symbols*, a two-year-old child can chant the numerals in the **code** from 1 to 10, but it takes some time before she can learn to distinguish the series 1-2-3 from the summing up of the concept of three-ness in a **context**.[35] That is, to see and to count three cows in a field or three birds on a tree limb is a summing up. And then in kindergarten she learns how to write the numerals, such as "3." These distinctions allow us to see how the serial order of *following sequences* is seen differently in the basic compositions.

THE AESTHETIC EQUATION SEEN AS A LIKENESS

Now let us summarize what we have said so far about the search for likeness by using matching, following, and cause and effect. Here too we can round off what we have said so far about larger issues of middle measure. Consider Hans Christian von Baeyer's essay about scientific discovery by way of the beauty of mathematical equations. Called "The Aesthetic Equation," the essay shows that a scientific equation, which has elegance, coherence, and inner unity, is one that is *proportional in the likeness* of its parts. So, for von Baeyer, it is beautiful.[36] Furthermore, these combining qualities are both the initial motives for, as well as the ultimate satisfactions of, creating a new equation for a new theory. He quotes Jacob Bronowski on likeness: "All science is the search for unity in hidden likenesses." Students can learn to be creative by searching for unapparent likenesses. For our core curriculum, we are proposing a method of balancing feedback as the way to see a hidden likeness that unites the three basic forms of composition in these arts and sciences. Bronowski in turn quotes the poet Samuel Taylor Coleridge's definition of beauty as "unity in variety." For von Baeyer, "science is nothing else than the search to discover unity in the wide variety of nature .... Poetry, painting, the arts are the same search." This sentence, couched as an assertion, brings together the arts and sciences in their mutual search for unity.

We are reviewing these three modes of composition as skills to be learned in middle school and beyond. Skills enable creative research. By chance we may stumble upon a new idea, but it takes a prepared mind to do the rest of the work. So far, we have discussed basic examples of taking things apart and then putting them back together into a new likeness. Furthermore, an acquired compositional skill can lead to new discovery, to creativity, in both the arts and sciences. This is the subject of Chapter 5 on "Middle Measure."

When we balance things and events, we are arranging them by the joint process of matching and following. The likeness is often expressed as a ratio between compared things and repeated events in a series. Ratio may not be an intuitive idea that is immediately grasped by middle-school students, but ratio is one of the most basic kinds of likeness as we shall see, one that is central to the three domains of compositions.

How is it that ratio is a basic measure of our lives, even if we do not realize it so often? Here is what von Baeyer says about likeness and ratio, both in science and in aesthetics. Notice his use of "equality": "In physics, the most primitive tool for expressing 'likeness' is the equality of two numbers." See Chap. 3, "The Equation." He says further: "The equality of ratios is to physics what rhythm is to poetry, and balance to painting (55)." Finally, he says that many discoveries in the physical sciences really find a hitherto unseen likeness between two ratios, and he cites Archimedes about a balance bar, which we shall explore in Chap. 2.

Notice that we are always seeking and joining unapparent sets of likenesses between ideas, and that the lever, the sentence, and the equation are basic means for connecting relations of apparently unrelated quantities and qualities into unities. Notice that to solve a likeness for weight and distance, we must use matching logic for finding equal weights and we must use a following logic for finding distances. Notice too that this abstract ratio depends explicitly upon balance. In remembering the playground seesaw, students can begin to solve this ratio between weight and distance intuitively by noticing that a heavier child can slide a bit closer along the length of the board toward the fulcrum in order to balance up with a lighter child sitting on the end. In order to solve for the ratio between weights and distance, you must use matching and following concepts. You are moving things around. You match up weights of corresponding numbers—5 pounds or 10 pounds. You count distances in orderly units of measure in which one number follows another in a *succession*. This sometimes called "iteration." So a student's kinesthetic, 3-D feeling of her balancing on the seesaw lends itself to the more abstract understanding of ratio as an abstract concept. In all of these examples and exercises, we notice with students how an everyday act of balancing, or even a difficult test of balancing in a physics lab, necessarily is seen as a kind of symbolic equation.

One of the most dramatic acts of creation, the finding of a hidden likeness in the history of discovery was also one of Archimedes' own. His sudden discovery of a likeness between two dissimilar ideas is so famous that it is now sometimes called a "Eureka moment!"[37] We describe this discovery in Chapter 5 where we discuss the idea of "combinatory play." In truth, furthermore, every time a student puts together the two sides of an equation, either in a sentence or in a formula, then there is a small discovery of a new combination between ideas. For sometimes there is no huge "Eureka" moment. Sometimes, and even more often, there are small successive insights that emerge along the way. More often than not, we do not aim for big discoveries. We are seeking realizations along the way.

When we seek a likeness or similarity in the world, even an unlikely likeness, we soon begin to find larger relations by noticing how things follow one after another, how they recur. Without an awareness of how things recur in patterns, there is not measure at all (See again Next Generation Science Standards for "patterns"). All measurements depend on recurrent likenesses, on matching and following one thing with another so as to reveal a pattern. The arts and sciences seem to be based upon patterns of recurrent likenesses. As we show in Chapter 5, all these measurements are certain kinds of "parallel constructions" that symbolize repeated balancing as different kind of symbolic equivalences. When we start looking for other likenesses, we are forming a patterned structure of recurring relations in space and time, what Bronowski called "unities." We are pattern-seeking creatures.

In all three domains we are balancing a proportion of likenesses by matching and following patterns, that is, by finding the correspondences and the successions that lead to new [sic] relations between ideas. The matching pattern and the serial pattern are combined in a right proportion. Notice that the longer the seesaw, the more extensive the mathematical or algebraic equation, the more expansive the sentence, the more the balance seems to become a recurring rhythmic balance of moving parts in a sort of harmony. For where you find an extensive array of moving parts, balancing one another, there you begin to see "scale" in a large sentence. So within each of the three kinds of searching and problem-solving, *dynamic balance* is seen as a moving proportion of matching and following principles in space and time.

NOTES

1. For an updated analysis, see Sister Miriam Joseph, *The Trivium: Logic, Grammar, and Rhetoric: Understanding the Nature and Function of Language*, ed. Marguerite McGlinn. (Philadelphia: Paul Dry Books, 2002).
2. Rembrandt van Rijn, *Child Being Taught to Walk*, ca. 1656. http://www.royalacademy.org.uk/ra-magazine/from-the-archive-life-drawing,1905,AR.html. For a full discussion, see Lawrence Wechsler, "Vanishing Point: David Hockney's Long and Winding Road" *Harper's Magazine* (June, 2005): 47–55.
3. For some recent scientific work summarizing the bodily movements of children, see Mark Johnson, one of the main proponents of embodied knowledge, *The Meaning of the Body: Aesthetics of Human Understanding* (Chicago: The University of Chicago Press, 2007), Chapter 2 "Big Babies.
4. See Michael Polanyi and Harry Prosch, *Meaning* (Chicago: The University of Chicago Press, 1975), 33.
5. John A. Kricher, *The Balance of Nature: Ecology's Enduring Myth* (Princeton: Princeton University Press, 2009). For a history of the paradigm of balanced nature, persistent since Aristotle, see Chapter 3, "Creating Paradigms."
6. See also New York State Education Department: *Elementary Science Core Curriculum, Grades K—4*. Online: http://www.p12.nysed.gov/ciai/mst/pub/elecoresci.pdf

7. See James H. Bunn, *The Dimensionality of Signs, Tools and Models: An Introduction* (Bloomington: Indiana University Press, 1981). Hereafter cited as *STM*.
8. George Lakoff and Mark Johnson, *Philosophy in the Flesh: The Embodied Mind and Its Challenge to Western Thought* (New York: Basic Books, 1999).
9. For example, see "Embodied Learning Blends Movement, Computer Interaction," *Education Week*, May 26, 2016. Online http://www.edweek.org/ew/articles/2012/10/10/07embody.h32.html
10. James Waack, fifth-grade teacher, Windom Elementary School, (Orchard Park, N.Y.), personal communication.
11. James Gleick, *The Information: A History, A Theory, A Flood* (New York: Pantheon Books, 2011), 22. See also Hans Christian von Baeyer, *Information: The New Language of Science* (Cambridge: Harvard University Press, 2004), 28–31, which demonstrates that information is the very language of science.
12. See Claude Shannon online for the basic diagram. Also Gleick, 246–248. Also von Baeyer, 115–120 about the economy of communicating by binary digits, bits.
13. Our arrangement into horizontal and vertical axes derives from the work of Ferdnand de Saussure, *Course in General Linguistics*. Roman Jakobson expands and applies Shannon's diagram to linguistics in "Closing Statement: Linguistics and Poetics," in *Style in Language*, ed. Thomas Sebeok (Cambridge, Mass.: 1960), 353. Hereafter cited as *CS*.
14. See *Next Generation Science Standards, For States, By States* (NGSS Release: April 2013), available for pdf download).
15. See von Baeyer's Chapter 18 and Gleick's Chapter 13, both called "Information Is Physical."
16. David N. Perkins, *Making Learning Whole: How Seven Principles of Teaching Can Transform Education* (New York: Jossey-Bass, 2009), 85–86.
17. *Common Core Standards and Strategies Flip Chart, Grade 5*, Michael L. Lujan, et al. (Mentoring Minds).
18. See, for example, Brenda H. Manning, *Cognitive Self Instruction for Classroom Processes* (Albany: State University of New York Press, 1991). See also The Waters Foundation online: "Systems Thinking in Schools."
19. See Ludwig von Bertalanffy, *General System Theory: Foundations, Development, Applications* (New York: George Braziller, 1968). Also see Bunn, *STM*, 140–141. For a recent overview see Fritjof Capra and Pier Luigi Luisi, *The Systems View of Life: A Unifying Vision* (New York: Cambridge University Press), 2014; on Bertalanffy, see 85–86.

20. In his discussion of economics, Jean Piaget discusses its "general theorem of equilibrium" as part of his assertion that equilibrium is a feature in several disciplines, and is therefore a basic principle of structuralism. *Structuralism*, trans. Chaninah Maschler (New York: Basic Books, 1970), 77.
21. Richard Feynman, *The Character of Physical Law* (Cambridge, Mass.: The M.I.T. Press, 1965). Hereafter cited as *CPL*. For this topic and many other related issues, see ReadWorks: http://www.readworks.org/
22. For his popular discussion, see Albert Einstein, "E = MC^2" in *Out of My Later Years* (Totowa, N.J.: Littlefield Adams, 1967), 51.
23. See online "Balancing Act- -Force, Torque, Rotation." http://phet.colorado.edu/en/simulation/balancing-act
24. 'Emile Benveniste, *Problems in General Linguistics*, trans. Mary Elizabeth Meek (Coral Gables, Florida: University of Miami Press, 1971), 110.
25. Plato, *Cratylus*, cited by Paul Ricoeur, *The Rule of Metaphor: Multidisciplinary Studies of the Creation of Meaning*, trans. Robert Czerny (Toronto: University of Toronto Press, 1975), 70. Much of what we say about sentences derives from this book.
26. For the usage of "is" in several languages as merely a filler, a "dummy verb," see John Lyons, *Introduction to Theoretical Linguistics* (Cambridge: Cambridge University Press, 1969), 322–323.
27. Patrick Leigh Fermor, *Between the Woods and the Water* (London: John Murray Ltd., 1986), 84.
28. Herman Weyl, *Symmetry* (Princeton: Princeton University Press, 1952), 3–4.
29. Howard Gardner, *Truth, Beauty, and Goodness Reframed: Educating for the Virtues in the Twenty First Century* (New York: Basic Books, 2012).
30. See Margaret Atwood, *Payback: Debt and the Shadow Side of Wealth* (Toronto: Anansi, 2008), 27.
31. Search *Wikipedia Commons*: http://upload.wikimedia.org/wikipedia/commons/7/75/Egypt_dauingevekten.jpg
32. Jean Piaget and Barbara Inhelder, *The Child's Conception of Space*, trans. F. J. Langdon and J. L. Lunzer (New York: W. W. Norton & Company, 1967), 9, 243.
33. See "Logic as Semiotic: The Theory of Signs," in *Philosophical Writings of Peirce*, ed. Justus Buchler (New York: Dover Publications, 1955), 108.
34. For an influential analysis, see William James, *The Principles of Psychology* (New York: Henry Holt and Company, 1890," vol. 1, Chapter XIV, "Association." For an analysis of correspondence and succession, in terms of a "throwing together" of ideas and signs of mental activity, see James

H. Bunn, "A Semiotic Model of Conjecture," *On Semiotic Modeling*, eds., Myrdene Anderson and Floyd Merrill (De Gruyter, 1991), 405–428.
35. See Susan Carey, *The Origin of Concepts* (New York: Oxford University Press, 2009), especially case studies in natural number.
36. Hans Christian von Baeyer, "The Aesthetic Equation," *The Sciences* vol. 30, no. 1, January/February 1990. Collected in his *The Fermi Solution: Essays on Science* (New York: Random House, 1993), 55.
37. See David N. Perkins, *Archimedes' Bathtub: The Art and Logic of Breakthrough Thinking* (New York: W. W. Norton & Company, 2000), 6–7. Perkins also discusses Arthur Koestler's coined word "bisociation," which is the combinatory act of bringing together two uniquely different frameworks of inquiry into a new unity (180–183). See *The Act of Creation* (New York: Dell, 1964).

CHAPTER 2

Archimedes' Lever

When we want to understand the composition of anything in the real world, we don't just look at it from the outside, and we don't just define it. We take it apart, if we can, and then we put it back together again, if we can. For example, Richard Feynman says that when you ask a first-grader what makes a toy dog move, you don't tell her that energy makes it move.[1] That is just a definition. You help a child to take the toy apart. You show what happens to the gears when the spring is let loose. You discuss ratchets. He says that this kind of skill in taking things apart and then combining them back together is a good way to start a science course.

Although we shall use some definitions in this chapter, we shall also find plenty of observations and exercises about how gears and other things move and interconnect. We feature a seesaw, because that playground device can show how basic tools are assembled with levers and how they are put together in combinations in order to make more complex machines. The laws of a balancing seesaw can show how a science course might begin.

So in this chapter we shall see how you can take apart and put back together the six basic tools and machines that are central to science and engineering.

Furthermore, throughout this book we shall widen Feynman's good idea about taking things apart and then combining them back together again. When we de-compose things and then re-compose them, we are learning about their composition, how they work; but just as important, as we shall see, this repetitive process amounts to the learning of a *skill*. We learn the rudimentary parts in order to be skillful at making new compositions. We recall that composites have the same root as compositions, and we remember too that any machine, equation, or sentence is a composition. An engineer's ability to design and build new machines from basic machines is an art of combination that derives from a skill in a certain kind of composition. Not only an engineer's ability but any student's ability to de-compose things and then re-combine them is part of a skill in balancing things that will be part of our regimen along the way.

For now, let's look very closely at the origin of the word "balance" because sometimes when we look at the historical origin of a thing, then we can see where a thing has come from and where it might be going. Later on, we shall look closely at the origins of the word "equivalence." In English, the word "balance" seems to derive from a balance scale. It is like the German word *Bilanz*. And both come from the Italian *bilancio*, which combines the Latin *bi* for two and *lancio* from the Latin *lanx* for "scale or steelyard": The Italian word means "a balance between assets and liabilities, whereas *Balance* refers to suspended objects which are not yet in equilibrium but are constantly and restlessly seeking it...."[2] If you think of the unfamiliar word "steelyard" as a balance scale like the familiar one in a doctor's office, you can see that it depends on a weight that slides along the long arm and continuously seeks the right counterbalance on the measured scale. So we can see how *bi* or "two" is the prefix both of something divided into sorts, like a binary digit, like a bit for short, and a pairing sought on a restless scale (*lancio*) of opposing either/or forces. Though its etymology is now hidden, our word "balance" derives from a combined word that unites two-ness and a restless scale. According to *Common Core Standards*, in fifth grade, students become familiar with this process of decomposing a word into a "prefix" and a "base word."[3] Along the way we shall also de-compose such words as "equivalent" and "parallel" into prefixes and suffixes. We can also ask students about the secondary sense given here: that we are always restlessly seeking balance. And in Chap. 5, we shall discuss balancing between assets and liabilities as a kind of middle measure.

We learn to make tools in order to make our work easier, and our work always involves balanced movements. We design and use tools that can be combined into more complicated machines with interrelated parts that incorporate balance principles in their composition. In this chapter, we study these balance principles that regulate the movements of six kinds of simple tools, beginning with levers, which may then be combined into machines. Of the three kinds of mental associations cited in the Introduction—matching, following, and cause/effect—we feature cause and effect here because all of these machines are governed by physical principles of motion. Of the three kinds of signs described in the Introduction—index, icon, and symbol—in this chapter, we feature the index because it is a three-dimensional (3-D) sign that communicates by touching, that is, by **contact** of the senses. When we work with tools and when we take apart a toy machine or a big machine to show how it has broken down and put back together, we are communicating by the manipulation of hands and fingers and minds. This kind of 3-D thinking with fingers and hands reinforces embodied learning. Take it apart and put it back together again with your hands and mind.

We shall see that the same physical principles of movement that regulate the ways that tools work also regulate the balanced movements of our own bodies. Or put it the other way round: We shall also see that the biomechanics of our own body movements are models for the composition of *prosthetic* tools (See below for a classroom exercise in prosthetics). When we transfer hard work from our bodies to a machine, we often speak of a tool as an extension of our own bodies, like a walking stick that helps a walker keep his balance. We can discuss tools as prostheses, as artificial limbs that improve balanced movements. Nowadays this kind of biomechanics underlies the making of new kinds of artificial arms and legs for soldiers disabled in recent wars. And as a related development, there has been renewed research in robot movements. Robotics is all about balancing arms and legs, and robotics is of course one of the most exciting new fields of discovery.

Energy

When our bodies and our machines do work, they spend energy. Machines are tools that corral, redirect, and expend energy, so they enable us to take advantage of the three main functions of energy. So here are some definitions: (1) Container tools such as buckets and pots let us *store* energy. (2) Machines such as railroad trains or tankers or pipelines let us *transport* energy. (3) Machines can also *transform* energy from one kind to another, like transformers on a model railroad train or like portable generators in a garage. Different kinds of machines can be assembled in order to combine the several functions of energy into composites like solar panels that collect and transform the sun's energy into direct current (DC) electricity, which is sent on to an inverter that converts DC electricity into alternating current (AC).

The human invention of tools is always devoted to the struggle to corral and to transfer energy as force, and to make it readily available for us to do work with less expense of our own energy.

Students study energy throughout the course of Next Generation Science Standards, Here is an excerpt for the fourth grade:

> Students are able to use evidence to construct an explanation of the relationship between the speed of an object and the energy of that object. Students are expected to develop an understanding that energy can be transferred from place to place by sound, light, heat, and electric currents or from object to object through collisions. They apply their understanding of energy to design, test, and refine a device that converts energy from one form to another. The crosscutting concepts of patterns; cause and effect; energy and matter; systems and system models; interdependence of science, engineering, and technology; and influence of engineering, technology, and science on society and the natural world are called out as organizing concepts for these disciplinary core ideas.

In this chapter, we feature tools that use levers, which pivot and rotate upon a fulcrum. That kind of work in the real world helps us to achieve a balanced leverage more easily than with our bodies alone. So we need to understand the interrelations of mathematics and mechanics in the composition of these tools.

Levers are 3-D objects "in the round." Like a seesaw, they pivot on a fulcrum. As we shall see in Chap. 3, two-dimensional (2-D) signs, like the equation with its equals sign, exist mainly as picture or graphic patterns on a flat plane. And in Chap. 4, we study one-dimensional (1-D) signs like the sentence that exist primarily as strings in a sequence. Tools like the fulcrum and its lever give us a lift in the real space of three dimensions. Toys like Erector Sets, Legos, and Tinker Toys let children combine and assemble things playfully. There the rules of combination are parts of their rules for assemblage. They are built-in 3-D **codes**.

In the Introduction's Sender-Receiver diagram (Fig. 1.1), we saw that the transporter of energy is gathered under the terms **contact**, and it involves the physical channeling of information. The transmission is caused by the physical contact of moving energies, and we note in passing that the definition of a "cause" is the physical transference of forces. Once we have come to understand how the six basic machines can be composed together, we can also understand that the six rules of assemblage comprise a **code** of mechanical compositions.

The laws of the lever will lead us to other simple machines, because they employ leverage in various ways. As we said, these tools are basic labor-saving devices that make working easier. They help us to restore balance to heavy loads. They also enable us to move faster. When we lift a weight with an arm, and bend and lift at the elbow, we are using the elbow as a fulcrum for a lever. We are lifting a weight against the downward pull of gravity. By studying basic laws of the lever, we can see how they are part of a larger set of principles that feature gravity as a kind of energy, and how we use its energy to help us do work and restore balance. And as we saw in the Introduction, the main conservation law of energy says that any exchange of energy must balance up. Most of the time, we use levers to work against gravity. So here we review the basic laws of gravitational energy as they enter into the real world of thinking with human-made tools and machines as extensions of our bodies. If the rules of assembling six kinds of basic tools into machines comprise a **code** of assembling instructions, then the **context**, or background framework against which the code is selected, is the field of gravity itself. Code and context go together in our Sender-Receiver diagram as choices in a set of possibilities. Further, as we shall see below, when information is actually being sent or transmitted in this 3-D **context**, then the transmitting energy is the actual pressure of gravity. And the feeling of resistance on the part of the receiver is the **contact**. Resistance, as we shall also see along the way, is a fundamental measure in balancing a lever on a fulcrum.

Here too we feature a real balance scale of exchanges, like the ancient Egyptian example cited in the Introduction, which is always in the background of our other Sender-Receive diagrams in later chapters.

Next Generation. Science **3. Forces and Interactions**
 Students who demonstrate understanding can:
 Plan and conduct an investigation to provide evidence of the effects of balanced and unbalanced forces on the motion of an object. Clarification Statement: Examples could include an unbalanced force on one side of a ball can make it start moving and balanced forces pushing on a box from both sides will not produce any motion at all. Assessment Boundary: Assessment is limited to one variable at a time: number, size, or

direction of forces. Assessment does not include quantitative force size, only qualitative and relative. Assessment is limited to gravity being addressed as a force that pulls objects down.

3-PS2-2. Make observations and/or measurements of an object's motion to provide evidence that a pattern can be used to predict future motion. Clarification Statement: Examples of motion with a predictable pattern could include a child swinging in a swing, a ball rolling back and forth in a bowl, and two children on a seesaw. Assessment Boundary: Assessment does not include technical terms such as period and frequency.

Throughout this chapter, we shall feature patterns of motion that are generated by counterbalancing swings of energy.

THE SEESAW AND THE BALANCE SCALE

A seesaw can tell us a lot about laws of levers. As a first exercise in leverage, you can build a seesaw in class that will demonstrate its engineering possibilities.[4] There are few better ways to begin to teach the physical concepts of ratio and proportion than by way of balancing real weights on a seesaw.

To begin, here is an old nursery rhyme:

> Seesaw, Margery Daw,
> Jack shall have a new master.
> He shall have but a penny a day,
> Because he can't work any faster.

As two children pushed themselves up and down on a seesaw with their arms and legs, they may have sung this song. For hundreds of years, the song has accompanied the rhythmic pattern of up and down. Like Margery on a seesaw, to push and to pull is the main bodily act of counter-resistance, and the feeling of natural pressure is called *kinesthesia,* a muscular feeling of the heft of things. When lifting a lever or when vaulting a bar, we experience a kinesthetic feeling of effort and resistance. What Margery may have to do with Jack is an unanswered question, but we know that both kids seem to be doing some sort of work, for Margery is at play expending energy, and potential energy is sometimes defined in terms of the capacity to do work. And an unnamed someone is measuring the capacity of poor Jack on a balance scale of time and money. "Time is money," says an adage. He makes less than a minimum wage because he can't work faster. The interplay of energy, work, and money will be issues in Chap. 5, for they will be huge issues in our children's lives.

This nursery rhyme about a seesaw doesn't feature play at all, but we shall have more to say about play and playgrounds in Chap. 5. The working model of a child's seesaw was surely the balance pan, a measuring device as old as the Egyptians (Introduction). Usually when we think of a balance scale, we imagine the balance beam resting on a fulcrum that is underneath, like the seesaw, but another way, as we shall see, was to use a rope hanging vertically that balanced a horizontal beam so that the center of balance was like a plumb bob (Fig. 2.1).

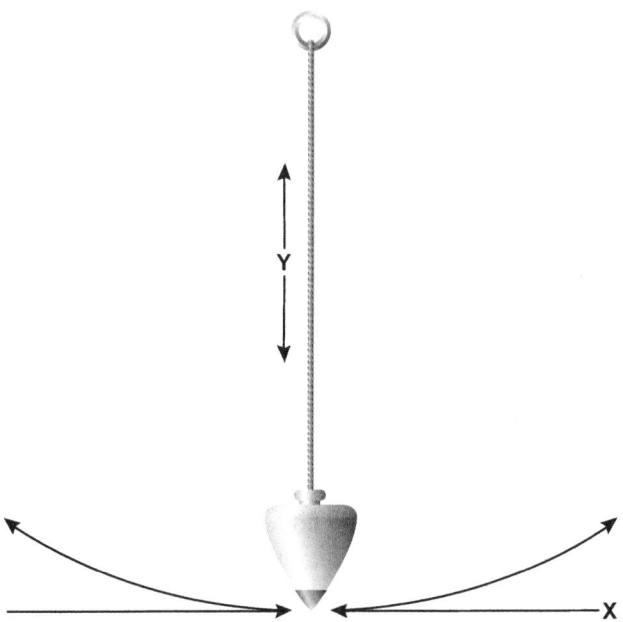

Fig. 2.1 Plumb bob, pendulum, and tangency
The horizontal axis can represent the horizon. Where the plumb bob brushes the horizon, there is the tangent point. The swing of the bob is its arc of rotation
The vertical axis can represent the center of gravity and also the center of symmetry
The plumb bob hangs straight downwards because of gravity. Its axis lets you measure the right angle, the center of gravity and the rotation symmetry

So now let's look briefly at the plumb line. Although it is not a lever, a lever depends on a plumb line as unit of measure.

The Plumb Line and the Pendulum

One of the oldest tools for measuring the relations between real things and their mathematical and geometrical ratios was a plumb line. Among stone-age builders in Egypt and in the Tigris-Euphrates valley, a plumb line with a hanging stone attached was used to measure vertical and horizontal walls. Here is a present-day definition: "A **plumb-bob** or a **plummet** is a weight, usually with a pointed tip on the bottom, that is suspended from a string and used as a vertical reference line, or **plumb-line**. It is essentially the y-axis equivalent of a 'water level'."[5] Notice the relation with a water level, which is sometimes called a "spirit level" by carpenters. We discuss water levels as levers later on.

How do you find the vertical angle for building a wall? When a plumb line hangs straight up and down, it divides the horizon, the ground on which to build, into two equal angles of 90 degrees. Here begins the wide usage of the right angle and the triangle in real-world measurement, and then later in abstract geometry.[6] We discuss right angles in Chap. 3. This discovery of a right angle is extremely important, because most real-world measures depend on its use. To reinforce this point, Lancelot Hogben says that, beginning in antiquity, the plumb line spotlights the use of the right angle of 90 degrees and how it "was to become a fundamental unit of angular measurement" (45).

Practical geometry begins with the measurement of *proportions* between angles and lengths of legs. In class we can correlate by using T-squares and protractors that help us to measure angles and legs in order to derive *areas*. In Chap. 3, we distinguish between flock numbers that count objects and field numbers that count areas. There is a big difference between counting and measuring. Angular measurements begin the extensive mathematics and geometry of measuring *areas*, seen as field numbers.

You can see how useful our Sender-Receiver diagram can be as it sets the pattern into an x–y axis, according to the laws of gravity seen as symmetries. Our information diagram, exhibiting balancing feedback, lets students understand how they can represent the exchange of energies across a balancing scale. Here the energy being exchanged is swinging gravitational force. A pendulum also can be used to demonstrate resistance, inertia, even friction. Furthermore, a pendulum's harmonic swing back and forth can be used to measure the passage of time.

Students can come to see that a plumb bob works like a kind of upside-down fulcrum, where gravity governs both tools, pushing them straight downward in a vertical line, the y-axis of our Sender-Receiver diagrams. A plumb bob hangs vertically, so it signals by gravitational cause/effect a center of balance for a thing being measured. Students can also notice that a plumb line attached to a horizontal beam is a kind of upside-down seesaw, where the plumb or bob is an upside-down fulcrum on the beam. You can demonstrate the interplay of potential energy at the peak of its arc and kinetic energy as it swings. You can discuss the opposing pulls of gravity downward and centrifugal force outward.

> Next Generation Science: 5-PS2 Motion and Stability: Forces and Interactions
> Students who demonstrate understanding can:
> Support an argument that the gravitational force exerted by Earth on objects is directed down. Clarification Statement: "Down" is a local description of the direction that points toward the center of the spherical Earth

In terms of Common Core Language Arts, you might also juxtapose Edgar Allen Poe's short story "The Pit and the Pendulum."

When a pendulum swings and when a fulcrum pivots like the center of a seesaw, students can see that each describes an arc of rotation. Principles of rotational motion are in the background, as Fig. 2.1 shows, and the common motif is simple harmonic motion. Hogben illustrates a plumb line, set swinging as a pendulum, in order to illustrate the principle of *tangency*. When a pendulum swings and touches a horizontal axis, it finds its tangency. Students can make a pendulum in order to think through its arcs of rotation. Then by demonstrating their circular arcs of rotation, we shall be able to link the plumb line, the lever, and some simple machines built upon circular rotation.

Archimedes Lever

> "Give me a place to stand, and I will move the earth"—attributed to Archimedes.

Now we begin to show why the seesaw and the lever are so important in the understanding of machines. In this section, we shall look much more closely at the principle of balancing in mechanics. We shall see how balancing is truly an act of rotating in a partial arc of a circle. And by way of a balancing scale, we shall understand the concept of ratios and proportions. There are many online classroom exercises that feature seesaws and levers, and we shall feature the first one, Archimedes' work, because we usually begin with the history of the question in order to see where we have been in the past and where we might be going in our future uses.

When Archimedes first studied the lever, with its ratios between weights and distances, he began to set the foundations for the study of the relations between mathematics and mechanics. Because mechanical tools help to make our work easier, the mathematics and mechanics of the lever are what we use when we begin to do the physical composing. That is why we stress a study of the plumb line and the lever: They reinforce the real relations between physics and geometry.

See Next Generation Science Standards below on

> Scale, Proportion, and Quantity
> §
> Natural objects exist from the very small to
> the immensely large. (5-PS1-1)
> §
> Standard units are used to measure and
> describe physical quantities such as weight,
> time, temperature, and volume. (5-PS1-2), (5-PS1-3)

Consider first the weights and measures of a hanging balance scale. Look more closely at any ancient model of a balancing scale of weights. For instance, Fig. 2.2 diagrams a typical working model of a pair of pans hanging from a beam and a cord.

Students can discuss how it is like a plumb line and bob.

Now let's consider that there are essentially two basic kinds of balance scales: One in which the pans and weights hang by a cord suspended from a horizontal beam *below* the beam, as in Fig. 2.2, and the other in which the pans and weights are supported by a beam *above* a fulcrum, like the central hinge below a seesaw. The first works by a kinesthetic feeling of pulling downward from a beam, and the other works by a kinesthetic feeling of being pushing upward, like your feet pushing up the other end of a seesaw, which causes the movement of the beam. These are basic feelings of resistance by contact. Primary school children learn about the basic

Fig. 2.2 Hanging balance scales
Here a vertical cord is connected to the center of a horizontal beam. The center of balance is the center of gravity as well as the center of symmetry. So the scales are bilaterally symmetrical
Notice that information is being balanced as it is exchanged from one side to another. We can visualize these verticals and horizontals as version of a Sender-Receiver diagram

physics of pushing and pulling as primal feelings of cause and effect. We stress these two kinds of devices because they are combined in the next demonstration about levers, as explained by an ancient mathematician.[7]

The writer begins by describing a horizontal balance beam, where the point of attachment is from a hanging cord as in Fig. 2.2. It works on the same principle as plumb bob. Then he compares it to a levered balance beam, to a fulcrum, which is set on a platform below the beam. In one device, the pans hang from below the beam, while the other pivots upon the beam like a lever. Perhaps he begins in this way because the ancients knew very well the measures on a hanging balance scale, such as

Ma-at's cited in the Introduction. So he tries to solve for levers by saying that the hanging beam and the lever are "equivalent." The point where the hanging cord is attached is the same point as the fulcrum that pivots underneath. One hangs from a point above, and the other stands on a point below. They are equivalent points at the center of balance, our large theme. He presumes we know how a hanging balance scale works, so he proceeds from there to demonstrate how a lever works.

Our next illustration (Fig. 2.3) shows how a balance beam serves as a lever, with the fulcrum centered at the cord's point of attachment (See *Archimedes Home Page* for an animated variation).

Note that both are at a center, which Archimedes would call the center of gravity.

The movements of the equal weights are explained by means of their movements as arcs on a circle. Although both weights are equal, the weight at a greater radius from the center moves more rapidly. Nowadays we would say that the outer weight has more speed. The commentator continues, "Now the greater the distance from the fulcrum, the more easily it will move. The reason ... [is] that the point further from the centre describes the greater circle, so that by the use of the same force, when the motive force is farther from the lever, it will cause a greater movement. For since under the impulse of the same weight the greater radius from the center moves the more rapidly."

In Fig. 2.3, the weight on the left side has been moved outward so its radius from the fulcrum has increased. The radius of the turning circle increases as you push the weight outward. We notice in this passage that the ratios begin to be solved by demonstrating the moving radii of circular motion. The writer says, "now the ratio of the weight moved to the weight moving it is the inverse ratio of the distances from the center."

To explain, we remember that a seesaw does not go up and down in a straight line; it rotates around the pivoting fulcrum of the lever, just like a pendulum swings in arcs. So this ancient student was thinking about rotating circular arcs in their relation to force and distance traveled.

In the diagram of arcs of force in Fig. 2.3, we notice that they rotate in opposition to each other as they move toward a balance. When we walk, our intuitive acts of moving our arms in opposite rotations, in order to maintain our balance, have a connection with an important concept in the composition of machines. In the physical world governed by gravity, when we work to turn an object in one direction, we feel a resisting force turning in the opposite direction.

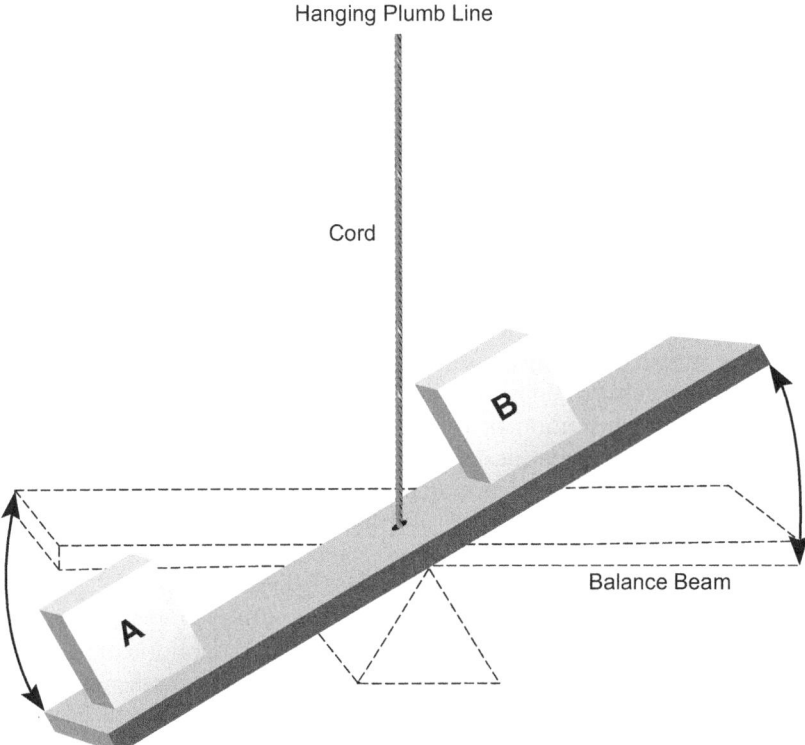

Fig. 2.3 Hanging balance beam and lever are equivalent
A and B are equal in weight. When block A is forced out along the balance beam, its radius of rotation is lengthened as it tips downwards
And when block B is lifted upwards, its radius is relatively smaller than A's radius
A hanging balance beam, like a plumb line, is equivalent to a balance beam that pivots on a fulcrum

Figure 2.3 allows us to see that all physical acts of balancing are seesaw-like. Balancing is an act that is performed as a small arc of rotation.
In this exercise, we also learn that the principle of cause and effect occurs intuitively as children feel themselves being raised and lowered on the balancing plank of a seesaw. Their minds and bodies are signaling by a real-world physical relation with gravity. This kind of sign is called an "index," in which the communication back and forth is done by a physical connection, based on feeling. We are beginning to see that our bodily balancing helps us to understand many principles of science.

The interrelations between these basic tools—the plumb line, the pendulum, the balancing beam, and the lever—can help students learn that these practical mechanics were the foundations of mathematics. In addition, in Chap. 5, we shall also note how the feeling of a pendulum's swing is central to artistic rhythms.

According to Norwood Russell Hanson, this ancient kind of beam balance is of the utmost importance for our later science, because the "physical process of addition" begins here; that is, with the idea that weights can be added onto the pans of a balanced beam, in such a way that you can say that three objects on one side may equal one object on the other, or that $d = a + b + c$.[8] Here the ancients used real weights to add up and to "take away" or subtract. The ancients used standard weights for their balancing acts, but each culture had its own standards or **codes** of weights.

Look at the illustration of the plumb bob and the pendulum again (Fig. 2.1). Because the vertical axis can be seen to divide the horizon into equal parts, it can also be seen as an important first slice of symmetry. The vertical line divides the design into a structure with bilateral symmetry and two 90-degree angles that are equal to each other. As Weyl was quoted in the Introduction about *Ebenmass*: *The center of gravity is also the center of symmetry. Balance and symmetry go together in nature, in art, and in science.* They are tacit components in figuring out the composition of patterns and designs as you take them apart and put them back together. You can design exercises that let students play with and design images of bilateral symmetry in nature, in science, and in art. All of us animals have bilateral symmetries of paws, wings, and fins because they propel us in directions off-angled from the vertical push-down of gravitational force.[9] When you are balancing up real-world things, you can discover that that their conserved energies are always also revealed as some kind of symmetry.

In classes, students can use 2-D cutouts of right triangles and compose four of them together at right angles to each other in order to find a pyramid. Or we can rotate one right-angled cutout four times and see that the rotation composes a cone. Rotation is one of the standard operations in symmetry operations. They can measure volumes, a standard CC task in the fifth grade, and they can see how they will work with conics in high school math. We can see then how a center of gravity, drawn as vertical line up and down from the center of the earth, is a first slice of several important operations in geometry (Chap. 3).

Here then begin the inverse proportions between the movements of weights and distances. *This movement and distribution of weights and distances that lets us see an inverse ratio is the basic law of the lever.*

Let's draw a distinction here: When we use the word "ratio," which has the same Latin root as "reason" or "rationale," we mean a mathematical expression, such as 5/2. When we use the word "proportion," we think of geometrical relations, or figures that have magnitude such as position, size, shape, and area. So ratio is a term that we shall use for mathematical compositions, and proportion is a term we shall use for measurements in the natural sciences, music, and other arts.

In the future, as we progress in our studies, both in this book and in the real world, we may find a lot of formulas and other kinds of expressions of inverse ratios and proportions. For instance, in physics, there are lots of inverse square laws that began with Isaac Newton's law of gravity. So now we can assert that any expression of an inverse ratio—as applied in the real world—will be based on a measure of relative balance. In Chap. 3, we shall find some equations that represent inverse ratios and proportions, and in Chap. 4, we shall find some balanced sentences that are expressed as inverse proportions. Why are inverse proportions so common in our methods of inquiry? Let students observe that we are always counterbalancing opposing forces of energy.

Notice that though the ideal might be a kind of static balance expressed as an equation, the real world issue is always about a dynamic balancing act in a world of change and contradictions (See Chap. 5).

Background: A central feature of physics is called "energy balance." In the following definition, energy balance is expressed in terms of systems theory: "The arithmetic balancing of energy inputs versus outputs for an object, reactor, or other processing system; it is positive if energy is released, and negative if it is absorbed."[10] Even though modern physical principles are characterized as inanimate movements, their understanding depends on human presumptions of balance. The basic principles of the equivalence of forces and of equal action-reaction depend upon our measuring of balance. In order to measure weights and distances on any scale, we first presume that they must balance, and we then presume that that they are equitable, that they can be written as equations. Though often unexpressed, equal balance is the basic premise and point of departure for any energy exchange.

So now we have a basic clue toward the solution of any real-world problem that is composed in three dimensions: *Look for its center of balance*. For example, as we shall see now, the center of balance of a lever is its fulcrum or pivot point.

Lever, Wheel and Axle, Pulley, Inclined Plane, Wedge, Screw

By featuring the six simple tools, we bring together the basic building blocks of machine technology and mathematical ratios. As a classroom exercise, you can introduce the six machines by screening a graphic enactment.[11] We compose more complex machines from these components.

A lever is a kind of balance beam where the fulcrum is off-angled to the effort and the resistance. Levers make our work easier. A simple classroom exercise requires a hammer and a nail. A claw hammer can pry up a nail because its off-angled arm lets the head serve as a fulcrum against wood. If the nail resists the claw hammer, you can use a crow bar with a longer arm to do the job. When you use a longer crowbar, you have moved the radius of rotation at a distance farther from the fulcrum, just like a smaller child moves outward from the fulcrum on a seesaw. If the nail still resists, you might use a much longer pry bar, five-feet long, to do the job. Although you might say to yourself, "This hammer is not long enough!" you do not need language to do the job by itself. You don't need to say, "Hammer! Hammer! Hammer!" There is no linguistic **code**, but there is a mechanical **code**, the tools that make up the six basic machines. Driving a nail with a hammer is one of the 50 dangerous things that you might let your children try out.[12]

Depending on the grade level, you can discuss the issues more technically. In the Next Generation Science Standards, exercises in "Push-and pull" begin in the first grade. These are embodied feelings of *force* that you put on an object, or that the object puts on you by its resistance, its massive weight. We are showing students how simple tools like the lever transport and exchange energy as force. We can cover the inverse law of the lever, beginning in the fifth grade. As we have seen, the ratio of the moving weight to the moved weight is the inverse of the distance from the fulcrum's center. Children have learned intuitively that a resisting weight moves more easily as they move the effort farther away from the center of the fulcrum, like the child moving farther out on the seesaw. You can begin to work through the mechanical advantage of a hammer as opposed to a longer crow bar.

You can also point out that the lever or the seesaw is not just moving straight up and down, but it is moving in a semicircle. The movement up and down is truly an arc of rotation. You can demonstrate by making pinwheels in order to show that the arc of a lever is the same kind of circular motion as windmill blades or propellers on airplanes. The six basic kinds of machines are all interrelated by the same rotational laws that we saw in the section about Archimedes' lever. In all such exercises, we are assembling composites—combinations of interrelated rotational patterns. As we said in the Introduction, all these exercises point to the idea that the lever, the equation, and the sentence are ways of *combining* ideas and things into new discoveries.

First-Class Levers

There are three kinds or classes of levers, and there are three parts to each class of lever. The parts are located (1) at the pivoting point on the fulcrum, (2) at the point of effort, and (3) at the point of resistance. As we shall see, a first-class lever has the pivoting point at the middle. A second-class lever has the point of resistance in the middle. A third-class lever has the point of effort in the middle.

A bending human arm is the prototype of a first-class lever: Weight or resistance is held in the hand. Effort is located toward the end of the lever where the biceps muscle is attached, and fulcrum is at the elbow. A seesaw and a balance scale are basic examples of first-class levers, where the fulcrum is at the middle. In both examples, the fulcrum is located somewhere between the resistance and the effort.

Another gripping example of a first-class lever is the oar on a rowboat: The rower's hand at the end of the oar provides the effort. An oarlock at the middle of the oar is the fulcrum or pivot point, and the water is the resistance. Let's consider rowing in terms of the Sender-Receiver diagram. We recall that in rowing, even when we grasp the oar handle, we are feeling the resistance at the other end, as the blade strokes through the water. We send a message of contact in a direction along the oar toward the resisting element, so it is as if we actually receive the message down at the other end where we feel the resistance. Brain and muscle coordinate in balancing feedback.

If you have ever rowed a boat yourself, you know that you need to coordinate your oars so that they move back and forth together so as to keep the boat heading in a straight direction. Your brain coordinates your sense of muscular balancing with your mental awareness of a good direction. You may have also noticed that as your oars stroke into the water, they make little curlicue ripples in the resisting water. If you look even closer, you can see that the ripples on one side of the boat are rotating in the opposite direction from the other. This is an example of balanced moments of opposing forces.[13]

This kind of counterbalancing rotational turn is technically called a "balancing moment." So:

"Clockwise Movements = Counterclockwise Movements."[14]

This principle turns out to be an extremely important physical law that applies to many machines. For instance, in order to understand the lift of airplane, you need to deal with moments of force that are at work in the plane's composition of weight.[15]

Second-Class Levers

An example of a second-class lever is a wheelbarrow, where the fulcrum is located at the wheel, the resistance is in the middle (seen as a weight in the barrow), and the effort is seen as the hands, arms, and back lifting upward. Another example of a second-class lever is a door hinge. Here the fulcrum is at the hinge; the resistance is again at the middle, where the weight of the door is centered, and the effort is located where a hand pulls the door open or pushes it closed. The closer you try to push the door to the hinge, the harder the work you must do. Correspondingly, if you push at the door closed at its outer edge, it is easier work. The harder you work the more energy you spend. If you combine two second-class levers together, you can make scissors or a nutcracker. The pivot or hinge is at one end, the resistance is in the middle, and the effort is at the other end.

Third-Class Levers

When we use a hammer to drive a nail, we are applying a third-class lever. The fulcrum is at the wrist; the effort works through the hand, and the resistance is at the nail penetrating the wood. Also, think of a fishing rod.

Tongs

Now we can begin to combine levers into moving tools and machines. When we combine two levers together, we can compose some very useful hinged tools. Scissors are composed of two first-class levers combined together. Nut crackers combine two second-class levers composed together. Tongs and tweezers are tools that are composed of two third-class levers combined together at a pivoting hinge. You may have seen or used fireplace tongs. You grab hot food or coal or logs with tongs. You grab an object in between their arms, but at a distance. Its fulcrum is a hinge located at the top ends of the arms. Its effort is located in the middle, and the points of resistance are at the ends. The arms widen and rotate from a fixed center of balance, much like a fixed pendulum. They are hinged pincers, like crab or lobster or crawfish claws, which grab something between the arms, where the weight or resistance is clamped at the ends of the arms.

Background: Ages ago, as long ago as the Iron Age, tongs were surely invented by the fireside to hold fiery coals at a distance, much like barbecue tongs hold and flip food cooking on a burning grill. Blacksmiths must have perfected tongs in order to grasp red-hot metals at a distance that would become forged into other tools. A blacksmith uses tongs to make another tool, such as a rim for a wheel or a horseshoe. Jacob Bronowski uses the example of tongs to show that its invention demonstrates an ability among early humans to plan ahead, to break down an operation into a series of steps into an orderly progression that reaches the sum of its parts.[16] Tongs were tools of discovery. Bronowski also associates this distancing as a kind of futures thinking, an ability to think forward, to anticipate a possible outcome, and he says this requires the invention of a language. The invention of tools required the thinking ability that goes along with language use. "Here's how to flake a stone tool with a burin." His reasoning is based on the idea that language is a kind of second-order tool that can think back upon itself and think forward too. Linguists call this use of language to think about language itself a "meta-language." We plan ahead with second-order tools (tools to make tools), so we put off immediate gratification for the pleasure of finding something out in a future (See Chap. 4, "The Sentence," for further discussion of this kind of futures surmise).

Tongs are second-order tools, that is, tools with which to make other tools. They keep our fingers and hands at a distance. As we shall see, a fundamental *displacement* characterizes a lot of exchanges of physical information and their transformation into tools. For example, a rock used by a craftsman has been taken out of its resting place in nature and has been transformed to a new kind of use. When a craftsman learns how to split rock with a tool, he learns that certain kinds of rock, like flint or chert or obsidian, split along their grains better than others like sandstone.

Dividers and Compasses: Basic Measures of Scale and Proportion

A **Compass**, a part of our geometry tool kit, is also a kind of stylized tong that measures angles and arcs on a 2-D plane. Imagine in the olden days a blacksmith rotating his tongs in the ashes of a fire and describing a circle. Here the fulcrum becomes at one end an axis of rotation, with one leg at the axis. For instance, the oldest existing map of the world shows Babylon at the center with water all around, and it is drawn with a pair of dividers, where one leg has punctured the center of a damp clay tablet, and the other has been rotated around so that it inscribed a circle. You can screen an exemplary online image with a smart board.[17] Nowadays, a compass, with its levered legs, is a tong displaced from its 3-D origins. It measures scale and proportion on a 2-D plane, like a map on paper. When you master the use of dividers and compasses, you see the fundamental, the extremely important relation between straight-edge angles and arcs of rotation. Angles and arcs go together in proportionate measures. Also, you may begin measuring the changing radius of a circle by increasing or decreasing the legs of the compass. When that ancient student computed the changing radius on a balance beam, quoted above, perhaps he was using a compass instead of a straight edge.

In order to understand scale and proportion as exact measures, you need to use a small thing to measure a large thing. You need a tool like this to build a model of your project. You need a physical object as transmitter, with a symbolic code built in. This is a second-order tool that uses a small part to measure the whole frame. Notice that compasses or dividers are levered tongs that have been abstracted or diverted away from the handling of real things of tactile experience. They measure images on a 2-D plane.

Calipers belong to the family of tong-like levers that include scissors, nutcrackers, and tweezers. Calipers can measure the volumes of 3-D objects, either their outsides or their insides. They can also be used as drawing tools, along with compasses, in order to measure dimensions on a 2-D plane. For a clever example, in the collections of the American Museum of Natural History, there is an odd pair of calipers shaped like an outstretched human body, which can measure both outsides and insides by means of one tool.[18] It is a witty example of a body-based tool, which has been transferred from real space to another context. For its outstretched arms are pointed inward to measure the outsides of figure, while its feet

Fig. 2.4 Body-based calipers
The inward pointing hands let you measure the outer diameter of an object, and the outward pointing feet let you measure the inner diameter of a hollow object like a pipe. Here the hinge pivots at the midsection

are pointed outward to measure the insides. The body is hinged at a middle pivot, so the two pairs of calipers can be widened or narrowed around a central axis of rotation. For a diagram, see Fig. 2.4.

Some anonymous craftsman saw that he could combine two separate hinged levers, clamped upside down together, into one tool. Then maybe he saw that the fused and opposed tools also looked like the arms and legs of a human body. That discovery was a small Eureka moment of playful combination (Chap. 5), and the craftsman liked the fusion so much that he composed the tool out of brass. Notice the physical components: A bilaterally symmetric human body, with outstretched arms and legs, can be seen as being composed of rigid rotating pendulums, hinged at a center of balance, and all together a neat little third-class lever.

Dividers and compasses are levered tools that can help map the geography of the earth or the astronomy of the stars. On a road map, for instance, you might find a distance scale that represents increments of 1 inch for 25 miles. So you could use your compass to compute a distance (Now a GPS in your car will of course do that calculation for you).

A map is a basic small-scale model that lets you predict where you are, where you have been going, and when you might arrive. Next Generation Science Standards feature modeling throughout the proposed curriculum:

Developing and Using Models

> Modeling in 3–5 builds on K–2 experiences and progresses to building and revising simple models and using models to represent events and design solutions.
>
> Develop a model to describe phenomena. (5-PS1-1)
> Scientific Knowledge Assumes an Order
> and Consistency in Natural Systems
> Science assumes consistent patterns in
> natural systems. (5-PS1-2)

As we consider tools and models in relation to the "consistency of natural systems," take the example of a gull-wing door hinge (See visual examples online). Here a kind of lever, a hinge, is seen as a kind of natural hinge, the rotator joint of a bird. Like a pair of compasses, the two doors are seen as wings that open and close. Here is a line diagram of a gull or tern that can be seen in terms of our Sender-Receiver diagram, drawn on an x–y grid (Fig. 2.5). The discipline that studies the application of natural systems to human uses, especially tools and machines, is called "bionics." There is no more basic bionic transfer than the transfer of arms and legs and such both for real and for the use of graphic descriptions, as in the arms of a sofa or the legs of a table (See the calipers, drawn as a human body, Fig. 2.4). The reason for this possibility of design is that nature loves pairs, and nature loves to put pairs in balance.

Summary of Levers

To summarize the work of the three kinds of levers, here is a passage from *Basic Machines* (I, 3):

ARCHIMEDES' LEVER 57

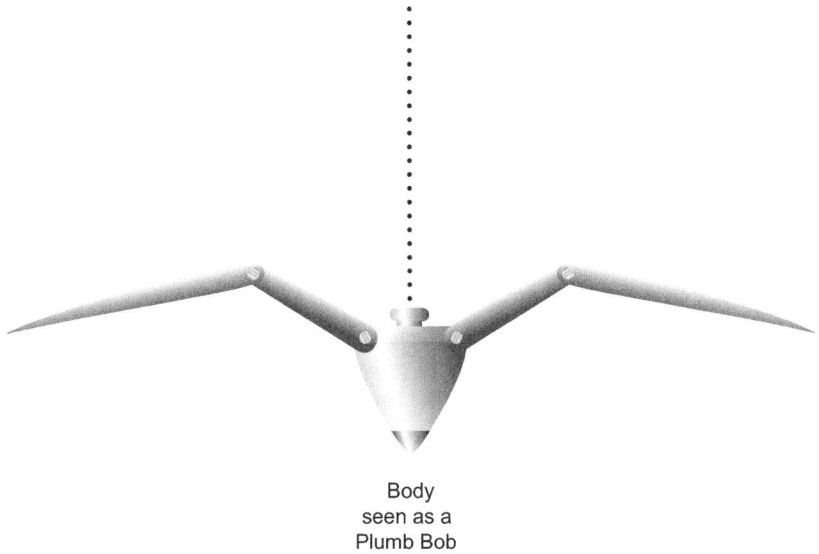

Body
seen as a
Plumb Bob

Here the diamond represents the gull's body, and it helps to situate the bird's center of gravity, as if it were a plumb bob hanging from a cord on a balance scale. If you position the center of gravity along a vertical axis, you can see how the bilateral symmetry of the two wings on either side are offset along a horizontal axis. Can you picture the two wings as if they were two halves of a seesaw, going up and down in alteratingrotations?

Fig. 2.5 Hinged gull wings
For balancing maneuvers, nature loves jointed or hinged pairs, such as wings, fins, arms and legs

> First- and second-class levers can be used
> to magnify the amount of the effort exerted,
> and to decrease the speed of effort. First-class
> and third-class levers can be used to
> magnify the distance and the speed of the effort
> exerted, and to decrease its magnitude.
> The same general formula [quoted above] applies to all
> three types of levers.

Mechanical Advantage

Mechanical advantage (MA) is an expression of the ratio of the applied force and the resistance:

$$M.A. = R / A.$$

Now if you want to write an equation that describes the *balance of physical forces*, you could write:

$$\frac{L}{l} = \frac{R}{E}$$

Let L the length of the effort arm
 l the length of the resistance arm
 R the resistant weight (force of gravity)
 E the force of effort (See *Basic Machines*, 1-4)

This balance of forces is called by NASA "The Law of Equilibrium:"

> A lever is in equilibrium when the effort and the load balance each other. The law of equilibrium is: The effort multiplied by its distance from the fulcrum equals the load multiplied by its distance from the fulcrum. This law of equilibrium is true for all classes of levers.
>
> For example, 2 pounds of effort exerted 4 feet from the fulcrum will lift 8 pounds located 1 foot on the other side of fulcrum .... This effort times distance about the fulcrum is the torque, the rotational force referred to in the gears (wheel and axle) tutorial.[19]

In sum, the law of the lever is: The load or mass is in inverse proportion to the distance moved.

Wheel and Axle

Once students begin to understand the relations between rotational, horizontal, and vertical motions, we can experiment with other basic machines that employ this principle about circular force, which is called "torque" above. For instance, a wrench is another example of a tool that uses rotation to turn a resisting object, like a nut on a bolt. The combination of a rotary device with a fixed piece that increases force or torque is called a wheel and axle (*Basic Machines*, Chap. 3, "The Wheel and Axle"). The fundamental purpose of a wheel attached to an axle is to redirect the direction of motion, from circular motion to horizontal or linear motion. Or vice versa. Almost everywhere you see a wheel in our culture, you can be sure that an axle is also at work. For instance, consider the way a doorknob works as a composite of wheel and axle. The size of the knob increases the torque that turns the small shaft inside the knob. If the knob comes off by mistake, you may learn how hard it is to turn that small four-sided shaft with your fingers. By increasing the diameter of the wheel, you can increase the force on the shaft. Just as a longer pry bar increases the force on a resisting object, so too a longer wrench rotates in a circle that increases the force on an object. Depending on the interests of those students who have a knack for this sort of balancing in the round, you can discuss mechanical advantage, moments of force, and balancing moments.

Classroom Exercise: Gears and Pulleys on a Bike

Here is a book called *Let's Ride a Bike* that is linked to Next Generation Science Standards. It defines and explains the parts and functions of a bike. For instance, it provides templates of sprockets of different sizes. It explains how one form of energy is converted into another.[20] After a child has taken apart a toy car, as Feynman suggests, perhaps beginning the science of taking things apart, by observing and then by reassembling them, she may move on to the composition of a bicycle. First she needs to learn how to ride it by keeping it in a moving balance. By trial and error, she learns how to pedal it and how not to wobble it back and forth but to keep it moving smoothly in a direction with a minimum of lurching the handlebars back and forth. She learns a dynamic balancing act by doing it over and over until she has the skill. She doesn't read a book, maybe called *Biking for Dummies*. She doesn't look at pictures. With a little guidance from a parent, maybe, she learns the skill tacitly by body, eye, and mental coordination. She certainly isn't told to memorize a formula for the dynamics of balancing. Michael Polanyi puts it this way about balance, our large topic:

> We cannot learn to keep our balance on a bicycle by taking to heart that in order to compensate for a given angle of imbalance a, we must take a curve on the side of the imbalance, of which the radius (r) should be proportionate to the square of the velocity (v) over the imbalance:
>
> $$r \approx \frac{v^2}{a}$$

He says that this kind of formulaic knowing is ineffective because we need to know the skill of biking tacitly.[21] (See Chap. 3 for formulas and equations.) The biker has tacitly learned the skill, and now she takes explicit pleasure in the rhythmic feeling of speeding balance.

Now back to the next steps of figuring out how the bike keeps her flowing. If a biker cleans her bike, she studies its parts. It's laborious to clean all the spokes on the wheels, but she may learn from this experience that the arrangement of the spokes is elegant, and she may see too that the skinny rim is a kind of bent-around lever that is held together by arrangement of spokes. A bike wheel is a perfect example of tension and compression. If she thinks of the toothed wheel on a bike as a kind of gear with ratchets, she will see that it is rotated on its axle by a chain, which is a kind of pulley. Each ratchet is a little lever. When she shifts gears on the bike to go up an inclined plane, a steeper hill for instance, then she switches over to the smaller toothed wheel, but she must pedal faster even as the resistance on the pedal is less (See *Basic Machines*, 3-2 to 3-3). The pedal on a bike, she learns, is a kind of crank which transforms rotary motion into linear motion in a direction. The crank is an amazingly important lever. A soon as we recognize how many machines convert energy via wheel and axle, then we know the importance of cranks.

Here is another example of a pulley, which is said to have been invented by Archimedes. A crane that lifts and transports large loads of massive energy is a big mechanical lever. You may have watched a crane at work in a construction site. One "arm" of the crane is attached to a rotating wheel base, while the top of the other arm has a pulley attached to it. The pulley serves as a rotating hinge and is fulcrum of the lever. A long rope is threaded through the pulley, and it usually has a grappling hook of some kind swinging at the end of the rope.[22] Other ropes let the arm move upward, downward, and sideways, as it lifts and lowers heavy weights. There is also a system of counterweights in place to keep the whole machine in balance.

A pulley allows you to pull a heavy weight with a length of rope that rotates around a wheel inside a block. The heavier the weight the more pulleys you need and the longer the rope you need to move the weight. You can see how leverage is achieved. The cost is that the distance moved is very small in comparison to the very long length of rope you need to pull. A basic pulley in a workshop is called a "come-along."

The Inclined Plane, the Wedge, and the Screw Are All Interrelated

When a heavier child on a seesaw sits on the ground, the child at the other end is sitting high in the air on an inclined plane. If she didn't hold on to the handlebars, she could slide down a slope, like rolling down a hill. Students can begin to see now how a lever is related to an inclined plane. On a highway system, any up-ramp or down-ramp is an inclined plane, on which a heavy car is being raised by a small force over a long distance. That is the mechanical advantage of an inclined plane; you can economize on force by increasing distance. A jeep or a tank can climb a steeper angle of a plane over a shorter distance, but not an automobile (*Basic Machines*, 4-1). Can you see the trade-off of mechanical advantage? You can either carry a heavy load a short way or carry a lighter load a longer way. There is a trade-off as you exchange kinds of energy and work.

A roller coaster in an amusement park is composed of a series of inclined planes and curves that use force plus gravity for its speeds and for riders' thrills. First the roller coaster gets slowly cranked up to its highest point. The ride begins on a car at the highest point of the ride. Here the potential energy of the ride is at its highest point too. As the car decreases in height, it increases in speed, and its kinetic energy increases, while it loses potential energy. Physicists and engineers can calculate "the rates of exchange" between the two kinds of energy as the car goes up, down, and around.[23] Our Sender-Receive diagram lets you see how energy can be exchanged, transformed, and conserved on a balance plane. Several web sites let you measure the differences in a roller coaster's energy, on a graph.[24] You can do this graphing as a classroom exercise.

Our feeling of vertigo in amusement park rides is the opposite of a feeling of balance. Playground games like seesaws and swings, and amusement park rides like roller coasters and tilt-a-whirls are designed to incite the thrill of intoxicating irrationality.[25] For Roger Callois, vertigo is one of the four fundamental kinds of games; the others are competition, chance, and mimicry or simulation. Games of vertigo "consist of an attempt to momentarily destroy the stability of perception and inflict a kind of voluptuous panic upon an otherwise lucid mind. In all cases it is a question of surrendering to a kind of spasm, seizure, or shock, which destroys reality with sovereign brusqueness" (23). Remember those shrieks of pleasurable panic when you careened down a rollercoaster. You can design playground exercises that summon these thrills of imbalanced vertigo. We consider play in Chap. 5.

A Wedge Slices into the Structures of Matter

A wedge combines two inclined planes into a very important kind of tool. When you split wood with a wedge or an axe, you drive the narrow end into the longitudinal pattern of grain in a piece of wood, gradually inserting the thicker plane of the wedge into the growth lines of the wood, thereby widening the split (*Basic Machines*, 4-1). An axe head is shaped like a wedge.

When you split along the vertical growth line of a piece of wood, you are doing the same kind of splitting into its structure as you would in splitting an atom or a molecule. In solving to overcome any resistance in matter, you first look for its grain, and then you look around for a probe or pry bar as a lever. When you are looking for the grained pattern in the structure of matter, you will eventually arrive at the structure of atoms, says Jacob Bronowski. He states an extremely important assertion about how the understanding of the physical patterns of a grain in a stone can be seen as the origin of understanding the structure of an atom. He says that this early kind of recognition is the very basis of the physical science of splitting and fusing the atom along the grains of its atomic structure: "Splitting and fusing the atom all derive, conceptually, from a discovery made in prehistory: that stone and all matter has a structure along which it may be split and put together in new arrangements."[26] Notice that slitting and fusing are processes of taking things apart and putting them back together again.

Here then is the very bedrock of the physical sciences. Look for the grain, the atomic pattern where it splits along its lines of least resistance. Then, with a tool, you can recompose it and transfer it into new arrangements for a future use, but you need a tool to take it apart and then to re-compose it.

Here is a very big claim about atomic patterns. The physicist Philip Morrison argues that all knowledge is modular because all knowledge derives from the presumption that the whole world is built upon atomic building blocks or modules:

The whole of our world—radiant energy and protean matter, crystals and cells, stars and atoms, all is built of modules, whose identity and simplicity belie the unmatched diversity of the worlds of man and nature. The world is atomic, which is to say modular; our knowledge is modular as well.[27]

Atomic modules compose the patterned substance and energy of the world.

The idea that knowledge is modular is less controversial now that we understand how computer coding works from the combinations of just two kinds of bits. Morrison claims that letters, words, sentences, and such are also modular. In this chapter, we are thinking about balanced compositions in a 3-D world. Modular thinking begins with 3-D compositions of the world's patterned structures. For instance, teachers can demonstrate in class with the structures of crystals. Matter has intrinsic structures or patterns, which you can find and then manipulate with a wedge-like probe. For instance, ice has a hexagonal structure of atoms that you can split along its grain with and ice pick. When you split a piece of atomic matter along its granular pattern, you release and transform its energy, and then you can redirect the energy as force by building it into a new assemblage like a tong. For even energy comes in structured chunks. When you split a log for firewood, your axe or hatchet or wedge will split the wood along its growth lines. You are seeking to release its energy as a future fire. You need a prosthetic tool, some kind of levered probe, with its own energy patterns, to find the modular patterns in things. So a tool like a wedge or a probe releases a kind of displaced and redirected energy along a grain of atomic force. We should always look for the grain in a thing because its pattern can tell us where and how it was composed. When you want to split a piece of matter, and then reconstruct it for another use, you need a wedge-like probe.

Like Bronowski, Richard Feynman also stresses the primacy of atomic structure with regard to the basics of science. Here is his long assertion, but it is not hard to understand, and it allows us see too how our three methods of inquiry can be brought together in practice:

> If, in some cataclysm, all of scientific knowledge were to be destroyed, and only one sentence passed on to the next generation of creatures, what statement would contain the most information in the fewest words? I believe it is the *atomic hypothesis* (or the atomic *fact*, or whatever you wish to call it) that *all things are made of atoms—little particles that move around in perpetual motion, attracting each other when they are a little distance apart, but repelling upon being squeezed together.* In that one sentence, you will see, there is an enormous amount of information about the world, if just a little imagination and thinking are applied.[28] (his italics)

By way of this sentence, Hans Christian von Baeyer stresses the importance of information theory in science, because it helps to understand how "brevity of expression" characterizes the formulations of science. In addition, we can feature that one sentence which compresses much of one science into the whole idea: "all things are made of atoms. ..." Notice he says that his sentence would contain the maximum amount of information with the fewest words. Further along in this chapter and others, we discuss a kind of "mini-max equation" that expresses a maximum of information with the fewest symbols. An equation does the job (See Chap. 3). Scientists celebrate this kind of simple brevity as a "law of parsimony."

As for our larger project about unifying the lever, the equation, and the sentence, consider this. Even though you would start with the premise of atomic structure, then you would need to go to a real-world workbench or a lab, with its specialized tools, to take things apart and to re-compose them, in order to test your sentence or equation. You still need a wedge-like probe, of some kind. And you would also use some imagination and thinking to broaden the implications of the sentence (Chap. 5). All three of our methods of inquiry come together here: some kind of balance scale at the workbench or lab to measure quantities, plus the equation for a formula, and the sentence as your beginning hypothesis against which any scientific proof must be measured. We test a hypothesis with 3-D tools in the real world of the lab; we formulate a 2-D equation of some sort, and we explain it as an assertion with a 1-D sentence. Feynman brings our three kinds of problem solving in this way:

> Physics is not mathematics, and mathematics is not physics. One helps the other. But in physics you have to have an understanding of the connection of words with the real world. It is necessary at the end to translate what you have figured out into English, into the world, into the blocks of copper and glass that you are going to do the experiments with. Only in this way can you find out whether the consequences are true. This is a problem which is not a problem with mathematics at all. (*CPL*, 55–56)

It is necessary to translate what you figured out from your physical experiments using mechanical and technical tools into mathematics and language. You need an understanding of the grammatical rules for words and sentences, and how they correspond, more or less, with the physical principles of the real world. Good thinking is multi-dimensional thinking, where the three forms of inquiry triangulate as a cloverleaf.

See Next Generation Science Standards for atomic structure:

PS1.A: Structure and Properties of Matter

Matter of any type can be subdivided into particles that are too small to see, but even then the matter still exists and can be detected by other means. A model shows that gases are made from matter particles that are too small to see and are moving freely around in space can explain many observations, including the inflation and shape of a balloon; the effects of air on larger particles or objects. (5-PS1-1)

The amount (weight) of matter is conserved when it changes form, even in transitions in which it seems to vanish. (5-PS1-2)

PS1.B: Chemical Reactions

When two or more different substances are mixed, a new substance with different properties may be formed. (5-PS1-4)

No matter what reaction or change in properties occurs, the total weight of the substances does not change. (Boundary: Mass and weight are not distinguished at this grade level.) (5-PS1-2)

That concept, in other words, is the principle of the conservation of matter and energy. As for the conservation of matter when it splits and fuses, to use a fulcrum on a balance scale as a teaching metaphor for balancing the chemical equations of atomic elements is perhaps the most familiar aspect of our program.[29] In this demonstration, the use of a physical lever has been displaced for use as a scientific metaphor in order to demonstrate how a chemical equation also balances up. Here the fulcrum of a balance beam is centered upon the equals sign (=) of an equation, so that equilibrium and equivalence are seen as identical. You need to test the chemical reaction in a lab in order to see that the elements and compounds are in equilibrium, even as the equations are in equivalence. So we understand that equilibrium and equivalence are in parallel but are not identical.

The Screw

By reviewing the grainy patterns in matter, we have come a long way from the everyday world of the wedge seen as two inclined planes fused together. To continue with basic machines, think of a jack screw. If you have ever had to change a tire on a car, you might have used a jack screw to raise the car. You rotate the handle in one direction, and the car lifts in a vertical direction. You can see too that a wheel and axle are also parts of the composition.

Here is a clear explanation of how the inclined plane and the **screw** are related (See Fig. 2.6).

"A screw is a modification of an inclined plane. Cut a sheet of paper in the shape of a right triangle and you have an inclined plane. Wind this paper around a pencil and you can see that the screw is actually an inclined plane wrapped around a cylinder. As you turn the pencil, the paper is wound up so that its hypotenuse forms a spiral thread. The pitch of the screw and paper is the distance between the identical points on the same threads measured between the length of the screw" (*Basic Machines*, 5-1). You can do this in a classroom exercise as an excellent example of the interrelations between 2-D plane geometry's right triangle and 3-D screw mechanics.

Let's look more closely at this screw and spiral in terms of primal mechanics. Although the technical term is cylinder, an everyday ancient precursor would have been a round log. Long before wheels were invented,

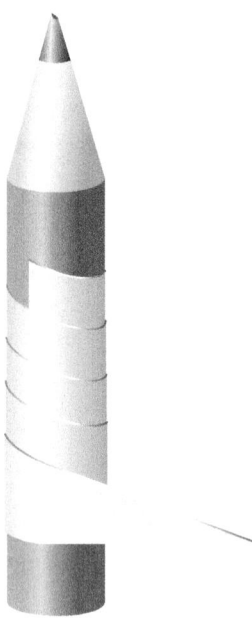

Fig. 2.6 Screw seen as an inclined plane in spiral form
Cut a right triangle (Chap. 3) out of a sheet of paper. Wind the paper around a cylinder, like a pencil. The hypotenuse of the wrapped right triangle makes a spiral line

logs were used as rollers to move heavy loads. A rolling log was both wheel and axle. You can imagine how ancient workers would keep placing rollers underneath a heavy weight to keep it moving. Now think about hauling a log roller into place with a rope. If the roller were on a hill (an inclined plane), and if by chance the roller got away from you and started rolling on its own, your rope might wrap around the log in a spiral. If you were able to pull back on the rope, the log might start spinning as the rope unwinds backward. The wrapped rope around the log has a mechanical advantage as it unwinds. You might even notice that the log spins on its own axis faster and faster, depending on the number of wraps, as the rope unwinds. You can re-enact this spinning in class with a piece of string and a pencil. You have discovered another principle of leverage. Notice too that the two primary parts are a rope and a length of wood, the ingredients of a balance beam and scale.

Classroom Exercise: Pinecones and Spirals

Students may apply these mechanical principles of screw and spiral to biomechanical principles of the spiral growth and form of plants, called *phyllotaxis*. We can ask students to think of other spiral growths in nature. How can they be applied to the inventions of newly imagined machines?

As we have seen, the most important aspect of a screw is its twist along a line. A screw in mechanics is based upon the same principles as a twist in symmetry studies. Here is an important example from bionics. A late nineteenth-century biologist named J. Bell Pettigrew described the mobile balancing acts of wings, fins, flippers as functional screws: "That the flipper of a sea-lion, the swimming wing of a penguin, and the wing of the insect, bat and bird, are screws *structurally*, and resemble the blades of an ordinary screw propeller."[30] Although Pettigrew did not know about airplane wings and propellers, his book helped the Wright brothers as they experimented with wings, by putting them together and taking them apart.[31] They experimented with wing warping by making one wing of a glider twist in the opposite rotation to the other. Much later, airplane propellers were designed with opposite twists. If you draw or exhibit a four-bladed airplane propeller, you can ask students how two of the opposing blades are shaped like the bilateral wings of birds. Then it only remains to discuss how the twisted wings provide leverage to help propel and uplift birds and planes through a resistant environment, the invisible air. *Balance and symmetry work together in animal forms and mechanical parts.*

Now students can see how the six basic machines are all interrelated, and how they can be combined together. They comprise a basic **code** of six modular combinations for the fulcrum and that begin with the lever. So many of these basic tools serve not only engineers but also hands-on experimenters in labs. Just as important, you can see from the illustration of a sheet of paper wrapped around a pencil how drawing on a 2-D plane reinforces the 3-D objects. You can see how geometry can illustrate the physics of motions (Chap. 3). The illustration also can reveal a discussion about the symmetry transformations of **Translate, Rotate**, and **Twist**. Here too we can see how these simple tools can reveal their relations with conic slices and with symmetry transformations of translate, rotate, and twist.

The Fly-Ball Governor

In the Introduction, we discussed principles of self-correction by means of balancing feedback. The machine prototype for balancing back and forth is the fly-ball governor. In the Industrial Revolution, it achieved fame as an invention that regulated the speed of James Watt's famous steam engine.[32] Gregory Bateson says that this kind of machine is a model for thinking about thinking, a circular process of self-regulation, but that is getting ahead of the story about mechanics. If you look at any illustration of a fly-ball governor online, you can see that it features several of the machine parts that we have been describing here. You can see that its two legs look like a hinged pair of dividers, which has its fulcrum at the top end. The balls at the ends of the legs whirl around in rotational cycles. A series of rollers lets the balls whirl up and down by means of centrifugal force, just like the slingshot that David used to fling a stone at Goliath. A slingshot is a kind of rotating plumb bob. The off-angled rotation of the legs provide torque for the little machine, which is very like the wheel and axle machine that converts horizontal motion into vertical motion, or vice versa. You can see how you can integrate the several kinds of machine parts into a more complex machine.

Bateson mentions that an earlier version of Watts's kind of governor was invented by Dutch wind-millers who used it to adjust for changes in wind directions. Theirs was based upon the principle of a conical pendulum, whose rotations we began with. Nowadays, wind turbines for cheap energy use the same principle of self-governance. Also, on sailboats, fantail stabilizers automatically steer a boat.

In the Introduction, we mentioned Norbert Wiener as the inventor of cybernetics, the theory of automatic self-governance. He used the Greek word for a helmsman who used the steering oar on a boat, *cybernos*, to reinforce the idea of a continuous kind of steerage that finds a middle course. You can tell what kind of a lever a tiller is. So his new theory was built upon an old mechanism. During WW II, Wiener modeled a variant of an automatic governor on an aircraft gun sight in order to predict the path of a swerving airplane. The gun sight aimed forward of the plane by tracking its back path. The mechanism predicted forward by tracing from backward. A lot of thinking predicts forward from back tracking, like the following sequence of pebbles laid down by Hansel and Gretel. The mechanism matched up the actual path of where an airplane had been with its projected future path, and it tried to find a point of convergence by balancing a middle measure of chance alternative courses, even as it swerved. We mention his invention because it is the prototype for the speed stick of video games. In the Introduction, we said that in any communication, a sent message is part of an implicit dialog between a sender and a receiver. It seems, however, that video games allow an interaction between the player and the characters in a setting. You learn the "mechanics" or codes, just like you learn the rules for chess, but now you apply them in a game that seems to fight back, so to speak. Luckily, the actors in the setting of the game, the heroes and villains, especially the villains, have not yet learned to learn how you, the player, think. If one survives long enough, an airplane pilot, or any opponent, begins to learn how you think, and s/he self-corrects in order to gauge your present and future moves. As you learn the rules of the game, you become better at it until you become expert, but so far the antagonists inside the video box haven't learned to become expert at your thinking. That future development is the stuff of robotics and computer modeling.

While discussing the interactions in video games, we can test this interactivity by asking whether there is more interaction between the sender and the receiver in a game of volleyball or badminton or tennis (See Chap. 5). If you think of the net as the middle point in the rectangle that outlines the boundaries, you can imagine its vertical line can represent the midpoint of a Sender-Receiver diagram. In those games, of course, there is a real ongoing interaction between the sender and the receiver, because in mutual balancing feedback, each player makes her own moves and anticipates the opponent's response. We can turn to checkers or chess or Go! in which each player moves a step on a board and then waits for a replay to her message. These yes-no steps on a board composed of antithetical colors imply that codes here are digital, while in the net games, the moves are continuous and analog. The board is a background framework or *context*, a significant set of patterns that also regulates the moves of the players.

To end this short section about cybernetic machines, it is worth mentioning that a fly-ball governor depends on analog coding because it is continuously self-correcting, but a thermostat in your house depends on digital coding and on-off, yes-no, switch for its mechanics (Bateson, 110–111). To summarize, let's recall that Paleolithic people first used a tool to make another tool, such as a burin used to make finely flaked edges on a knife blade. These have been called second-order tools, which require us to plan ahead, to look into a possible future. Some think too that this skill allowed Paleolithic people to develop a more supple kind of language use, for sentences are the best means by which to plan ahead, to imagine future states. The fly-ball governor is a second-order tool that regulates the speeds of another machine. In itself, it does not plan ahead, but its components regulate the speeds that are possible in the parent machine. As we have now seen, this machine can be abstracted so that it can be turned from a 3-D machine in real space and it can be represented on a 2-D plane of diagrams such as a picture of Watts's model, or even a moving picture of it that you can find readily online.[33]

Certainly the most important transfer of Watts's 3-D machine governor to 1-D language was Alfred Russell Wallace's transfer of the concept as he described an as-yet-unexplored self-balancing principle of nature. He sent the description to Charles Darwin in a letter. Each was working independently on a principle that as yet had no name. Here is a short excerpt:

> The action of this principle is exactly like that of the centrifugal governor of the steam engine; which checks and corrects any irregularities almost before they become evident; and in like manner no unbalanced deficiency in the animal kingdom can ever reach any conspicuous magnitude, because it would make itself felt at the very first step, by rendering existence difficult and extinction almost sure to follow.[34]

Here Wallace applies the new concept of centrifugal governance, the prototype of balancing feedback, in order to describe one of the most important principles of biology, which did not yet even have a name though it did seem to have a balancing factor. He transformed a sophisticated tool of the Industrial Revolution into a model of scientific discovery. While a tool is a means to an end, a model of discovery invents a possible outcome for which you do not yet foresee the real end. The machine model allowed Wallace to apply checks and balances as a principle of auto-correction to the workings of nature.

When Darwin read Wallace's letter, he immediately began to write his great book about evolution, and a new future line of research opened for biology (See Next Generation Science Standards: "Natural Selection and Evolution"). As Gleick says, "Evolution itself embodies an exchange of information between organism and environment" (9). We can ask students whether the principle is just a word, a concept, an idea, which stands for a non-verbal exchange in the environment that is self-correcting. In any case, Wallace transferred the mechanics of a fly-ball governor to serve as a model of discovery for an unknown concept. A tool is a means to an end. A model is a figment of an imagined end. When we are trying to discover something new, don't we imagine that the end point comes before the means of achieving that end? We imagine futures with sentences, but we enlarge the realm of language with visual thinking and with real models and machines. Wallace used a mix of different kinds of thinking in order to compose a new self-balancing concept in nature. Although Wallace introduced a new concept about species interacting within the environment, his idea of small magnitudes of change stressed almost invisible balancings within nature that were going on continuously all the time. Evolution occurs as species make **contact** with environmental changes. These changes occur in the present, but they make no predictions about future changes. For evolution does not predict futures. We can make predictions with tools, like a barometer, which we begin to consider now.

Water as Lever

Although not often seen in this way, water can be used as a kind of fluid lever. For instance, a water screw is an ancient machine used for pumping water from a lower level to a higher. Some say that Archimedes also invented it, and it is thoroughly described as a useful tool in Vitruvius's *Ten Books of Architecture*.[35] It combines an inclined plane with a screw. A hollow tube is composed with a long rotating screw enclosed inside it. When the tube is set an angle with one end placed in a source of water to be pumped out, and the other end set a higher elevation, one can turn a handle and pump the water up and out of the tube. Vitruvius says that the right triangle's inclination should be set so that the parts correspond with the lengths of the Pythagorean theorem (See Chap. 3): the height at the top of the screw consists of three lengths; the horizontal base consists of four lengths, while the screw, seen as the hypotenuse, equals five lengths (See Chap. 3). The angled water screw is a kind of gear that uplifts by leverage. There are plenty of illustrations and descriptions online.

Although water both yields and resists a pressure, it will support a boat as long as the boat's center of gravity is well designed for stability. The fulcrum of a boat is the center of gravity at its keel. If you have ever stepped into a small boat, you feel immediately that it is tippy. You need to avoid stepping too far on one side or other of the boat, or else you might spill into the water. If the boat overturns, it pivots in a severe arc of rotation. If you sit right in the middle, shifting your weight as need be, you find the boat's center of balance. It is surprising how many students have never experienced this feeling of stepping into a tippy small boat. The boat is working like a floating fulcrum.

A boat is a perfect model of a balanced mechanical composition that exhibits a tense harmony of opposing energies. It balances oppositions between its weight and its buoyancy. It resolves oppositions between the thinness and density of its walls. It uses curves that bend and stretch away from the long straight line of its directional aim along the keel. A boat can be seen as a floating balance of beautiful forms in tense opposition. A boat is a dynamic form of balance that floats on the great primal form of flow. Even a gigantic cargo ship, stacked high with containers, or a super tanker, weighted down low with oil, can be seen as beautiful. A tense harmony of opposing forces or energies will be a basic definition of composed beauty in Chap. 5.

In the *Wikipedia* definition, we saw that a plumb line and a water level or spirit level had a similar use in building. The plumb line helps a builder find a vertical line at its center of gravity, and a water level helps set the exact horizontal line. We recall that the center of gravity is the center of balance, and that is also the center of a vertical slice of symmetry that divides something into equal parts. In science, this center of balance is also expressed as the equivalence of opposing forces. So let us review some of the implications of water and balance.

Vitruvius saw that water is not exactly level like a plane but that its surface is spherical, and its center is at the center of the earth. "Perhaps some reader of the works of Archimedes will say that there can be no true leveling by means of water, because he holds that water has not a level surface, but is of a spherical form, having its centre at the centre of the earth" (243). If you have ever used a carpenter's spirit level, you can see through the little window that a spherical bubble moves back and forth so that you can find the center of the bubble is the center of balance and the true horizontal along the balance beam of the tool. The bubble in a spirit level is a kind of fulcrum too because it shows the pivot point at the center of a convex arc. The spherical arc of a bubble mirrors in small the large sphere of the earth.

Since time immemorial, people have known that water flows downhill to its lowest level. But it also flows back uphill as evaporation, in a water cycle that can also be measured in terms of balances. In Next Generation Science Standards, fifth graders learn concepts of water flow through an ecosystem. In grade 4, they learn about weather. Early on, students learn that they can experience a water level by looking closely at a still pond, or lake. So fifth graders can better understand large principles of water balancing in an ecosystem, its atmospherics, once they have learned the small principle of water balancing in a bathtub or a coffee cup.

Classroom Exercise

Archimedes also worked with water balancing. You can tell the story of the king who wanted to know whether his new crown was made of pure gold. Review his famous "Eureka!" moment of discovery that eventually became his law of buoyancy. Archimedes' law of buoyancy says that when an object is put in water, its weight displaces an equal amount of water. So a boat will float if its own weight displaces an equal weight of water. It is then buoyant. It is balanced.

In a submerged submarine, for instance, the air pressure within must balance with the large amount of water pressure without.[36] A submarine contains tanks that contain both water and air. When the sub's tanks are filled with water, it sinks below the surface of the water because its density is greater than the surrounding water. It also stores compressed air, which, when released, allows the sub to rise upward. So hull designers of ships and airplanes always measure the differences between the thinness and thickness of the steel walls, as opposed to pressures from the surrounding medium. Sailors must not let a sub sink too far downward, else they are in peril of having the walls of the sub collapse under increasing outward pressure from the sea. They must seek a balanced middle measure between the opposing forces. Water has mass because it is composed of atoms and molecules. Because water is composed of matter, and has density, it can be used as a kind of yielding spring that raises and lowers other things.

Air as a Lever

Air too is composed of atoms and molecules that have density. So air can be put to work as a lever. Students can work with a famous experiment attributed to Robert Boyle, that the dense pressure of a gas at a constant temperature is inversely proportionate to its volume in a closed space. In the seventeenth century, when people discovered this principle, they first had to conclude that air is dense, that it is truly matter, that it is not just the locale of airy spirits. Many students will have worked with a bicycle pump, so we can work with that tool to see when the arm pushes downward, how the decreased volume increases pressure within the chamber so that air flows into the tire. Pressure increases when volume of the matter decreases, and as volume increases, pressure decreases. This law is usually expressed as an inverse proportion: $p = 1/v$. A barometer works by this principle: where pressure varies inversely with volume.[37] For a related exercise, specifically related to weather, students can make a water barometer that measures air pressure.[38] Although a falling barometer can tell us that the weather is changing now, it can also let us predict that it may be getting worse.

All of these tools give us leverage in the present. They are extensions of our limbs that make our work easier by means of levering. Using a fulcrum for a task gives us a momentary fulcrum, a temporary balancing, in our everyday tasks. Furthermore, by inventing a new lever for a task, whether a tong or a calipers or a new kind of wheel, or a model of discovery, we probe ahead into a possible future that still is part of our real world of three-space.

Isaac Newton's Three Laws of Motion

Next Generation Science Standards: Middle School, Forces and Interactions

> MS-PS2-1. Apply Newton's Third Law to design a solution to a problem involving the motion of two colliding objects.
>
> Clarification Statement: Examples of practical problems could include the impact of collisions between two cars, between a car and stationary objects, and between a meteor and a space vehicle. Assessment Boundary: Assessment is limited to vertical or horizontal interactions in one dimension.
>
> MS-PS2-2. Plan an investigation to provide evidence that the change in an object's motion depends on the sum of the forces on the object and the mass

of the object. Clarification Statement: Emphasis is on balanced (Newton's First Law) and unbalanced forces in a system, qualitative comparisons of forces, mass and changes in motion (Newton's Second Law), frame of reference, and specification of units. Assessment Boundary: Assessment is limited to forces and changes in motion in one dimension in an inertial reference frame, and to change in one variable at a time. Assessment does not include the use of trigonometry.

In order to summarize what we have said about balancing tools based on a fulcrum, and in order to set up some issues about equations to be discussed in the next chapter, let's consider Newton's three laws of motion in relation to tools and to the movements of the human body. For these basic tools extend from principles of motion at work in our bodies, and for that matter, in any animal body.

Let's say again that these laws of motion are also balance laws: "Emphasis is on balanced (Newton's First Law) and unbalanced forces in a system, qualitative comparisons of forces, mass and changes in motion (Newton's Second Law), frame of reference, and specification of units." It's good to memorize these laws, perhaps by using your own terms. Here they are:

1. Every object persists in its state of rest or uniform motion in a straight line unless it is compelled to change that state by forces impressed on it.
2. Force is equal to change of momentum (mV) per change in time. For a constant mass, force equals mass times acceleration. $F = ma$.
3. For every action there is an equal and opposite reaction.[39]

Here is a shortcut for remembering the three laws: 1: inertia, 2: acceleration, and 3: equal action-reaction.

With Newton's laws of motion, we have perhaps the most famous expressions of equivalence, which we shall study in Chap. 3. In order to demonstrate the coherence of our three compositional systems, how they go together and reinforce each other in actual practice, recall that all motions of mass and energy in the physical world, from the cradle to the playground to the lab, include all three of Newton's laws of motion. Exercises in the Next Generation Science proposal cover these laws in successive grades of middle school.

Once you have understood these three laws, you might see that the third law includes the first two: Every action requires an equal and opposite reaction. We have enlarged this principle to say: for every rotation in three-space, there is an equal and balanced rotation in the opposite direction. Here is the physical basis of equal measure. Notice that this sentence is explicitly a dynamic balance law, based on a Sender-Receiver exchange of elements in action. Notice that design principles of equality, opposition, and proportion are involved.

As we study these laws, please recall the formula for balancing ratios, described above:

$$\frac{L}{l} = \frac{R}{E}$$

You can see how this equation is an expression of Newton's third law. But notice an important point here as we think about equal action and then reaction. In order to gauge the equal forces, you need to find the balancing point, the fulcrum, the pivot, which divides the contrary opposing forces. Where is the instant point of reversal where the turn occurs? Our Sender-Receiver diagram helps to reinforce the point that to solve a balancing problem, it helps to locate the fulcrum at the center. As we shall see in Chap. 5, this point of return is central to the arts as well as the sciences.

Here is an example of how the three forms of composition—the lever, the equation, and the sentence—go together. Newton's second law of motion is expressed first in his own kind of language: "A change in motion is proportional to the motive force impressed and takes place along the straight line in which that force is impressed."[40] How, exactly, are change in motion and a change in force to be thought of as proportional? How would you compose this in a simpler sentence? (See Chap. 4, section on Proportion). Notice that Newton's word "impression" indicates an accurate sense of physical contact. Our current use of the word "impression" has only the slightest feeling of physical pressure.

And then here is the algebraic equation for the second law: $F = ma$. Notice that it also incorporates Newton's first law, about inertia, and motion in a straight line. James Trefil and Robert Hazen express the balance nicely with a balanced sentence: "The greater the force, the greater the acceleration, but the more massive the object, the smaller the acceleration."[41] You need a lot more force to propel a car up a ramp than a motorcycle. Since this law too is one of the most familiar in science, it pays to remember its formula. "The equation conforms to our intuition that an object's acceleration is a balance between two factors: force and mass"

(*TS*, 48). Balanced sentences work best when they are expressing balanced or opposed ideas. In the explanation of Newton's three laws of motion, we can see how scientists work back and forth among our three basic forms of composition to explain the three concepts.

In terms of work, we see that these laws of motion can be composed in "mini-max" terms of inverse ratios or proportions. We express them as equations and we express them in sentences (An equation often strives to say more and more with less and less signs, a law of parsimony, while a sentence usually opts for a balance of more and less. See Chap. 4). A massive object requires more force and moves slower than a small object's acceleration. A lever requires a longer length to move a more massive object. On a pulley, a longer length of rope is required each time you add another block to the tackle. We are making our work easier with one of these tools that give us leverage over a resisting environment, but while the work may be less effortful, it takes a little bit longer to complete the task. We take a little more time to move an object in space. We trade off speed and distance and time. When balancing things in our work, we are always compensating for opposing forces.

This avoidance of effortful work by way of levering tools is part of a large principle called "least effort," and it applies to the ways we think as well as the ways we move objects around in the real world of objects. According to Daniel Kahneman,

> A general "law of least effort" applies to cognitive as well as physical exertion. The law asserts that if there are several ways of achieving the same goal, people will eventually gravitate to the least demanding course of action. In the economy of action, effort is a cost, and the acquisition of skill is driven by the balance of benefits and costs. Laziness is built deep into our nature.[42]

We shall see in the next chapters that we "balance" these extremes by seeking a middle measure. However, we are not always lazy, but often we work hard, with lots of effort, to achieve a worthy end.

In conclusion, let's see how Newton's laws translate into human and animal motions. For they will help us to understand how we move by way of resistance in an environmental framework, and how tools give us leverage in our work. Here is how a biologist transfers Newton's third law to an animal's movements. In *Animal Locomotion*, James Gray shows how Newton's third law of motion works for animals within an environmental framework:

'For every action there must be an equal and opposite reaction.' Translated into biological terms, this can be expressed by saying that, in order to subject the body to a forward propulsive force, the animal must simultaneously exert an exactly equal but opposite backward force against its external environment; the animal moves forward because the environment resists the movement of fins, legs, or wings relative to the body.[43]

Life forms counterthrust in a *resisting* environment. Life forms must *leverage with limbs* against the opposing forces in their environs, whether on land or see or air. Here then, with animal bodies, is the origin of mechanical leverage. Mechanics begins with the biomechanics of propulsion. Life forms are the pivot points, the centers of balance between opposing environmental forces of action and reaction. Their evolved designs let them twist and shake and pivot in their locales. Recall that the point of resistance is one of the essential parts of a lever. A child pushes against the ground to lift herself upward on a seesaw against the downward pull of gravity. A fish swims forward by pushing backward in water, its resisting environmental context. A rocket shoots forward because the backward force of the propellant confronts the resistance of its airy environment, while the total energy is conserved or balanced before and after. These laws of motion do not just apply in physics textbooks; they also enter into environmental laws of balanced force. The limbs of animals, their legs, their fins, their wings, work as levers to propel them forward in a direction. Now we can see how we compose six basic tools into machines that use environmental resistance to complete our work.

Notes

1. Richard Feynman, "What Is Science?" in *The Pleasure of Finding Things Out*, ed. Jeffrey Robins (New York: MJF Books, 1999), 179.
2. Karl Menninger, *Number Words and Number Symbols: A Cultural History of Numbers*, trans. Paul Broneer (Cambridge: The M. I. T. Press, 1969), 175.
3. See *Common Core Standards and Strategies Flip Chart*, "Vocabulary and Strategies," Panel 8. Hereafter cited as *Flip Chart*.
4. On seesaws, see https://www.teachengineering.org/activities/view/nyu_seesaw_activity1
5. See *Wikipedia*, for "plumb bob". https://en.wikipedia.org/wiki/Plumb_bob
6. Lancelot Hogben, *Mathematics for the Million* (New York: Norton, 1968), 45.

7. See E. J. Dijksterhuis, *Archimedes*, trans. C. Dikshoon (Copenhagen: Ejnar Munksgaard, 1956). Find it online at *Archimedes Home Page*: http://www.math.nyu.edu/~crorres/Archimedes/Lever/LeverLaw.html
8. See Norwood Hanson, *Perception and Discovery: An Introduction to Scientific Inquiry*, ed. Willard C. Humphries (San Francisco: Freeman, Cooper & Company, 1969), 49–50. Hereafter cited as *PD*.
9. See James H. Bunn, *The Natural Law of Cycles: Governing the Mobile Symmetries of Animals and Machines* (New Brunswick: Transaction Publishers, 2014). Hereafter cited as *NLC*.
10. *McGraw Hill Science and Technology Dictionary.* https://books.google.com/books/about/McGraw_Hill_dictionary_of_scientific_and.html?id=9t83ABfTBvQC
11. A graphic description of the six machines is at Idaho Public Television: http://idahoptv.org/sciencetrek/topics/simple_machines/facts.cfm
12. See Gever Tulley and Julie Spiegler, *50 Dangerous Things (you should let your children do)* (New York: New American Library, 2011), 6–7.
13. For a diagram and description of a rowboat at work, see Bunn, *NLC*, 10.
14. For this equation and other descriptions of machines, see *Basic Machines*, US Navy Training Manual 121199 (Washington, DC 1994), 3-3. For an online description of balancing moments, suitable for students 11–14 years old, see *School Physics*: http://www.schoolphysics.co.uk/age11-14/Mechanics/Statics/text/Balancing_/index.html
15. See NASA's website: https://www.grc.nasa.gov/www/k-12/WindTunnel/Activities/balance_of_forces.html
16. Jacob Bronowski, *A Sense of the Future: Essays in Natural Philosophy* (Cambridge, MA: M.I.T. Press, 1978), 128–129. For a discussion see *Wave Forms: A Natural Syntax for Rhythmic Language* (Palo Alto: Stanford University Press, 2002), 26–27.
17. Find the image and a description in the British Museum archives: http://www.britishmuseum.org/explore/highlights/highlight_objects/me/m/map_of_the_world.aspx. See also Bunn, *STM*, pp. 88–91, for a description of horizons by way of this image and other maps.
18. For the image see "Dancing Leg Calipers" http://americanhistory.si.edu/collections/search/object/nmah_904332.
19. See NASA online "The Lever": http://www.ohio.edu/people/williar4/html/haped/nasa/simpmach/lever.htm
20. See online: Science A-Z: Focus Books Teaching Tips. *Let's Ride a Bike.*
21. Polanyi, "The Logic of Tacit Inference," in *Knowing and Being: Essays by Michael Polanyi*, ed. Marjorie Grene (Chicago: The University of Chicago Press, 1969), 144.
22. See the online article in *Wikipedia*: https://en.wikipedia.org/wiki/Crane_(machine).

23. Albert Einstein and Leon Infeld used a roller coaster in *The Evolution of Physics: The Growth of Ideas from Early Concepts to Relativity and Quanta*, ed. C. P. Snow (Cambridge, England: Cambridge University Press, 1938), 44–50. For a discussion of Einstein's roller coaster see also von Baeyer, "Einstein at the Ex," in *The Fermi Solution*, 75.
24. See http://www.pbslearningmedia.org/resource/hew06.sci.phys.maf.rollercoaster/energy-in-a-roller-coaster-ride/.
25. See Roger Callois, *Man, Play, and Games*, trans. Meyer Barash (New York: Free Press of Glencoe, Inc., 1961).
26. Jacob Bronowski, *The Ascent of Man* (Boston: Little Brown and Company, 1973), 24.
27. Philip Morrison, "The Modularity of Knowing," in *Module, Proportion, Rhythm, Symmetry*, ed. Gyorgy Kepes (New York: George Braziller, 1965), 1.
28. Richard Feynman, *Lectures on Physics* (New York: Addison-Wesley, 1963), volume 1, 1–2. Quoted by von Baeyer, *Information*, 16.
29. For example, see the online program about learning to balance chemical equations at Jefferson Labs: "It's Elemental; Balancing Acts". http://education.jlab.org/elementbalancing/index.ht.
30. Pettigrew, *Design in Nature* (New York: Longman, Green, 1908). See my discussion *NLC*, 217–220.
31. See http://www.wrightbrothers.org/History_Wing/Wright_Story/Inventing_the_Airplane/Warped_Experiment/Warped_Experiment.htm.
32. For a brief history see Gregory Bateson, *Mind and Nature: A Necessary Unity* (New York: E. P. Dutton, 1979), 107–114.
33. http://en.wikipedia.org/wiki/Centrifugal_governor
34. For fuller descriptions, see Bateson, *Mind and Nature*, 175–176. Also Bunn, *NLC*, 291–294.
35. Vitruvius, *The Ten Books on Architecture*, trans. Morris Hicky Morgan (New York: Dover Publications, n. d.), 297.
36. See *Basic Machines*, Chapter 10, Hydrostatic and Hydraulic Hydraulic Machines."
37. See the discussion of a mercury barometer in *Basic Machines*, p. 9-6, because it features Archimedes' displacement, gravity and air pressure.
38. See http://kids.earth.nasa.gov/archive/air_pressure/barometer.html
39. NASA's website explains the three laws for middle school students in terms of airplane flight: https://www.grc.nasa.gov/www/K-12/airplane/newton.html
40. Robert P. Crease, *The Great Equations: Breakthroughs in Science from Pythagoras to Heisenberg* (New York: W. W. Norton, 2008), 46, Chapter 2, "Newton's Second Law."

41. James Trefil and Robert M. Hazen, *The Sciences: An Integrated Approach* (New York: John Wiley & Sons, 1995), 43–50.
42. Daniel Kahneman, *Thinking, Fast and Slow* (New York: Farrar, Straus and Giroux, 2011), 35.
43. James Gray, *Animal Locomotion* (New York: W. W. Norton & Company, 1968), 4.

CHAPTER 3

The Equation

After returning from kindergarten one day, a child may tell you, "I learned about plusses and equals today." Then when she recites, *1 + 1 = 2, 2 + 2= 4, 3 + 3 = 6*, all the way up to *5 + 5 =10*, we know she is learning something exact about the meaning of "equals." She learns that *4 + 4 = 8* is always exactly right, not "sort of" or "kinda" right. Throughout her schooling, she repeatedly learns about exact equivalence by means of this new code of moving numbers along line plots, and around tables and graphs. She learns that numbers may be grouped into matching bundles, and she learns that the number system follows an exact unvarying sequence: *1, 2, 3, 4, 5*. She learns to match and to follow (Introduction). She learns that the symbol of equivalence in mathematics, algebra, and geometry always means that the combination must be exactly right. Also, from kindergarten onward, she learns by means of those methods of inquiry to be intent on rigorous analyses of exact numerical truths. When we "balance" a pure mathematical or algebraic equation, we expect that all the signs will always come together in a clear pattern whose combinations can be checked at each step along the way. There is no place for doubt or uncertainty in the equals sign.

To begin, let's look more closely at the idea of balancing an equation. We can see that the phrase "balancing an equation" has been carried over from the real-world feeling of physical balancing on a scale (Chap. 2). So the idea of a mathematical or algebraic equation has been abstracted from a three-dimensional (3-D) tool and reduced to a two-dimensional (2-D) plane and strung along a one-dimensional (1-D) linear sequence (In the *Common Core Curriculum*, fifth-grade mathematics students will become familiar with these dimensional abbreviations). At the outset then, we can begin to define an equation as an abstract balance scale laid out in an iconic pattern on a 2-D plane. In the next pages, we shall look much more closely at this idea of abstract proof.

In Chap. 2, we learned to look for the center of balance on a scale, and now we are moving toward the idea that we should seek the center of balance in any composition. So in this chapter, we consider balancing an equation, with an equals sign at its center as middle measure. In Chap. 5, we explore the idea that in arts and ethics, we are usually balancing opposing forces with middle measures.

An equation is probably the most important sign system in mathematics because it is a paragon of a brief proposition expressed as one symbolic code. Recall Feynman's phrasing quoted in the last chapter: "… what statement would contain the most information in the fewest words?" This most/least principle of inverse equations is now one of the main principles of information theory: to say more and more with less and less. We shall study this idea of an equation's symbolic brevity along the way. The equals sign itself (=) was invented in the sixteenth century as a shorthand for equivalence, as a way to avoid needless repetition of words.[1] With its two dashes, one on top of the other, it was seen as a sign of parallel composition. So the equals sign is a symbolic code that makes the bi-relations much more brief than writing it in a language. In the next chapters, we shall have more to say about the patterning of parallel compositions.

Ever since Isaac Newton used equations to express his universal laws of gravity, the use of equations, with their spare, objective, and even beautiful brevity, has been the preferred sign system of many scientists and engineers (See Feynman and von Baeyer, Chap. 1). For equations allow us to cross over from the purity of mathematics and then to count and to measure things and their motions in the real world and in the lab. We shall explore this idea of a crossover from the proofs of pure mathematics to real world measures all along the way.

COUNTING AS ACCOUNTING: HOW THEY WERE INVENTED TOGETHER

In the Introduction, we said that the balanced lever, the equation, and the sentence could be taught together as a unity, because in the later lives and careers of students, they will often use these three kinds of inquiry together. A good way to introduce this unified idea is to show students that counting, writing, and measuring were also first invented together as a unity. We just said that sometimes we learn a lot more about a concept when we try to figure out where it came from and where it is going.

First, let's look again at the Sender-Receiver diagram in the Introduction, Fig. 1.1, our unified model of communication that is common for the fulcrum, the equation, and the sentence. As we shall see now, it seems that mathematics was first invented as a way to record and to exchange goods with equal certainty. So to think about the developments of counting, we presume that a sender is recording the count of goods, while a receiver is checking the sender's information against a tally of the real goods. So in the fact checking, there is already a rough and ready form of balancing feedback.

In the *Common Core Curriculum*, the study of history is central to the Social Studies sections. By studying the history of a question—where did an idea come from?—we can often tell how it is used today and how the idea has changed or has been modified over time. So where did the general idea of a numerical equation come from? Most authorities agree that in the ancient Middle East, counting and writing began as methods of keeping exact records of the storage and trade of foods like grains. Principles of exchange and distribution of goods depended on keeping accurate records of these stocks and trades. These were principles of accounting records that depended on equity, another *equi* word that stands for fairness and impartiality (Chap. 5). But the equals sign had not been invented yet. At first, the ancients matched up their tallies with other kinds of signs. They were originating a new **symbolic code**, long before numbers and writing were invented.

An influential thesis about the origin of writing says that counting preceded and then gave rise to writing.[2] This development happened in several stages over thousands of years in the Middle East. First, we know that the trade and exchange of goods was very old in the Middle East and elsewhere. For instance, even in the old stone age of the Paleolithic era, obsidian, which is a shiny black and dense mineral, was exchanged and traded as a valuable stone tool over many millennia and through many cultures over many miles. Its hard and glassy density allowed it to be chipped cleanly along its crystalline grain. But most anthropologists agree that a need to measure quantities of grains and cereal goods was solved by using 3-D tokens to stand for certain stuffs. As early as **8500 to 3000 B. C.** of the Neolithic era, 3-D clay counters of different sizes and shapes were used to stand for, to designate, kinds of food and produce. A new **code** was being invented for tallying things, and a 3-D token was the earliest unit of accounting. An ovoid shape came to indicate one jar of oil, while three shapes indicated three jars. There was assumed a basic system in which there was a one-to-one equivalence (*HWC*, 124–125). Much later, a system of geometric shapes was invented that stood for different numerals, so that the counting system was separated from the grains designated. Schmandt-Besserat calls this separate invention a process of "abstraction" (*HWC*, 101). About 3700–2600 B. C., a further process of abstraction developed when traders as senders invented a way to record transactions for receivers by enclosing shaped tokens inside a clay envelope, shaped like a pod. She says that these tokens were "geometrical" shapes: cones, triangles, and squares. Even later, 2-D pictographs were stamped on the outside of the clay envelope in order to confirm the 3-D tokens that were inside. The tokens were enclosed inside like peas in a pod, while a visual/iconic sign was impressed on the outside of damp clay and then fired. Then even later in time, about 3100–3000 B. C., people realized that they didn't need either the stamped 3-D envelope or the tokens inside, so they stamped or incised pictographs on a flat piece of wet clay. By using an online review of this process as a classroom exercise, students can graphically match up the tallies.[3] Notice that a flat clay tablet now emerged as a standalone background **context**. And signs that were impressed on the clay as icons gradually developed into more abstract 1-D symbols. So a new **code and context** (Introduction) emerged as an information system of mathematical numbering. And a new tacit principle of equivalence emerged when numbers stood for any kind of goods, whether grain or jars of oil. We can see that a gradual process of increasing abstraction allowed a system of counting to emerge that was completely separate from its origin in measuring foodstuffs. The counting system became increasingly removed from the world of the sense experience of cereals toward an economy of abstract enumeration that was quick and easy to record.

Schmandt-Besserat also says that the process of recording and storing goods was "institutionalized" by a priest-like caste, which "ritualized" the process as well (*HWC*, 106). She illustrates with a line of worshippers delivering jars for the use of a deity, Inana. Priest-kings regulated peoples into kingdoms under the rituals of religious orders. Students of the Common Core Language Arts will have become familiar with different kinds of rituals as they study myths and folktales, from the fifth grade onward. With the growth of larger cultural institutions like kingdoms and organized religions, the notion of more abstract principles of equivalence became necessary. Writing accompanied counting as a process of finding more abstract equivalences (see Chap. 4).

To sum up this section, here is a useful overview about the historical development together of trade goods and arithmetic:

> In trade, we find the four arithmetic operations: addition to find a total, subtraction to strike a balance, multiplication for replication, division for equal partition. Logically prior to these operations, though not chronologically, are a number of more primitive notions. There is exchange or equivalence: two sheep for a goat. There is assignment of abstract measures of value: everything has a price. In this way, equivalent classes of values are set up. The abstract representatives of the equivalence classes, coins, are originally perceived to have intrinsic value, but gradually this value tends to become symbolic as one moves toward paper money, checks, credit lines, bits in a computer memory.[4]

Notice too that money is an information system concerning value with its own codes and contexts. But, some say, it is not just another information system. Some even say that money is a "universal equivalent." In Chap. 5, we discuss an ethics and an economy in which, some say, everything seems to have a price. As for this passage and for what is to come, we can ask students about the apparent progression here of forms of symbolic value. Is there an increasing degree of symbolic abstraction in this history?

From Objects to Abstractions

Now we come to a very important point regarding equivalence, and it is the principle of abstraction itself. Consider the idea of "threeness." Abstract numbers came about when a one-to-one equivalence between tokens and objects became insufficient for more complicated records: not just one token for one measure of grain. In history, as we have seen, this abstraction away from real tokens toward pure symbols, from concrete numbers having to do with weights and measures toward abstract operations with their own principles of addition, subtraction, multiplication, and division, was a huge shift in ways of thinking. For with abstract numbers, and with writing, you weren't necessarily thinking about goods, but you could be thinking about pure numbers without contents. When counting with numbers by themselves, we are thinking in an abstract framework, a **code** of purely grammatical relations and operations. Pure mathematics and pure algebra, as we shall see, are strictly hypothetical transformations, having nothing essential to do with a real world.

The ancient Middle Easterners moved from real objects to the pictures of objects, to abstract numbers, and then to representations of things by recording words in a string on the clay. For another example, in both Egyptian and Minoan hieroglyphics, the visual sign for "balance" was a simple stick figure: It was composed of a horizontal line representing a beam, a vertical line centered above the beam representing a cord, and two triangles drawn underneath at each end of the horizontal line representing the hanging pans. Sometimes the icon represented numbers, but at other times, it seemed to represent a person who may have been a "scribe" or "accountant."[5]

Flocks and Fields

In the history of counting, there is an extremely important distinction that developed between counting things as opposed to measuring areas. When early peoples learned to count, they counted their flocks of sheep, their cows, their pots of grain and oil in order to keep track. They were checks on trustworthiness. Their equivalences between real-world stuffs were supposed to be symbolically verifiable and accountable. And somewhat later in the Neolithic period, they learned to measure their fields and their lands (Hogben, 40). When counting flocks, they matched up token objects and things. However, when they measured their fields, and their temples and pyramids, they moved toward a more abstract concept of equivalence. This method of measuring fields, not individual things, was a huge shift in the history of counting. For instance, they needed to know the vertical heights of a wall and the horizontal lengths of a room. They needed to measure storage bins, temple walls, and palace dimensions. By measuring vertical and horizontal lengths, either strips of land or lengths of bricks, they were measuring *areas*. They were not matching up bundles of things. When they combined verticals and horizontals to seek an area, they were working with *proportions within a field*. *Area* was an entirely new and extremely important concept. For an example of proportion, see the section on Thales below (Cross ref: Common Core Grade 5 on area).

The Right Angle

By measuring the proportions between verticals and horizontals in buildings, ancient surveyors of the Middle East featured for the first time the use of the right angle as the fundamental concept of equivalent and proportionate areas. With a right angle you can measure a big area by means of a little abstract code. *There is no more important fundamental measure of geometry than a right-angled equivalent measure.* As we shall see below, dividing a square into two equal parts of an equilateral triangle was the fundamental basis of Euclid's geometry of the right angle and its variations.

In Greek etymology, the prefix *Geo* (earth) + the suffix *Metric* (measure) = *Geometry*. The use of the right angle as a basic unit of geometry became the basic unit of measuring area. The right angle became the fundamental measurement of equivalences and proportions, as they measured the *geo*, the earth. Now for the first time, a representation of the background **context** comes into play as the essential shaper of the measure. Although Paleolithic cave painters, for instance, used a wall as background, their use of the background was not featured. Although they sometimes placed the hump of a bison, for instance, on the hump of a wall, they did not otherwise draw attention to the larger setting. They featured figures of aurochs and other animals, but not the walls. But Egyptians and Sumerians, thousands of years later, measured the background "wall" itself. When they drew 2-D pictures on the sand, seen as a flat surface, they created the first visual models of larger areas of equivalence. A *model* was then, and still is, often used as a visual *hypothesis*. Here, for the first time, a hypothetical area, a cyberspace of "as if," was featured as a background field. They made up a model of an imagined space. The abstract study of geometry, with its ideal figures and equivalences, then came about. In Next Generation Science Standards, for each grade there is a section called "Develop a Model...." (Cross ref. Common Core Grade 4, "Geometry" on angles.)

Ancient Units of Equivalent Measures: The Knotted Rope[6]

A length of rope was the first ancient tool that measured accurate equivalences and proportions upon an area of earth. In the river valleys of the Nile and the Tigris-Euphrates, ancient surveyors measured out ditches, canals, and storage rooms. They were called "rope stretchers" because they used long ropes that were knotted at equal intervals. This stretched rope was another kind of abstract tally in which the intervals between knots allowed for the measure of equivalent distances on the ground. There weren't numbers on the knots. No fixed unit was attached to each unit. They were just abstract tallies. Nobody knows who first discovered the brilliant way of bending a stretched rope into a right triangle. But the

3-4-5 **following** sequence of knotted intervals allowed the easy **matching** of an exact right angle anywhere on a background. Even when we change the lengths of the rope, and thus when the following sequence of 3-4-5 knots changes in lengths, the right triangles retain the same proportions. So right triangles are proportionate to one another in shape even though their lengths may be unequal (We shall check this statement when we discuss Thales's measurements of the Great Pyramid, below). You can find plenty of images on the internet that demonstrate this knotted figure, and it is a useful classroom exercise to perform on a schoolroom floor. Notice how handy the rope can become as a coded 3-D sign system. You can fold up the rope and tuck it into your belt. It is a small-scale mnemonic, a substitute memory device that is very like a pair of dividers (Chap. 2), which can measure the proportions of different areas.

CLASSROOM EXERCISE: THE PYTHAGOREAN THEOREM

Cross ref. Common Core Curriculum Standards,

> "Grade 8 » Geometry » Understand and apply the Pythagorean Theorem. » 7 Apply the Pythagorean Theorem to determine unknown side lengths in right triangles in real-world and mathematical problems in two and three dimensions.

(See also principles of congruence through symmetry transformations: translation, rotation, reflection. Also note volumes and their formulas.)

The development of geometry as a study of figures in 2-D and 3-D spaces can be shown by demonstrating what is probably the most famous and influential theorem of all rational measurement. It featured a right angle of equivalent measure, and it derived from the 3-4-5 knotted rope. The English mathematician and philosopher Bertrand Russell avows, "No proposition in the whole of mathematics has had such a distinguished history... [because] everything in geometry, and subsequently in physics, has been derived from it by successive generalizations."[7] What an amazing summary in one assertive sentence (We study declarative sentences as assertions in Chap. 4). He then goes on to explain the historical development of the proposition. Russell was also working with the idea that if you can find out the ancestry of a thing, then you can figure out its logical development as a sequence of related discoveries. Russell's claim was expressed in a summarizing sentence about the historical development of mathematics, geometry, and science, all working together. As we have seen, the theorem's extremely abstract formula of triangular equivalence was derived from the "field number" of measuring the real world. With its example, we see the movement from stretching rope to an abstract geometry of equivalences and proportions.

For a basic bodily experiencing of this angular measure, let's cite Jacob Bronowski's introduction to the Pythagorean theorem, as he sets up "the primitive constants of natural laws":

> There are two experiences on which our visual world is based: that gravity is vertical, and that the horizon stands at right angles to it. And it is that conjunction, those cross-hairs in the visual field, which fixes the nature of the right angle; so that if I were to turn this right angle of experience (the direction of 'down' and the direction of 'sideways') four times, back I come to the cross of gravity and the horizon. The right angle is defined by this fourfold operation, and is distinguished by it from any other arbitrary angle (*AM*, 157).

Students may discuss the metaphor of a crosshairs. We notice that it is an image of a centering, a crisscross, and so it is an essential way to experience the centering focus of the vertical and horizontal lines on our Sender-Receiver diagram. These two perceptual experiences surely govern our assumption about a center of balance that coincides with our own center of gravity. This kind of bodily visual experience is a tacit recognition of *embodied knowledge* because we use our bodily perceptions to measure verticals and horizontals (See Introduction). Implicit in this description of what he calls a "universal experience" is the feeling, the sensation, of the sun's constant influence. Notice that it is our perception of the sun's gravitational force of up-down that defines the vertical leg of the angle, and it is the apparent slant of light, perhaps as the sun sets on the horizon, that defines the flat plane of the other leg. So a right angle can be seen a fundamental matrix for further real-world measurements. Physical laws are seen here to derive from our bodily experiences of nature.

It is extremely important to begin with this original model of *visual* equivalence, because too often students only learn the much later sign system of mathematical equivalence, as expressed by algebraic symbols ($a^2 + b^2 = c^2$). Here is a redrawing of Hogben's image of the Pythagorean theorem that shows the image of squares, both big and little ones. See Fig. 3.1

In a classroom exercise, we can draw this image on a smart board and let students work out different variations. As we study this visual image, we can see that when we measure the angles, we are also figuring out the

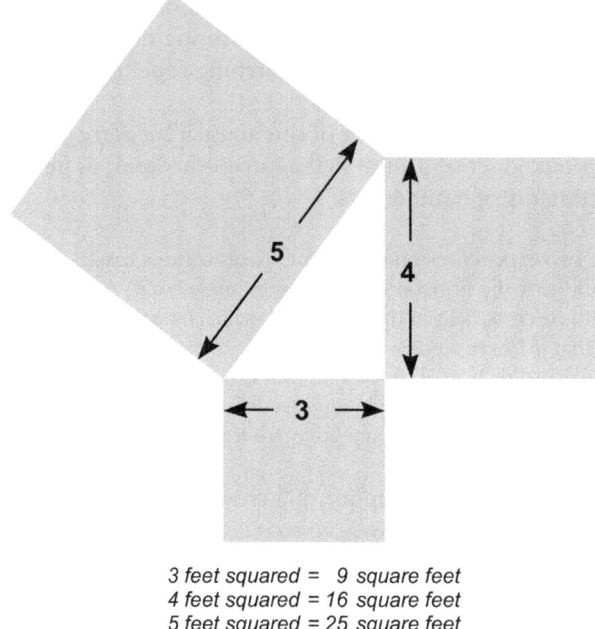

3 feet squared = 9 square feet
4 feet squared = 16 square feet
5 feet squared = 25 square feet

Fig. 3.1 Squares drawn upon a Pythagorean triangle

areas by counting with numerals. So a tacit combination of the two kinds of equivalence, flocks and fields, is working together.

If we did not know this developmental history of this proposition, we might presume that the Pythagorean theorem (and other square laws that were later developed from it) was a universal principle that itself governed the movements of things, forces, and energies. For instance, Russell states that Newton's inverse-square law of gravity is a derived universal principle. The principle expresses in coded signs a dynamic balance, seen as a middle measure, which inheres in the areal relations between bodies and forces. However, even though the symbolic equation shows us how to represent things that balance in motion, it does not itself do the governing. The equation is a shorthand-coded expression; the symbol is not in itself an abstract governor that is doing the balancing. It is a concept that measures our perception of a universal balancing act, a constant natural law, but the generalizing concept, though immensely important to remember, does not exist as a thing. To presume that an abstract equation is governing the physical balances is an act of crossover confusion. It displaces the physics of balancing up forces and substitutes a mathematics of balancing signs made up of purely abstract integers. So a grammar of signs can stand in the way of, and substitute for, a semantics of real-world forces. Along the way, we need to pay attention to this kind of substitution.

Star Lore

In building the great pyramids, Egyptian surveyors apparently used the knotted stretched rope in combination with measurements of the sun and the stars in order to achieve amazingly accurate alignments of the four angled corners of the pyramids onto a north-south axis. For instance, here is a passage that describes a scene of the god Thoth who holds a coil of rope and a golden mallet with which to drive pegs into the ground:

> I have grasped the wooden peg; I hold the handle of the mallet; I grasp the cord with Seshata [goddess of the stars and wisdom]; I cast my face toward the course of the rising constellation; I let my glance enter the constellation of the Great Bear [our Big Dipper]; I establish the four corners of the temple.[8]

In this description, the god Thoth is given a speech in which he derives the four corners of his temple, with its off-angled areas, by measuring the angles of the constellation. But who is doing the actual measurements? We can ask students why ancient astronomers would displace their own workings onto a god's apparent intervention. What is the point of the ritual?

In Next Generation Science Standards, there is a section for each grade called "Earth and Its Systems," so here we review another kind of real-world problem.[9] Once the ancient surveyors were able to measure the heights and angles of their temples, their ziggurats, and pyramids, they began to measure the heights and angles of the sun, the moon, and the constellations as they apparently moved around the sky. Many ancient peoples had studied the movements of the stars around the night sky in their significant groups and patterns, and they ascribed different stories to account for their arcs and returns in their observed cycles of rotation. For instance, the constellation Orion, the hunter in one myth, appears in the night sky in late summer, and he marches across the sky until springtime, when he gradually disappears. What is he doing? Where is he going? Ancient peoples matched and followed the stars, trying to figure the causes and effects of the movements of heavenly bodies. Narratives, told in sentences, could account for the presence and absence, the movements of the constellations. The ancients tried to match up the order of things with an order of symbolic stories. Thinking with language in stories enhances the visual thinking, especially when we use language to represent absent things that appear in our memories, imaginations, and dreams.

The location of the North Star or Pole Star or Polaris is startling because it apparently does not move at all from our field of vision. So the god Thoth (above) could design his four-cornered temple by finding its fixed northern orientation. Also, because the Pole Star seems to remain still, and because it points north, many peoples in history have used it to find their own movements in relation to it. The pole star is an **index**, that is, a physical indicator of an eye's embodied aim as it points northward.[10]

Let's pause for a moment and consider the North Star in terms of a center of balance, our point of departure for the several Sender-Receiver diagrams. We can review with students how it is located at the north celestial pole. It seems to remain relatively still because the earth's globe seems to rotate around it. Its true rotation cycle is unapparent. Because the North Star is a pivot point of global rotation, it can be seen as the central axis of a vertical line drawn from it down through the center of the Earth, and even further down through the Southern Hemisphere where there is a similarly located South Star.

Other neighboring stars, like the constellation Big Dipper, seem to rotate around the North Star. They do not wander because they are held by their mutual induced gravitational pull into a combined orbit (The center of gravity between any two astronomical bodies is their center of balance, an equivalent measure between the two, as if they were on a seesaw, Chap. 2). In a time-lapse photo, you can see the apparent motion of these stars as if they were rotational circles drawn around Polaris (See *Wikipedia* photo for an image that depicts the stars as circular lines around the pole star). Even though the Big Dipper slowly rotates around Polaris, you can still find it in its place by following an apparent line up from the outer edge of the dipper. So on clear nights at least, you, like the ancient trackers and mariners, can always orient yourself northward. Nowadays you might be baffled if you spot a star that stays in almost exactly the position throughout the night, like Polaris, and also on successive nights at different times. These may be geosynchronous satellites. For the etymology, decipher the prefix "geo" and the suffix "synchronous."

Some teachers may want to discuss William Shakespeare's Sonnet #116, in which he defines the constancy of love in terms of the pole star as a constant guide to wandering pilots who seek its fixed point.

The apparent movement of the sun and the stars in their daily rotations and seasonal changes was also the main calculator that helped ancient peoples account for the intervals of passing time, as well as space. The great movements of heavenly bodies in the sky helped ancient people to prefigure, to anticipate, the timing of their movements on earth, such as migrations. When is the best time to sow seed? When is the best time to reap a harvest of grain? When are the lambs born? When are the calves born? Where should I be when my child is born? People learned to remember and they learned to predict more accurately as their domestic needs matched up with the apparent movements of the great star charts. The repeated rotations of the great star clusters seemed to tell ancient peoples when to act. Reading the great star charts in space helped them to be ready to act in time. The patterned flocks of stars in space helped them to see the whole sky as a background field, a context of movements. With these repeated patterned motions, they could predict future sequences. Star lore had real-world influence as a way of forecasting what will happen sooner or later, so the measurement of passing time became as important as counting flocks and measuring fields in space.

Furthermore, many ancient peoples were also taught by their priests to believe that the constellations were not only gigantic measures that told them *when* to act, but also people were told that the constellations seemed to govern *how* they *ought* to act on earth. This is another way of displacing an interpretation of sign systems onto another frame of reference. The constellations were ritualized into remote governors by means of a false equivalence. Just because things may happen in a following sequence does not necessarily mean that cause and effect must also be working. Although 3 follows *1* in a following sequence, it does not mean necessarily that one (*1*) caused three (*3*). Of our three kinds of associations discussed in the Introduction, **matching, following,** and **cause/effect**, the latter two are often confused together. Those of us who read our horoscopes in the daily newspaper are also tempted to believe the same displacement. Ancient rituals of sun worship, aided by the interpretation and predictions by the sun god's priests, rendered the star world into a sacred space whose equivalent was the temple in small. The temple in small was often seen as an *equivalent model* for the sky god's large framework. That is why so many ancient temples face east toward the rising sun, the dawn, and why so many ancient temples are oriented toward the dawn's slant of light at one of the solstices. Students will study myths and rituals throughout the Language Arts sections of the Common Core. Students may want to discuss the differences between the words "forecast" and "divination."

METHODS OF STAR MEASUREMENT

For ancient stargazers, it was extremely important to be able to measure the locations of stars and their constellations at different times of the year. How did the ancients measure the angle off a star? Diggins speculates that a device was invented when they were able to divide up a circle into six equal arcs (52–53). They may have used a string and a peg to draw a circle in the sand or any other flat background. Then by rotating the same length of string through the original center of the inscribed circle, they found that only six points of six arcs met at the circumference of the original circle. So a model seems to represent in small a large-scale stellar field. We can perform a classroom exercise and watch the symmetry of a six-leafed floweret emerge. We can use a compass from our drawing kit, and can derive the familiar floral pattern. Draw a circle of any diameter. With your compass, find the radius of the circle. Place your compass point at any point on the circle and draw the radius as an arc from that point to its limit on the circle. Start at that point and repeat the radial arc. Repeat until you get six symmetrical leaves. This act is an early act of *rotation symmetry*. Visual thinking and geometry go together as skills.

Later, ancient astronomers discovered that they could measure the angular directions of star movements by inventing a hinged tool with a movable pointer that pivoted around a semicircular device that was divided into six angled florets. It was a hinged lever that did not measure things; instead it was an abstract tool that measured the angles and proportions of stars in relation to the earth (Chap. 2). Even later in history, a related tool, an astrolabe, helped people navigate on the sea and on the land by way of angular measures of the stars. The ancient stargazers were then able to record angular units of measure and store the starry records in their temples. The Mesopotamians counted in patterns of six and ten, so the circle began to be divided up into those modular increments. Even today, many compasses have the old six-petal flower superimposed upon the circular grid. You can screen an image on a smart board. Called a "compass rose," its florets represent the six main points of the compass. And since they also thought that a year was composed of 360 days, the circle could be similarly composed. So units of time and units of space were also super-imposable. They were made *equivalent* under multiples of six. By the way, the old navigational tool called a "sextant" means six-parted. Next Generation Science Standards:

> MS-ESS1-1. Develop and use a model of the Earth-sun-moon system to describe the cyclic patterns of lunar phases, eclipses of the sun and moon, and seasons. (Clarification Statement: Examples of models can be physical, graphical, or conceptual.)
> MS-ESS1-2. Develop and use a model to describe the role of gravity in the motions within galaxies and the solar system.
> Clarification Statement: Emphasis for the model is on gravity as the force that holds together the solar system and Milky Way galaxy and controls orbital motions within them. Examples of models can be physical (such as the analogy of distance along a football field or computer visualizations of elliptical orbits) or conceptual (such as mathematical proportions relative to the size of familiar objects such as their school or state).

As students consider the influence of the sun on the seasons, cited above in Next Generation Science Standards, we can define "equinox" in terms of equivalence, for *equi* means "equal" in Latin and *nox* means "night." The joined word means that in an equinox, the lengths of the days and nights are equal. During the fall equinox, the sun rises and sets in the same location, so you can find east and west exactly at those times.[11]

THE X-Y GRID AND THE "PHENOMENA OF NATURE"

According to Russell's history of the development of the Pythagorean theorem, René' Descartes was the first thinker to combine geometry with algebra. He devised a visual model of a background field that eventually developed into what was called the "Cartesian grid" (64). In our terms, the transformation of a field to be measured into a new kind of grid or graph amounted to an invention of a new code and context for measuring both places in space and movements in time. If you move east on a flat landscape three steps in a horizontal direction called x and if you move north in a vertical direction called y, you can find the shortest linear distance back to your point of departure by expressing the algebra as $r^2 = x^2 + y^2$. Descartes' grid later became the standard basis of a graph with an x and a y axes. It is the basis for our Sender-Receiver diagrams. So this new method of finding equivalence became the basis of Descartes's graph method of coordinate geometry. According to Morris Kline, this "association of algebraic equations with curves and surfaces... ranks as one of the richest and most fruitful veins of thought ever struck in mathematics."[12] Anytime we use a graph, we now know in addition to its technical uses, where it came from.

> See Common Core C: Grade 5 » Geometry » Graph points on the coordinate plane to solve real-world and mathematical problems. »
> Use a pair of perpendicular number lines, called axes, to define a coordinate system, with the intersection of the lines (the origin) arranged to coincide with the 0 on each line and a given point in the plane located by using an ordered pair of numbers, called its coordinates. Understand that the first number indicates how far to travel from the origin in the direction of one axis, and the second number indicates how far to travel in the direction of the second axis, with the convention that the names of the two axes and the coordinates correspond (e.g., x-axis and x-coordinate, y-axis and y-coordinate).

Geometry can help us to compute both "real world and mathematical problems." Kline introduces his chapter on coordinate geometry with this passage written by Descartes: "I have resolved to quit only abstract geometry, that is to say, the consideration of questions which *serve only to exercise the mind*, in order to study another kind of geometry, which has for its object the explanation of the phenomena of nature" (302). Both the Common Core and Next Generation Science Standards stress real-world discoveries, "the phenomena of nature," as well as abstract problem solving.

CLASSROOM EXERCISE

In this exercise, students can work on a real-world problem of graphing the shape of the constellations on an x-y grid.[13] For instance, in the section about mathematics and constellations, Fuson suggests an excellent classroom exercise which shows how to plot the pattern of the Big Dipper on a graph:

(0,3) (2,4) (4,3) (5,2) (5,0) (7,0) (8,2)

First, we recall that the point of origin for charting any point on a graph is numbered "0." If we were working with both positive and negative pairs of numbers, then the graph would depict a cross with the 0 at the intersection. Then if we wished, we could superimpose it on our Sender-Receiver diagram. The 0 would intersect at the same point as the pivot on a fulcrum, the equals sign (=) of an equation, and the verb "is" in a sentence. If we are working simply with positive pairs of numbers, we would use just the north-east quadrant of a grid.

Geometry Before Euclid: Thales Measures the Great Pyramid

Cross Ref Common Core C: Grade 8 » Geometry » Understand congruence and similarity using physical models, transparencies, or geometry software.

We have said that the ancient surveyors of the Middle East understood the fundamental importance of the right angle as a measure of equivalent areas. Both in Greek and Roman histories, as well as in modern histories of mathematics, the Greek mathematician Thales is often credited with transporting these ideas from Egyptian geometry to Greece. Where did geometry come from, and when and where did it go? His most famous discovery is told in the story how, while visiting Egypt, he measured the height of the Great Pyramid on the spot. By reviewing this set of measures, we can accomplish two goals. First, we can show students how geometry differs from the other kinds of symbolic equivalences that we have mentioned so far. And second, we can show students how Thales may have taken the lengths of two different triangles, each with its own vertical and horizontal measures, and shown how they were in *proportion,* even though their lengths are not equal.

First, we now begin to see that geometry was not, at the outset, an isolated internal "grammar." It was not like algebra, which is a logically pure grammar. Geometry had real-world practical influence. Its lines, as we have seen, derived from physical measurements of gravity and horizon, sun and shadow. Although abstract geometry has been taught, ever since Euclid, as if it were pure lines and angles, the story of Thales shows a different origin in a real space of buildings. By way of the ancient surveyors' use, we can see that the straight vertical line of geometry derives from their straight-up walls. In a straight vertical wall, they found what we call a center of gravity. As we saw in Chap. 2, a plumb bob can measure a center of gravity, a center of balance, and also a center of symmetry, seen as a center of bilateral equivalence. Then too, when they made a flat floor, they inscribed a horizontal line that derives from the physical world as well, from the seen horizon itself, as well as from the plumb line and the straight edge of a stretched rope. As we saw in Chap. 2, a plumb bob shows us the center of gravity of a point in space, which can be drawn as vertical line; and now we can derive a horizon from the off-angled right angle. The abstract point in pure geometry derives from the abstract slash marks and knots that demark intervals on the land or in the sky. We stress that geometry is the most *visual* of our symbolic systems that represent equations and proportions.

So, unlike algebra or language, the symbolic measures of geometry had an important intrinsic relation with the laws of nature and culture. For example, when Galileo said that the book of nature was written in mathematics, he did not use algebra for his computations of the universe, for, as Dick Teresi says, "its characters are triangles, circles, and other geometrical figures."[14] Galileo was thinking with geometrical shapes and measures like the ancient Sumerians and Egyptians. We recall that Galileo's greatest scientific discovery was his calculation about the speed of falling bodies in which he assumed a center of gravity for his calculations. And of course his most famous invention was an improved telescope that he turned to the moon, in order to understand its perfection, and he found it full of pits, pocks, and other imperfect irregularities. Bronowski says that Galileo was the first to use "the scientific method" (*AM*, 200–218). Nowadays, we know that there is not just one scientific method.

We have said that the ancient surveyors knew that the proportions of the right angle were a basic building block, and that they could do useful things with its variations, which have found their way into the later geometrical axioms. And ancient history tells us that the Greek philosopher Thales was apparently the first to show how two proportionate triangles, one small and one large, could be used for abstract reasoning. The story goes that one day he asked his Egyptian guide how high the Great Pyramid was (Diggins, Chap. 11). Nobody knew. Thales knew the length of the pyramid's base, because many people had paced it. So he knew one leg of a right-angled triangle. He knew that shadows cast by the pyramid changed through the course of the day. For sundials were used all the time. He knew that as he stood straight and tall there in Gaza, his vertical height was two paces (or just about six feet). So when his shadow cast a length of two paces, he was looking at an equilateral triangle, with his height as the other leg. That is one small triangle, which could serve as a model, but how did he use it to measure the large triangle?

And how could he find an unknown height even when the right angles of the pyramid and those of his shadow were proportionate because their shadows changed constantly, corresponding with the length of the day? He fixed his attention first on the right triangle because the 90-degree angle would remain unchanged both for the pyramid and for his own shadow. And he could measure the proportionate lengths of the pyramid and of his shadow as they got longer later in the day.

THE EQUATION 101

Here is how Julia Diggins describes the proportion:
"*Height of Object* (Ho) is to *Shadow of Object* (So) as *Your Height* (Hy) is to *Your Shadow* (Sy)."
Here it is written as equal ratios: "*Ho: So: : Hy: Sy.*"
Here it is written as an equation of fractions:

$$\frac{H_o}{S_o} = \frac{H_y}{S_y}$$

As a classroom exercise, you can compare the measurements of Thales's height to the question of the pyramid's height and you can compare the known length of the base to the length cast by Thales' shadow. There are several online demonstrations that create the visuals. Thales had used an abstract principle of corresponding proportions that compared a small triangle with a large one. Proportionate triangles depend upon equivalent angles.

SELF-EVIDENT AXIOMS OF EQUIVALENCE

How is it that the basic idea of an equation is such a universal notion? It is an abstract concept with many uses or applications. But is it self-evident? In a movie produced by Steven Spielberg, the character Abraham Lincoln says to a young man who wants to be an engineer that equal rights for all people spring from the ancient mathematician's first principle of reasoning: "Things which are equal to the same thing are equal to each other." He says that this mechanical principle is a "self-evident" truth because it works. [15] We can ask students about the phrase "self-evident." Is self-evidence a kind of habit or belief that we suppose must be true? If you do not have a stable belief upon which things are based or balanced, how can we solve what we don't know? If self-evidence is not one of Euclid's phrases, where would Lincoln have learned it? Recall Thomas Jefferson's "We hold these truths be self-evident...." Is it self-evident that most people want things to be fair, to be balanced, to be just? (See concluding chapter, "Seeking a Middle Measure.)". Notice that in the movie, the character Lincoln takes a first principle of belief from geometry, and he transfers it to the real world of free and equal men. Is it "not fair" to take a principle about ideal figures and to make them equal to social states?

"It's true because it works." He calls it a "mechanical" not a mathematical law. We can ask students the difference. Notice in passing that Lincoln's sentence is an assertion based on the self-evident axiom of work in the real world. This kind of apparent assertion is often seen as a peculiarly American philosophy, called pragmatism, that says in so many words, "Show me how this works in the real world of trade, of business, of physical laws." We can ask students how that assertion might be different from a starting point that says, "Let us suppose ...." A supposition, we know, is not the same as an assertion. It poses a hypothesis.

Because Euclid's *Elements* was the most basic book about geometry in the ancient world, it was used as a textbook for 2000 years. As a young lawyer, Lincoln apparently carried a copy around in his saddlebags.

Euclid begins with five axioms that may or may not be self-evident, because they are unproven at the outset. Euclid claims that these axioms, as he called them, are unproven and not capable of being proved. You have to begin somewhere (We have suggested that a good beginning is to look for the center of balance in a composition). In addition to the first principle, "Things which are equal to the same thing are equal to each other," Euclid opens his book with four other common principles of belief about things that are equal:

2. If equals be added to equals, the wholes are equal.
3. If equals be subtracted from equals, the remainders are equal.
4. Things that coincide with one another are equal to one another.
5. The whole is greater than the part.[16]

Equality seems to have become a common notion of belief ever after Euclid first spread geometry through the world. "Equality is an indispensible idea. It is like water to the fish—everywhere at once, but easy to ignore and difficult to define." (Berlinski, 22.) Because equality is a concept that everyone seems to understand but that is still hard to define, we can help nail it down by centering on "equals." If water is a fish's total environment, and air is a bird's, what is ours? What is our total **context**? Is information our total environment, as Gleick suggests (Introduction)? Is it language? What is equality anyway? Is it merely an "inside" grammatical connection, a dummy relation like an equals sign? Is equality an assumption about the world "outside" too? In algebra, in mathematics, in sentences, in beliefs, what is it? Is it a universal concept? (In Chap. 4, we shall see that universals like equality are usually expressed in sentences as predicates.) Is equality a great universal first principle that is a given about the world? Are all our proofs based on this common notion of belief, even though we may know more about than we can define it? Is it a kind of pre-judgment? Does all our reasoning derive from this first principle of equality, often expressed as balance? Does equality have the same meaning here as "similarity," a term often used in Common Core Mathematics? Or does it have the same meaning as "Matching, as discussed in the Introduction"? In Chap. 5, we continue to discuss some of these issues of equality within the context of justice and equity.

Proofs in Algebra

In an essay, Alfred North Whitehead studied the different "patterns" of meaning that characterized geometry, mathematics, algebra, and language.[17] He showed that each kind of inquiry invokes patterns in different ways. It's important to see how they differ, because the different patterns can characterize the equation, the lever, and the sentence (The composers of Next Generation Science Standards feature "patterns" throughout).

Consider again the patterns of an algebraic equation. As we have said before, it is all inner grammar, with no necessary reference at all to the real world "outside" of a formula: "$a = b$." Its learned grammatical rules of composition, its codes, are self- contained and logically rigorous. As Whitehead explains of algebra, "It is essentially a written language, and it endeavours to exemplify in its written structures the patterns which is its purpose to convey" (107). This is an extremely important statement about algebraic patterning. In an algebraic equation, the pattern of its inner grammatical composition is the intended pattern. Its design is entirely composed of its inner layout. An algebraic equation demonstrates its own iconic pattern of assemblage. Although this kind of formula is composed of symbolic letters and numbers, its pattern is made clear by its visual associations on the line of the formula. An algebraic formula is primarily a 2-D visual pattern composed with symbols in a lineup. Most often, of course, we use an algebraic equation as a method for representing physical things that need to be balanced, as in the substitution of weights and measures for solving the amount of work down in the transport of energy when working a lever.

In the Introduction, we spoke of the beauty of an equation. A mathematical equation can exhibit the beauty of an abstract thought moving in a symbolic pattern that is removed from any one particular instance or any balanced set of things. Some scientists believe that if an equation reveals a hidden symbolic unity, if it has an internal clarity and a simplicity, then it is a good indication of the power of a new discovery. This satisfactory feeling of beauty, however, is not a proof. An aesthetic equation must be tested in the lab or in the field with the tools of hands-on analysis. So what do we do when we want to prove something? What is proof?

According to Ian Stewart, one of Euclid's main innovations was the very concept of mathematical "proof."[18] "Euclid refuses to accept any mathematical statement as being true unless it is supported by a series of logical steps that deduces it from statements already known to be true" (22). Mathematical proof is composed as a strict series of steps that follow one another in a series, beginning with the first assertion, equivalence. That is why Euclid begins with his five basic presumptions, from which his later deductions are composed. And yet Stewart asserts, physicists, astronomers, and engineers view this kind of strict mathematical proof "with disdain," because "observation" is the truer gauge (23). That big claim is just like Descartes' vow of only doing calculations about the real world of nature. That claim about observation is also what Feynman said about seeing how things work by taking things apart and of putting them back together again with your hands, quoted at the beginning of Chap. 2. It is a method that is sometimes called "empiricism." The "internal logic" of mathematical proof is not enough to calculate the motions of the moon, for instance (Stewart 24). We need the outside demonstrations of experiments to make a proof work as a physical truth in order to render logical steps and physical observations equivalent. We need real-world balancing feedback to check up on the initial logic. But maybe Euclid's word "coincide" is a more accurate term for the bringing together of real-world physics and abstract computation. The grammatical logic of a mathematical equation must match up with the outer references to an outside world. Is the equation true or is it false? How do we prove an equation? We need our several different kinds of balanced inquiry to make sense of the real world.

Here is a Common Core section from "Engage New York" Algebra 1:

Lesson 10: True and False Equations
   Student Outcomes
   § _Students understand that an equation is a statement of equality between two expressions. When values are substituted for the variables in an equation, the equation is either true or false. Students find values to assign to the variables in equations that make the equations true statements.
   Classwork
   Exercise 1 (5 minutes)
   Give students a few minutes to reflect on Exercise 1. Then ask students to share their initial reactions and thoughts in answering the questions.

Exercise 1
a. Consider the statement: "The President of the United States is a United States citizen."
Is the statement a grammatically correct sentence?
What is the subject of the sentence? What is the verb in the sentence?
Is the sentence true?
b. Consider the statement: "The President of France is a United States citizen."
Is the statement a grammatically correct sentence?
What is the subject of the sentence? What is the verb in the sentence?
Is the sentence true?
c. Consider the statement: "."
This is a sentence. What is the verb of the sentence? What is the subject of the sentence?
Is the sentence true?
d. Consider the statement: "."

Is this statement a sentence? And if so, is the sentence true or false?

We see again how any unified composition should be a composite of both sensible observation and intelligible concepts. We handle it in the real world with our hands or with tools and 3-D models. We visualize it, perhaps by drawing it with a diagram on a flat plane, or by rendering it into an algebraic equation. We write and speak about what we have done, and what we hope to do with it. When they are combined, they constitute a good working proof. Balancing feedback is built in as a compound proof, because we incorporate a cloverleaf of methods of inquiry.

It pays to review the point we made in the Introduction. The "inner" logic or grammatical connecting rules of mathematics and algebra do not have anything necessarily to do with the meanings of the "outer" world. Their codes of composition are pure symbols and letters arranged into logical patterns. As Norwood Hanson says, "To put it another way, definitions in mathematics are *syntactic* rules, not *semantic* rules. They instruct you about how certain symbols are related to each other, not how symbols are related to objects. They are concerned only with the business of *formal substitutions* and not at all with *material application* [his italics]. Knowing that '2' is substitutable for '*1 + 1*' does not provide the slightest clue to about what '*2*' may be applied to (266)." It pays to review the definitions of syntax and semantics because different people use them in slightly different ways. In Chap. 4, we define syntax as a set of rules for slotting words and phrases in a sentence in a certain following order (See Fig. 4.1 for a diagram about "the slots of syntax").

Hanson, furthermore, then goes on to show that several of the mathematical rules for addition, whose symbol is "+," work according to commutation, association, and distribution principles:

$$x + y = y + x$$
$$(x+y)+z = x+(y=z)$$
$$(x+y)z = (xz)+(zy)$$

According to Common Core Standards, students should learn these formal rules by the fifth grade. [19]

We know that the four "basic laws of arithmetic" are addition and subtraction, which are opposites of each other, and multiplication and division, which are also opposites of each other.[20] For instance, to commute means that "two integers can be added or multiplied in either order without affecting the result," as in $x+y=y+x$, above. But subtraction and division cannot be commutative acts because a definite **following** sequence shapes the final pattern. You cannot write $5-2 = 2-5$. You cannot write $6/3 = 3/6$. We can see that commutation, association, and distribution are purely grammatical rules, having nothing to do with the real world of semantic meaning, in Hanson's terms, but they have everything to do with the ways that the symbols are related to each other by the inner logical groupings within the strict patterns of mathematics and algebra.

For Hanson, the "=" symbol for what he calls "equality" are these possibilities:

if $x = y$ then $y = x$
if $x + y$ and $y + z$, then $x + z$
$x + x$, for all x (Hanson, 267)

Here we can review the distinctions between symbols of operation and symbols of equivalence. Symbols like +, −, x, ÷ are operational, while symbols like = and ≠ are relational. We can ask students to review the idea that addition and subtraction are opposites, while multiplication and division are also opposites to each other. We can see then how and why so many equations are set up as inverse formulations.

Notice that Hanson's word is also Lincoln's word "equality." Notice too that Hanson uses a sentence with "If-Then" clauses. This is the very syntax of the hypothesis, and it reminds that, for some, mathematics deals only with hypothetical propositions, the world of "as if," not with stuff. Let us gather together into a small group to suppose an answer. Let us make up a possible solution from a series matching and following series of deductions.

Now we look more closely at the *positioning* of the letters in the algebraic formulas above. You must figure out the sequences and the transformations by *visual thinking*. They are picture diagrams where the order, position, and sequence are significant (Peirce, 98 ff). An algebraic equation is basically a picture of a grammatical pattern. As we noted, Peirce's word for a picture thinking sign is "icon." For Peirce, the algebraic figures themselves are not icons; they are numerical symbols that work by conventions that we learn. But their patterned relations within the equation are iconic; they signify by their visual relations on a plane, like a diagram or a grid. Their visual context lets us see the large pattern. Peirce says they are based on "likeness" (106–107). If an index communicates in the present instant by a real physical connection (Chap. 2), an icon works by a resemblance made in memory as we match up an image with an object, like a drawn map represents its landscape, or like a stick drawing of a balance scale can represent balanced numbers and weights. To understand an icon as such, we match it with an image drawn from our past memories.

Peirce's classification of signs is a little bit tricky. For instance, we might think that a photograph is an icon because it depends on visual thinking, but Peirce would say that a photo is primarily an index because it sends a real message transmitted by light rays contacting within the camera, and then the message is impressed as electronic signals on our eyes and brains. All signs are mixed when put in use.[21]

In the patterns of algebra, we understand the **context** in which the numerals and/or letters are placed in a position and in an order. In the Introduction, we noted that in a sentence the orderly sequence of the words in their grammatical positions has nothing to do with an actual sequence of meanings (semantics) in the outer world. "The quick red fox ran down the road." The road is not following after the fox in reality, just in the grammatical sequence of sentence structure. But with algebra, the matching pattern of the position, order, and following sequence *is* the meaning. Here we can review the early use of the primary geometric shapes as tokens. Play games with geometric tokens. Abstraction is very old.

In order to stress the important consequences of this progress toward equivalences seen as proof, consider also Albert Einstein, who cautioned, it was a "fatal error" to forget that Euclid's geometry, which opens with its logical axioms, was first based on the real sense experience of bodily objects, as we have shown.[22] Why was it a fatal error to forget the real world of our experiences of solid bodies? For Einstein, it was too easy just to follow the formal dictates of the clear and simple axioms, and too easy to forget that testing with our sense experience in the real world is also required. This kind of testing and "balancing up" in the real world is the fundamental action for living in the real world, and it is called empirical thinking or "empiricism" for short. The word derives from the Greek for experience. Einstein, in other words, was reinforcing the importance of remembering that good thinking and acting combines both the sensible and the intelligible aspects of a composition, as we have stressed here and in the Introduction. And in Chap. 5, on Middle Measure, we take up Einstein's very similar thinking about "combinatory play."

As Einstein noted, Euclid's axioms and geometrical proofs, at the outset, were not just logical rules. They derived from the outside world of our sense experiences of "the phenomena of nature," as Galileo put it. The idea that thinking must begin with certain "self-evident" first principles or axioms, in Euclid and other Greek philosophers, probably derives from Aristotle.[23] For our purposes in understanding equivalence, Aristotle's three basic "laws of thought" are useful: (1) Principle of identity: $A = A$; (2) Principle of non-contradiction: $A \neq A$; and (3) Principle of Excluded Middle. The truth of the principle of non-contradiction is not just a law of logic but apparently a law about the world: "the same attribute cannot at the same time belong to and not belong to the same subject and in the same respect."[24] Although the principle of non-contradiction works for logic and for algebra, it is misleading in the world of human affairs, where we must live with and compensate for opposite forces and contradictory situations all the time (See Chap. 5).

Aristotle's three laws of thought may be a bit too complicated for many middle-school students. But the notion of self-evidence is obvious to many students. "That's obvious," we often say. Where does the idea of self-evident equality come from anyway? Where and how does it begin? Is the basic idea of balanced equality or equivalence a self-evident idea, as the character Lincoln says? Have we demonstrated in Chap. 2 that we tacitly learn about balanced equivalence on a seesaw or on a walk in a park? Didn't we learn the meaning of equivalence to be a bodily feeling of resistance to opposing forces in the real world of play and work? Is that feeling a kind of bodily self-evidence, a tacit testing in the real world of our own embodied experiences? Doesn't balancing in the real world serve as the tacit fulcrum for symbolic equivalence?

So when we say that an idea is self-evident, what do we presume? Here is a big leap from a feeling of bodily resistance to a premise about physics: The scientist and social philosopher Michael Polanyi is thinking through some of the presuppositions about the conservation laws and the "equilibration of forces," or what we have called "balancing up":

> We can measure one force only in terms of another; but what is often forgotten is that it is only because we assume that they must all balance that we can possibly establish the *quantity* of the one in terms of another. We must *assume* an equation before we are able to determine the values of any one of the variables involved.[25]

That is, in order for us even to think about the very principle of the balance of forces, our large thesis, we must presume that there is a more basic starting principle of equivalence upon which to measure those balanced force and energies. So is an equation one of the primal principles of belief, a "given," like Euclid's axioms quoted above, something that must be assumed but never finally proven mathematically? Yes. Curiously enough, although an equation should be clear and exact, *1 + 1 always = 2,* its beginnings as a basic concept of belief are not so clear. What comes first: the idea of an equation or the feeling of balanced forces? "It's true because it works." Is this proof enough? No.

What comes first is the physical principle of the conservation of energy: that the forces must balance up, always. For instance, Feynman studies the forces that balance on a lever in order to show how the conservation of energy works as balanced gravitational forces (*CPL*, 72–73). First, he describes the law in sentences; then he diagrams a lever with weights and heights, and, and then he gives the equation. Again, all our methods of inquiry reinforce one another.

Note of Caution About Equivalence

When we begin to apply the methods of algebra and mathematics to the real world of things and fields, it pays to be cautious. For instance, the ideas of space and time are physical concepts that we use when measuring field numbers. We can divide units of space and time, but only as units within the laws of mathematics. We cannot divide them in reality because we now know space-time is a continuum. Space and time are words that we use in sentences and equations. A physicist once said, "… it is meaningless to say literally that a velocity, for instance, is equal to a length divided by a time. We cannot perform algebraic operations on physical lengths, just the same as we can never divide anything by a physical time." [26] How can he mean what he says? We can say Velocity = Length/Time. We do this all the time. We can say Distance = Speed × Time, if we want to figure out how fast we are going in car. We say that we are speeding at 50 miles per hour. Or we can divide by Time: Time = Distance/Speed. Dividing time into units is crucial in everyday speech and measure. But notice that in dividing time in an equation, we do not divide matter. We divide matter along its patterned grain with a wedge-like probe (Chap. 2).We are only marking time into *following* intervals that we can measure on some kind of grid, like a clock. For instance, we divide time into units of one hour in a 24-hour day. We divide an hour into units of 60 minutes all the time. For a minute, look more closely at the division of an hour into 60 minutes or a minute into 60 seconds. Our clocks are arranged that way, but who says that 60 minutes is the divisor? What is so special about the number 60? Why is it such a significant *bundle*? Again, the answer about units of equivalent times may be found in ancient history.

The Sumerians were first to use divisions of 60 (*HC*, 24). They found that the number 60 could be divided up in many *equal* ways. You can divide it by 1, 2, 3, 4, 5, 6, 10, 12, 15, 30, 60. Nowadays, we use the base 10 for most of our calculations, but they used 60. We don't know that they divided time that way. But we do know that they used 60 and 10 for bases to multiply for larger numbers. By the way, their way of illustrating what we see as the number 60 was a picture of a large wedge with a round circle in the middle. They did not have numerals like ours. But they did understand that the number represented units in which equivalence was measured by multiplication and division. These were then applied to real goods. You get accurate counts of things, like 360 baskets of grain or 120 pots of oil. So a farmer whose crop was 360 baskets could be taxed exactly 36 baskets by the accountants:

> There can be no doubt that abstract counting was invented to cope with the development of business, trade, and taxes, in the first cities. A more precise method of counting became necessary once a workshop produced quantities of pottery and tools. But it was the tax system that had the biggest impact on counting. Every month, each Sumerian had to deliver to the ruler specific amounts of fish, grain, or animals. Because of this, the palace accountants had to come up with a way to keep track of large amounts of goods (*HC*, 22).

In the Common Core Social Studies Sections, students may study taxation systems.

Just to reinforce the caution about equivalent numbers of 60, recall the 360 degrees of a compass, with which you point a direction. Space can be divided into numerical units, just so long as we remember that this is a mathematical calculation, not a real division of something (Cross-check tongs and dividers in Chap. 1, "The Fulcrum").

Zero, The Ultimate Abstraction

The measurement of flocks and fields was increased dramatically when the very concept of *nothing* was invented as a counting device. We recall that ancient numbers were not themselves used to count with. Instead they were labels that recorded the results of doing sums within some sort of an ancient framework, like an abacus *(An abacus is a matching and following device which sorts abstract units into ranks and files)*. Hogben says, "In the whole history of mathematics there was no more revolutionary step than the one which the Hindus made when they made the sign '0' to stand for the empty column of the counting frame."[27] So it stood for a kind of empty place marker on an imagined frame. Zero was an act of displacement on a hypothetical framework or background **context**. For instance, there is a tradition of using figurate numbers, like the placement of abstract dots in significant numbers like a triangle of 10 digits (Hogben, 82–87.) Place four dots as the base; then stack three dots on top of the four dots; then place three dots on top of the four dots; then place two dots on top of the three dots; then place one dot as the apex of a shaped figure number. You can ask students to invent some others and to count that way. This structure of digits in shapes was a kind of figurate graph. The shape, made out of dots, revealed iconic relations. They were early examples of nesting or chunking principles in a theory of groups. So eventually zero was also used as a sign of a displaced base, like the base 10, 20, 40, 60, 80, 100. In sum, as Hogben says: "if your base is 10, you require only nine other signs to express any number as large as you like" (Hogen, 39).

And when zero finally meant nothing, then it reached the ultimate abstract equivalence: 0 = nothing. It became the ultimate empty copula in algebra and mathematics. Only then could it represent empty space.

So we see that it is risky to cross over from a method of mathematical equivalence to an apparent division of space, time, and length or width. Goods can be divided up into accurate and equivalent portions like 36 bushels owed to the temple or palace, but the field numbers are trickier measures. To summarize, we can say that equivalence in mathematics is a matter of picturing figures in abstract groups, but that equivalence in goods and foodstuffs is a matter of moving real things around in a storeroom and transporting them from one place to another.

Matching and Following Exercises in Review

To match numbers in groups and to rank numbers in following sequences, and then to combine them correspondingly and successively, is perhaps the most common exercise for finding equivalences.

By the fifth grade, students may learn to write equations of two kinds: a situation equation "shows the structure of the information in a problem. A solution equation shows the operation that can be used to solve a problem" (Fuson, 187).

Here are some of the highlights from the Common Core Math: COMMON CORE: 2.NBT.A.2 |.

"Bundles": As early as the second grade, students learn to match separate large numbers into bundles. For instance, the number 826 can be bundled into 8 hundreds, 2 tens, and 6 ones. The units are matched. Or 100 can be bundled into 10 tens.

"Skip counting": Primary-school students also learn to count in "skips" along a number line in a following series. They learn to count by 5s, by 10s, by following along a drawn series of numbers.

> Cross Ref. Common Core--Grade 4 » Number & Operations in Base Ten.
> "Number and Operations in Base Ten ... Recognize in a multi-digit number, a digit in one place represents 10 times as much as it represents in the place to its right and 1/10 of what it represents in the place to its left." (*Flip Chart.* Panel 2).

In addition, students use matching and following principles when they learn how to add two sets of numbers together by starting with the base 10. For instance, students learn to add 73 + 6, first by finding the base-10 number of 70. Subtract 3 from 73, and move the 3 to the next number 6, and add it so that it equals 9: 70 + 9 = 79. With a little practice, you can do it in your head.

Throughout their early grades, students learn in the Common Core to multiply with "times" tables. They don't just learn anymore that 3 ×

$4 = 12$. Instead the operation and the equivalence mean that you add the number *3* together *4* times in a following sequence. And you see the table laid out before you. Students learn then that multiplication means adding a number together multiple times in succession. You don't just learn the grammatical rules of multiplication. You learn the underlying logic of matching and following in a succession, in a series of groups.

Once students have figured out the logic of multiplying by successively adding numbers, they can figure out an underlying numeral that is not self-evident, but that still regulates a following series of numbers: *1, 4, 7, 10, 13* Or: *1, 3, 9, 27, 81* (Hogben, 90). They are on the way toward an understanding of logarithms.

By the fifth grade, students understand "Associative Property of Addition": "Changing the grouping of addends does not change the sum. In symbols, $(a + b) = c = a + (b + c)$ for any numbers *a, b, and c*. See also "Associative Property of Multiplication" (Fuson, vol. 2, Glossary, S14). To group is a matching or bundling operation. See also "Commutative Property of Addition:" "Changing the order of addends does not change the sum. In symbols, $a + b = b + a$ for any numbers *a* and *b*." See also "Commutative Property of Multiplication." To commute means to reverse. Non-commutative operations are marked as being irreversible. You can't invert the order. In general, to commute means to substitute or exchange one thing or another. Here the exchange is purely a change in the order, so to commute is a reversible following operation. These are basic patterning exercises that involve matching and following associations.

The Cartesian method of using a graph posits grid frames to bundle the units with matching principles, and it lays them into a framework of following series. Similarly, the use of "line plots" depends on the two associative principles: matching x's up and down on a vertical line, with y's in following frequencies on the horizontal line. For instance, *Common Core* mathematics in the fifth grade studies fractions. Here is an example from Engage New York:

> Make a line plot to display a data set of measurements in fractions of a unit (1/2, 1/4, 1/8). Use operations on fractions for this grade to solve problems involving information presented in line plots. For example, given different measurements of liquid in identical beakers, find the amount of liquid each beaker would contain if the total amount in all the beakers were redistributed equally.

Proportion in Review

Common Core Ratios & Proportional Relationships begin in Grade 4 through Grades 6 & 7. In grade 6: Ratios and proportional relationships, and early algebraic expressions and equations. In grade 7: Ratios and proportional relationships, and arithmetic of rational numbers. In grade 8: Linear algebra and linear functions.

To sum up here, proportion means in general a relation between the parts and the whole of a thing. In mathematics, proportion is usually expressed as a certain kind of ratio. A "direct proportion" means a ratio between parts and whole of a thing that remains constant as a thing undergoes change (See Chapter 1 "The Fulcrum" for ratio). As one value or amount increases or decreases in an equation, another increases or decreases at the same ratio. If you are being paid $15 an hour, how much do you make in 8 hours? You can add 15 eight times, or you can multiply 15 by 8 to get the answer. The proportional constant is 15. The equation is often written as $y = cx$, where c is the symbol for the constant proportion. Sometimes the constant in an equation is written as k. In others, the symbol is seen as α.

An inverse ratio in an equation means that as one value or amount increases, the other decreases constantly (See Chap. 2.) Or if one value or amount decreases, the other increases at the same rate. To understand these inversions, we tacitly use balancing feedback. Maybe the most common calculation of this inverse proportion is the conversion of speed and distance in terms of miles per hour. If you are speeding at 50 miles an hour and the distance to be traveled is 10 miles, then time it takes to travel is y. But if you speed up to 60 mph, then the time is $y = c/x$. This equation is often written as $y \propto x^{-1}$.[28] But students will need to know in this equation that the superscript is a power operation.

In general "inversion" means that you can **match** one thing with another, often its opposite, by way of the oppositional rules of addition and subtraction, multiplication and division; and you can turn a thing upside down, or downside up; or inside out or outside in. You can reverse a thing's position or its order in a **following** sequence. In mathematics, inversion means that you can reverse a ratio between an antecedent number and a consequent:

$$a + b = b + a$$

Another basic kind of inverse operation is the ratio

$a/b = c/d$, which can be written as $ad = bc$. This inverse operation gives us the important rule of cross-multiplying fractions on a diagonal (Hogben, 89). The issue of fractions becomes more interesting when you combine them into numerals of measuring fields with units of measuring flocks.

When an inverse proportion is applied in the real world, its equation means not just a numerical ratio but also an equivalence that involves a varying balancing act of some real-world stuff (Chap. 2). As we noted in Chap. 2, maybe the most economical formulation of an inverse proportion in the lab is Boyle's law of gases that says in a closed system the pressure of gas is inversely proportional to its volume. Pressure increases as volume decreases, or pressure varies inversely with volume. The equation can be written as $p \propto pk/v$, or $pv = k$. We can see how an inverse ratio in mathematical equations can seem as an inverse proportion in measured volumes.

In a balanced sentence characterized by *chiasmus*, an inverse ratio is set up as balanced oppositions (See Chap. 4). "He went to the country; to the town went she." Here the constant term is the verb "went." The usual coordinate conjunction for expressing opposition "but" is omitted here. Chiasmus is an important device for expressing a basic and abiding contradiction. We live amid contradictions, but often we try to balance them in a middle measure. Although we speak of balance in the construction of a sentence, we usually mean that a sentence describes a moving proportion that involves space and time, as we shall see next in Chap. 4.

To conclude, we can ask, just why is it that inverse proportions are so prevalent in equations of opposites of more or less, maxima or minima? Here's an answer. To represent inverse proportions in our three methods of inquiry—lever, equation, and sentence—is a very exact way to calculate and adjust for the opposite extremes of "balancing feedback." An inverse proportion in an equation expresses with exactness a balancing pattern between opposing forces, both in nature and in culture. And you can apply the formal rules of algebra and mathematics to represent the proportions as ratios.

NOTES

1. See https://en.wikipedia.org/wiki/Equals_sign.
2. See Denise Schmandt-Besserat, *How Writing Came About* (Austin: University of Texas Press, 1996). Hereafter cited as *HWC*. For a useful summary and a good drawing of the evolution of tokens towards cuneiform writing, see her online essay "From Reckoning to Writing": http://en.finaly.org/index.php/Reckoning_before_writing.

Also see a review of the book, Ivars Peterson, "From Counting to Writing," *Science News*, March 8, 2006: https://www.sciencenews.org/article/counting-writing. See also Bunn, *STM*, 83–86. See also Denise Schmandt-Besserat, *The History of Counting* (New York: Morrow Junior Books). Hereafter *HC*.

3. Here is an online review: Mathematical Association of America. Frank J. Swetz, "Mathematical Treasures: Mesopotamian Accounting Tokens." http://www.maa.org/press/periodicals/convergence/mathematical-treasure-mesopotamian-accounting-tokens.
4. Philip J. Davis and Reuben Hersh, *The Mathematical Experience* (Boston: Birkhauser, 1981), 90.
5. For a number of these illustrations and discussion see Arthur Evans, *The Palace of Minos: A Comparative Account* (New York: Cambridge University Press, 1935; online edition 2013), vol. 4, 658–662.
6. See Hogben, pp. 47–49. Also Julia E. Diggins, *String, Straightedge, and Shadow: The Story of Geometry* (New York: The Viking Press, 1965), Chapter 5 "The Rope Stretchers."
7. Bertrand Russell, *The ABC of Relativity* (New York: Signet Science Library, 1958), 63.
8. Diggins (46) does not provide a source for this quotation, but apparently it comes from a scene and epigraph at the temple at Edfu. For a similar translation and description of this scene, see Martin Isler, *Sticks, Stones, and Shadows: Building the Great Pyramids* (Norman: University of Oklahoma Press, 2002), 173.
9. See also *Engage New York* online: https://www.engageny.org/resource/grade-1-ela-domain-6-astronomy.
10. Peirce, 109. See http://en.wikipedia.org/wiki/Pole_star.
11. Online: http://earthsky.org/?p=26181.
12. Morris Kline, *Mathematical Thought From Ancient to Modern Times* (New York: Oxford University Press, 1972), Chapter 10 "Coordinate Geometry," 302.
13. See Dr. Karen C. Fuson, *Math Expressions: Common Core*, Volume 2 (New York: Houghton Mifflin Harcourt, 2013), "Math and Constellations," 231–232.
14. Dick Teresi discusses how it is misleading to translate Galileo's discoveries into the equations of algebra, in *Lost Discoveries: The Ancient Roots of Modern Science—from the Babylonians to the Maya* (New York: Simon & Schuster, 2002), 58.
15. Steven Spielberg, *Lincoln* (2012). See wikipedia, http://en.wikipedia.org/wiki/Lincoln_(2012_film). For a critique, see *The Catholic World Report*: http://www.catholicworldreport.com/Item/1822/spielbergs_ilincolni_politics_as_mathematics.

16. For a discussion see David Berlinski, *The King of Infinite Space: Euclid and his Elements* (New York: Basic Books, 2013), 21.
17. Alfred North Whitehead, "Mathematics and the Good" in *Essays in Science and Philosophy* (New York: Philosophical Library, Inc., 1947).
18. Ian Stewart, *Why Beauty Is Truth: A History of Symmetry* (New York: Basic Books, 2007), 22.
19. See *Common Core Standards*: http://www.corestandards.org/Math/Content/3/OA/B/5/.
20. For a discussion and exercises see K. A. Stroud, *Engineering Mathematics*, 5th edition (New York: Industrial Press, Inc. 2001), 11–13.
21. See Bunn, *STM*. For an extended discussion of Peirce's several different kinds of signs, especially the mixed status of icons.
22. Albert Einstein, "Physics and Reality," in *Out of My Later Years* (Totowa, NJ: Littlefield, Adams & Co. 1967), (67–68). This is not meant to suggest that increasing abstraction in the development of mathematics is futile. See Raymond L. Wilder, *Mathematics as a Cultural System*, (New York: Pergamon Press, 1981), "Evolution toward Further Abstraction," 3–32.
23. See online *Stanford Encyclopedia of Philosophy*, "Aristotle and Math."
24. Aristotle, *Metaphysics*, 1005b10-20; cited in Lakoff and Johnson, *Philosophy in the Flesh*, 375.
25. See Michael Polanyi and Harry Prosch, *Meaning* (Chicago: The University of Chicago Press, 1975), 175.
26. P. W. Bridgman, *Dimensional Analysis* (New Haven: Yale University Press, 1922, revsd, 1937), 29.
27. Hogben, 39. Schmandt-Besserat says the Sumerians invented it. See Charles Seife, *Zero: The Biography of a Dangerous Idea* (New York: Viking, 2000).
28. Weisstein, Eric W. "Inversely Proportional." From *MathWorld*—A Wolfram Web Resource. http://mathworld.wolfram.com/InverselyProportional.html.

CHAPTER 4

The Sentence

In the last chapter, we discussed the origins of numerical equivalence in the context of its ancient history. Now we introduce sentences in a similar way by thinking about the origins of verbal equivalence in terms of the developments of language, in very ancient history. As in the two previous chapters, we study the historical origin of a thing so we can better understand where it is going by seeing where it came from.

The earliest use of verbal equivalence probably began when Paleolithic peoples learned how to match up a spoken sound with the meaning of some event or thing. It began as they learned to match a sound with a seen image, as we might sound out the spoken letters for "F-O-X" in order to point to the idea of a reddish, bushy-tailed creature. This learning how to match up an image with a sound was probably the first use of verbal equivalence. We assume that each tribe or ethnic group had its own agreed-upon notions of what equaled what. Just as the German word for "d-o-g" is *Hund* and the French word is *chien*, so in early ages the words for "c-a-v-e b-e-a-r" or "m-a-s-t-o-d-o-n" were different for each speaking group. We don't even know what spoken sounds were used to equal the idea of a mammoth, a caribou, a saber-toothed tiger, or a cave bear. The actual beasts are lost to us, along with their matched-up sound sense; they live no longer; only their visual images abide in cave paintings and in our books.

Another very early use of symbolic equivalence was a visual relation made between a remembered image in the mind and a drawing. We know that some Paleolithic peoples could draw these animals accurately and beautifully, as any number of early cave paintings will show. These artists, who were probably shamans, drew an image held in their shared memories, and they used a tool to record a matching picture so that we recognize them for what they were despite our not knowing their names.[1] They drew finger drawings by inscribing an indented line in the soft walls; they also drew with brushes. In the last chapter, we called a visual image an "icon." Because an iconic picture works by matching up an image in our memories, it usually reflects on the past. In this chapter about sentences, we will use his term "symbol" for a verbal sign, which, as we shall see, leans primarily forward onto a future placement within a string of noun, verb, and object. How so? Words in sentences lean toward what happens next. Each word is a little promise, as we shall see.

Paleolithic peoples were not only able to etch and to sketch accurate pictographic images of animals, but they could also apply another kind of visual sign that equaled an idea. This kind of visual sign was much more abstract than a picture of an animal. It was just a slash mark, a line. Apparently, it was a kind of tally. There is evidence that some of them knew how to etch abstract linear marks in patterned groups sliced on bone in order to represent lunar calendars. The following series could be bundled into a pattern. One slash line equaled one day. Apparently, they slit line marks in a bundled series in order to stand for repeated intervals in time, grouped to record the passage of 30 days so as to represent the passage of successive moons.[2] Why so? Everybody's life is governed by time, even Paleolithic peoples, who needed to know the timing for seasonal migrations, or lengths of pregnancies, for instance. As we shall see here, symbolic thinking is concerned with passing events, with time and timing. An abstract slash line etched on a bone could equal a day in a lunar calendar. A slash mark was not the picture of a day, so it was not an icon. The slash mark was an abstract symbol of a day in passing, so it was forward looking. But because an abstract line can represent almost anything, it is not a picture of a thing as such. It can stand for anything that you want it represent, so it is an abstract aid to your memory. You can design classroom exercises for different kinds of counting with abstract "tally sticks." Sunrises, moon changes, and seasons of the year may have been measured as sequences following one another. Each slash was an abstract aid to memory, a mnemonic, and each slash represented the equivalence of an interval in time.

And put all together, you can see a series of **matching** and **following** equivalences. You etch a slash mark to equal one day. If you can group the series of abstract slashes into patterned intervals of 30, which represent phases of a moon's changes, then you are thinking in bundled sets, groups, or slots. If you "bundle" slash marks together into regular units of 30, then the pattern is iconic, like a line plot or a formula. Matching and following go together in a rudimentary mathematics. Some say that the very origin of number signs among the Egyptians and Babylonians was the need to tally the passages of time (Hogben, 34).

Old stone-age people transferred a real occurrence, an agreed-upon interval of time passing, and they transcribed that occurrence onto a background frame of some sort, like a bone, or later on a piece of clay slab. The linear symbols were parts of the **code**, and the background frame helped set a pattern of an arranging **context.** An abstract visual symbol was transferred to another background, a bone for instance, much as we would use a chalkboard, a writing tablet, or a computer screen. A virtual background that helped shape the patterns of signs could represent a real space. This is an important discovery: A symbol system was invented, a code, together with a symbolic frame, a context, which itself helped to shape the figures into slotted patterns or groups, just like an abacus. The background helps to fix and to shape the figures into their patterns. Here we stress the extremely important idea that language, drawing, counting, and writing are done within a symbolic framework or background, a match-and-follow context, which helps to shape the patterns of the figures. A cave wall was the first cyberspace for the projection of an image. That is, a cave wall or a bone was an imagined in-between world where signs worked *as if* they were real. They called upon their memories and imaginations. Their cyberspace of *as if* represented important compositions that may have stood for a real event, such as a hunt. Does that mean that they were fictions? Students can discuss the difference between a hypothesis in science, a supposition in philosophy, an assertion in a declarative sentence, and a fiction in literature or film. Any set of symbols requires a background frame to help the figures to get arranged into significant contextual patterns. And the measure between a figure and its ground is called its "scale." So now we have set up a figure-ground relationship between any symbolic code and its context. And we notice that real experiences have been set aside and composed, transferred, and transcribed, within a new realm of memory and imagination, the world of *as if.* So we learn that symbolic equivalences are always slightly displaced into a model, a fiction, or a diagram, much like the cyber space of a "magic circle." (See Chap. 5.)

Beginnings of Linguistic Equivalence in Early Childhood

In the Introduction, we spoke of matching and following principles as essential methods of connecting one observation with another in our minds. We compose associative patterns in our minds by matching, following, and cause/effect. We tacitly use equivalence when we begin to see that one thing is matched with another as an equal.

Verbal equivalence began for us as children when we began to learn our own languages, spoken to us by our parents. However, this origin of equivalence in each of us was not even recognized as such, even while it was first being used. Nevertheless, verbal equivalence tacitly began with the ability to speak words with other persons, our parents, and then within our larger families. Without realizing it, we children were part of a family contract, a tacit agreement about the equivalence of certain sounds with certain ideas. Each of us learned a family language, with its own cultural and ethnic slants. This spoken family circle was our first virtual reality, our first "magic circle" that was set aside for us as a playing and learning field. We discuss magic circles in Chap. 5.

Later, in school, another kind of magic circle, we became part of a larger public contract when we learned to agree about the standard meanings and uses of words. The culture shock of learning a public language, in conflict with our own private usage of speech patterns, has its own domain of balancing what we may suppress and what we may highlight. We learn that the grammars taught in schools have fixed rules about what stands for what, and what properly goes where, but the languages we learned at home and the languages we hear all around us in the world are unfixed and always changing. The rules of grammar cannot really fix languages into unchanging compositions because everybody is always changing a language just a little bit differently each time we speak it. Any language changes over time because each of us is always slightly misusing its words.

Language begins, among children, as a learned habit of equivalent *pointing*. In linguistics, this idea about language as a kind of pointer is called *deixis*, the Latin word for pointing. Instead of just babbling, a little child learns that the sounds can refer to a parent. With lots of smiles, we are encouraged to match up a sound, which points to "Ma-ma." You can point to a dog, even one that is absent, by saying the word. By saying the word "d-o-g," you can summon briefly the image of an animal that maybe isn't even there. For some people, there is a little bit of magic in summoning an absent creature by way of language. There is a little bit of a flicker effect in the combination of an absent thing and a present symbol. There is even more magic for us in using the word "mastodon," because it summons, if only fleetingly, an extinct animal. So imagine yourself a shaman who summons up an absent image in order to make it present itself fleetingly by torchlight on the totally dark wall of a cave. What pointing magic is there? What kind of summons? What kind of virtual reality is a flickering cave wall? Imagine yourself walking through those dark winding passages with only a torch to light your way. Isn't that torch-lit series of flickering images very like a moving picture, a movie, or a flick?

If you point to a thing and speak a word at the same time, you are usually thinking in a noun-like way. Nouns are thing-like symbols and are found in the subject of a sentence. As we shall see, in a descriptive sentence, a noun usually points to a something, while the predicate is a general concept that helps shape an onward assertion. As we shall see, a thing-like subject is combined with a concept-like predicate into an unusual composition called a sentence. Only when noun and verb are connected together as a complete sentence do they amount to a completed statement.

When a child first learns a language, when she learns to say "Ma-ma" or "Da-da," she learns to make a certain sound represent or stand for an idea. Growing up, we tacitly make the sound and the sense to be equivalent. We learn to make the sound equal to the sense, and an object and a symbol are seen as "equivalent," as Jerome Bruner puts it.[3] The principle of equivalence is assumed. It is a tacit relation. It may never even be questioned if a child doesn't learn another language.

If you have ever experienced a very small child learning a language, you recall that it is an everyday, all-day, process of her trying out the words in their rhythmic sound slots, and an equally continuous process of your correcting and reshaping her pronunciation and grammar. The dialog implies balancing feedback back and forth between speaker and listener, all day and every day. When a child begins to learn to write a language, the feedback continues, but it is now explicitly a dialogue of correction, encouragement, and self-correction.

Most linguists agree that the combination of the sound, a phoneme, and the sense, a morpheme or word, is what they call "arbitrary," because the relation between a sound and its sense is not really one of equivalence. The relationship is a symbolic convention, an agreement. That is what a symbol is, a learned convention. In linguistics, the carrier vehicle, the sound part of a word, is sometimes called a "signifier," and the meaning or conceptual part is called the "signified." These terms come from a Swiss linguist, Ferdinand de Saussure, who argued, "The bond between the signifier and the signified is arbitrary."[4] So despite what we presumed as children, sound and sense are not truly equivalent. There is no necessary equivalence between the sound and the sense. The sound of a dog barking is not the sound of the word "dog." Or if written, there is no inherent relation between the letter as a signifier and the read meaning. The letters "d," "o," and "g" have no real equivalent relationship with the idea. Words are like "amphibious" animals; they can exist in different environments, like land and sea, like sound and sense.

Rules of Grammar

Please consider our opening Sender-Receiver diagram again (Fig. 1.1). We can sort some of the various amphibious junctions on a vertical axis of **code** and **context**. The sound of a phoneme combines with the meaning of a morpheme into the equivalent of a syllable; syllables combine into words; words combine into phrases; and phrases combine into sentences. Sentences combine into the larger group of sentences that shape the final **context** of a paragraph or essay. "Use context (e.g., cause/effect relationships and comparisons in text) as a clue to the meaning of a word or phrase" (See *Common Core Flip Chart*, Panel 9, Standard (L5.4a)).

Each of these amphibious combinations follows rules of composition that a young child learns tacitly along the way (See Fig. 4.1).

A child does not even know that the rules of putting together morphemes into words are not the same rules as the rules for combining words into sentences. See Common Core Standard (RF.5.3): "*Know and apply grade-level phonics and word analysis skills in decoding words.*" *Flip Chart*, Panel 3). Not even many adults know, or need to know, that you cannot derive the rules of a higher order of composition from those of a lower. For instance, the rules of grammar that we use for composing sentences are not the same rules that we use for making words. There is a rising scale of combining rules along the vertical axis. But the rules become less rigid as you combine words into sentences, organize sentences into paragraphs, and paragraphs into a larger context of an essay. Each code fits into its next higher context.

Many linguists agree that children learn longer patterns of grammatical construction into which they "slot" words as part of a larger context.[5] "And the words slide into slots ordained by syntax."[6] (See Fig. 4.1.)

THE SENTENCE   125

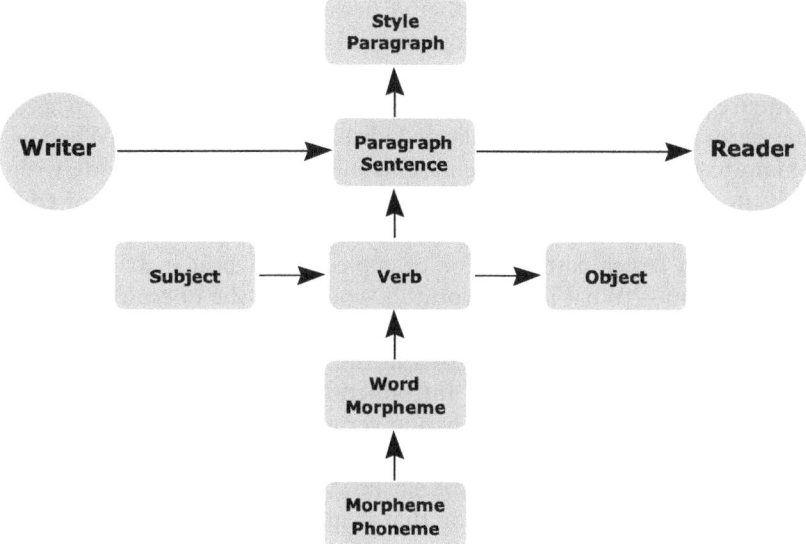

Fig. 4.1 Reader-writer diagram for slots of syntax
You see here two axes: The vertical axis represents the codes for combining grammatical units. Notice how there are different codes for each of the combinations in rising order along the vertical axis. There is a separate code for combining phonemes into morphenes, and for combining morphemes into words, and for words into sentences. Each code serves as context for its next higher level. Notice that you cannot derive a higher set of codes from the lower set. The codes for constructing sentences cannot be deduced from rules for composing words from morphemes. But the codes become freer as you go from sentences to paragraphs to styles
The horizontal axis represents the actual action of speaking or writing a sentence or group of sentences. These actual combinations of code and context, when they are spoken or written as actions, are the slots of syntax

Syntax governs the rules for laying out words of a sentence in a prescribed sequential order. Children hear their parents and others use syntax in pre-slotted patterns, which also include their patterns of sounds. In speaking words in sentences, the sound pattern is just as important as the grammatical pattern. When a little French child greets you on the stairs, and she smiles and says *"Bon jour!"* you hear the rhythmic tones in her singsong slots. (If you are learning a foreign language, at the outset you probably here the rhythmic patterns of sound better because you can't understand the meanings of the strings of words so well.) This kind of tacit agreement carries over to the learning of words strung together into phrases and sentences. Nobody tells a child about the construction of sentences as she learns to speak more complicated ideas in strings of words. When listening to their parents, children are learning a conventional **code** without knowing that it is a **code,** and they are hearing the choice of code words in a rhythmic **context** without knowing that the words are being slotted into larger patterns. For example, if you hear a 3 ½-year-old child exclaim—"What in the world!"—you know she doesn't know the meaning of "world", but you know she picked up from her parents the sound-sense pattern of words used in the right context of a surprising exclamation. As we said in the Introduction, when a child first learns a language, she is not taught nouns and verbs in space and in time. Speech flows from her parents' voices in everyday instruction without benefit of nouns and verbs. And the speech flows in modules of information, little slotted patterns of inflection that shape the stream into meaningful patterns.

So we come to see that a balance of information is regulated by the rhythmic sounds as well as the ideas carried by those sounds.

A 4-year-old child may say of a fat old panting dog, "Maisie's life is harsh." The sentence sounds funny because the dog's life has been one of a beloved pampered pet, and the child slightly misuses the expression, which she must have heard just recently: "Life is harsh." But she has transferred a general assertion, and she has made it her own creation. Even though she learns a language bit by bit as it comes from her family and friends, she soon learns that she can turn a set of words to her own uses. A whole system of relations, a new code, has become her own possession. She has transformed a learnt adage from her memory into her new concept of things and lives. Her skill in mastering a language is beginning. We can ask students whether there is not a lot of pride, of self-possession, in this new power of usage. Now in middle school, she learns how to take apart the language and to see how a noun works, how a verb works, and how a sentence works when it is put back together. She is taught to study these modules of thought patterns as formal rules of assembling parts of the code into a context.

So to summarize, remember that we said in the last chapter that the rules are not the game. Let's say that grammars are the codes of a language, held in our memories, but syntax prescribes the larger slots of sound and sense that come into play while the game goes on; that is, the words in their order, pronounced or written (Fig. 4.1).

META-LANGUAGE

Along the way, a parent often corrects her child's pronunciation and usage in a back-and-forth kind of feedback. Speaking about language itself is a crucial part of learning, as we shall see later. The use of language to talk about language is a facility that some linguists call "meta-language." You can use language to talk about language. That is a big word for an everyday occurrence. "It goes like this…" You can discuss various family words with the prefix "meta," which meant "about" in Greek: metaphor, metaphysics. In literary criticism, there is even a phrase, "meta-theater," which refers to a play that refers to itself, like the play within a play in *Hamlet*, or a film that refers to other films along the way. Nowadays the overuse of meta-language has become so common in some circles as to be a cliché: "That is so meta-."

This issue of speaking about language with language to refer back to itself brings us to one of the main differences between learning about fulcrums and equations, as opposed to learning about sentences. Herbert Read cites the child psychologist Jean Piaget in saying that a child learning a language, as we have seen, begins tacitly; that is, she learns without being aware that she is learning.[7] At first, s/he doesn't learn nouns and verbs, subjects and predicates (Common Core Language Arts Grade 3, and following). That is a later act of analysis. Read quotes Piaget from his *Language and Thought of the Child*: "The line of development of language, as of perception, is from the whole to the part, from syncretism to analysis, and not vice versa." Students can discuss this difference between parts and whole, codes and contexts. Some will have heard about "whole foods." Others will have heard "holistic" in different contexts. And they will certainly know the word "analysis," but few will know the term "syncretism." "Syncretism" is an odd word to use here, because it means the act of reconciling opposing ideas. Although the word could be part of our own vocabulary for a way to unify stressful oppositions into a middle measure, Piaget's use covers over the notion that children learn languages without realizing that they are reconciling oppositions. "Synthesis" might be a better substitute.

A middle-school student learns to analyze an algebraic equation by beginning with the various coded relations, all of which are totally new. But when s/he studies the parts of speech, she turns and analyzes her own speech, which she has been using holistically from childhood, and then she must analyze its parts as broken-up nouns and verbs as objects or actions. Then too, the phrase "vice versa" always applies in issues of balancing oppositions, just like "on the one hand" or on the other. This back-and-forth combination of analysis and synthesis is a basic definition of learning a skill. We take things apart and then we put them back together again, as Feynman recommends, quoted at the beginning of Chap. 2. We decompose and then recompose them. Taking apart a composition and then putting its parts back together, as we have seen, is central to all three of our methods of inquiry. Now we shall see that the most important act of synthesis with language is our act of bringing together words into sentences.

The Sentence

Common Core Language Arts stress the importance of sentence composition by featuring "progressively" more complex sentences throughout middle school.[8]

As we review these three methods of inquiry, we introduce an important distinction between the ways in which an algebraic equation and a sentence relate things differently in their following sequences. In Chap. 3, we said that even though a sentence is a following sequence of words, the sequence has nothing to do with meaning. It is purely the grammatical sequence of subject followed by verb followed by object. In the structure of a sentence, there is no causal order in the succession of the parts of speech. In the sequence of subject—verb—object, the words follow one another in a coded grammatical sequence, not a real physical sequence in space and time. The pattern of subject, verb, and object is mere convention. For instance, Whitehead says, in the nursery rhyme, "Humpty Dumpty sat on a wall.... The wall is in no sense subsequent to Humpty Dumpty" (107). The wall of building blocks is underneath Humpty, who perches in precarious balance on top, not behind it. The inner grammatical codes for stringing together the parts of a speech into a following sentence have nothing to do with the actual arrangements of elements in the physical world of space and time. In the physical world, although objects may trail after one another in a following sequence, there is no such real thing as a sequence of subject followed by a verb and followed by an object. That following sequence is a grammatical rule, not a physical rule. However, algebra is crucially different, he says. "In the usage of Algebra the pattern of the marks on paper is a particular instance of the pattern to be conveyed to thought" (108). For example, $a + b = b + a$ is an inverse pattern caused by an inverse operation.

The grammatical sequence and the logical operation mirror one another. As we saw in Chap. 3, algebra, by itself, is all patterned form with no messy content, with no smashed Humpty Dumpty. Where is the symbolic system causal, and where is it casual?

Now consider that a sentence uses *both* outside and inside symbolic references. Ever since Aristotle drew this distinction, it has been understood that some kinds of words point to the world of meaningful concepts outside the sentence itself, while others work inside the sentence to make grammatical connections, like "the," "a," "and," and "is." As the linguist Morton Bloomfield says, "Words have "two major roles" in language use. They can point outside to the world of things and "concepts," or words can point inward toward their "internal relations" within sentences: "The first convey meaning: they name; the second convey grammatical function: they connect or relate."[9] The words that point outside themselves suggest real structured interrelations in space and time, while the grammatical relations guide the structural patterns of the sentence. Similarly, when we study the diagrams of fulcrums that depict actions in real space, and when we study algebraic equations that depict logical or mathematical relations, we can see also the connections between inner and outer pointers.

Now let's try to state just how important a sentence is. As we said in the Introduction, a sentence is the fundamental unit of speaking and writing in languages. *"The sentence is the basic unit of discourse."* Languages are made up of sentences, so to be competent in a language, you need to understand how a sentence is grammatically composed. *To combine a noun with a verb into a sentence is to point the way toward a new thought.* In order to plan ahead, toward any possible future, in order to describe a discovery, you need to be skilled with composing sentences, because sentences are the main ways we think about and speak to ourselves and to others about what may lie ahead in thought and deed. When we plot a sentence to move toward the next sentence in a paragraph, we are also thinking about the larger context that is gradually unfolding. Words won't do the job by themselves; neither will pictures, nor mathematics. For example, based upon mathematics, you can study forecasts about the growing numbers of human populations or the declining rates of animal or plant populations, but you need sentences to understand what the numbers add up to. You can add up the numbers of people who were employed in the past, as opposed to the numbers projected into a future, but you need sentences in order to understand the implications. Only sentences, spoken or written, let us consider where we have been, where we are at present, and where we are going. So we need to understand how sentences work as they combine parts of speech into balanced equivalences. If sentences are the main vehicles for letting us plan ahead, they themselves are usually forward looking, so their stance of balance is not so much a static state; instead, it is often a kind of dynamic pointing, a staging ground, poised on the verge of the next sentences with their own forecasts. Even while a sentence completes a thought by joining a noun and a verb, it is always "on the way" to understanding. Later on we shall call this inclination of sentences to point forward as kind of attentive "hovering." As writers, we should always know our plot as we unfold it in sentences, but our readers only surmise the plot as they read it unfolding as a narrative. When we are reading, as we shall see along the way, we are usually hovering in suspension.

Classroom Exercise

When we grope for a word, when we seek just the right one that will fit into our impending slot of a sentence, then we are on the verge of a choice that is sometimes stressful if we can't find just the perfect fit. We can discuss Emily Dickinson's poem that begins:

> Shall I take thee, the Poet said
> To the propounded word?[10]

It is helpful to screen this poem on a smart board in order to go through it word by word, stanza by stanza.

This poem is strictly "meta-," because it is a poem about making a poem. It is self-referential. While one word may be proposed, hanging "suspended," stationed with other possible candidates as the poet keeps searching, there then comes un-summoned the perfect fit for the vision. Coincidentally perhaps, John Keats's word for that state of poetic suspension is "stationing."[11] (See Chap. 5, where this kind of hovering or balanced suspension characterizes a lot of art.)

If you are speaking the word, you combine phonemes and morpheme into the complete pronounced meaning. As you speak, you fit the word into the higher slot of a sentence. You fit that sentence into an even higher slot of sentences and paragraphs. In Fig. 4.1, the horizontal axis implies that you string the parts of speech into a basic sequence of words that follow one another. In English, subject, verb, and object string along one after the other in a direction. When you actually speak or write the sentence, you can visualize the process as matching along the vertical axis and following along the horizontal axis.

Noun and Verb, Subject and Predicate, Link Together

By the eighth grade, students should be in command of standard English usage:

Conventions of Standard English:
Common Core SS.ELA-LITERACY.L.8.1
Demonstrate command of the conventions of standard English grammar and usage when writing or speaking.

Consider this assertion about the importance of a child learning subject and predicate together: "When we observe the highly instructive process of a child's gradual advance in the acquisition of language, we see how decisively important the emergence of the subject-predicate is. It liberates speech from the here and now and enables a child to treat events distant in time and space or even fictitious."[12] The ability of a child to learn how to connect subject and predicate is liberating.

The importance of combining a noun and a verb has been known ever since the Greek thinker Plato said that just stringing together a list of nouns was not sensible enough. A string like "a lion, stag, horse" never makes a "statement." A statement, he said, "gets you somewhere by weaving together verbs with nouns. Hence we say it 'states' something, not merely 'names' something...."[13] This statement about a "statement" is worth flagging. As a statement or assertion, a declarative sentence takes a stand, and it also gets you somewhere, shows you the way, points the way. Notice that a sentence gets you to another idea by a weaving together, by matching and following. In sentences and in life, we are always poised on the way. That is why Peirce called a verbal sign a future-pointing "symbol." Words, sentences, and books are symbols that point forward, even when they use the past tense. They communicate because we have learned their conventions of a prescribed syntactic order. The Greeks apparently used their word for "symbol" to mean a kind of convention or contract, an agreement (Peirce, 114). A symbol can mean a connection. Because symbols get you somewhere, their bearing is on the "indefinite future" (112). We shall stress that sentences usually bear on the future of their unfolding context within the frame of other sentences about to happen.

As an aside, consider too that Plato's metaphor of weaving is based on what was probably the first background grid system in ancient history: A fixed weaving frame of strung vertical and horizontal strands was real context. (See Chap. 3 on grids and graphs.) Students can discuss other very early non-verbal forms of grid-like composition, such as basket weaving or knitting.[14] We see over and over that when we compose any figures into a pattern, we need a background framework that helps us slot the figures into a patterned design. So the ancient origin of all grid systems, from the ancient abacus to Descartes's coordinate geometry to computer diagrams, an origin which also includes the verticals and horizontals of our Sender-Receiver diagrams, may have been a weaver's frame.

We have said, and we shall see, that when we find oppositions and contradictions in our daily lives, we usually seek out an equal measure by a mental balancing act back and forth. (See Chap. 5.) A good phrase for this mental process, we have said, is "balancing feedback." When we give voice to those stressful oppositions in words, we see that they are usually general terms: truth vs. falsehood, power vs. weakness, rich vs. poor, freedom vs. necessity, order vs. chaos, pleasure vs. pain. These general terms are concepts, which do not exist in the real world as things, except as classifications. They are categories of thought in language. And they usually are slotted into the predicate of a sentence: "My neighbors are not rich. We are all middle class." "Maisie's life is easy, not harsh." Because the subject in a descriptive sentence is often something that exists truly as a substance or thing, its combination with a non-existing predicate is also an amphibious combination, like a phoneme and a morpheme. A sentence allows us to identify a single individual while including a general concept by way of the combo of subject and predicate. "Lincoln was wise." "Johnny Nolan lies too much." "A lemur is an animal and not a vegetable." "The world is a wonderful place." "The world is miserable."

As we saw in "The Equation," the widespread idea about "equivalence" in geometry as a primary starting point seems to derive from Euclid's beginning propositions about equal things. "Things which are equal to the same thing are also equal to one another." Equivalence is the beginning presumption of geometry and algebra. However, as we saw in Chaps. 2 and 3, the conservation principle of balancing up energy underlies the concept of symbolic equivalence. In Euclid's sentence, the verb "are" serves to point the equivalence. Where does equivalence stand as a starting point in terms of sentences? How do we use the concept of "equal to" with words and sentences? As we saw in the Introduction, in English the verb "is," or its parts of speech as in "are" above, serves both as an equal connector and as a transporter of balanced ideas. Now we look more closely at the composition of sentences as combined structures of balanced equivalence. However, in this book, we do not try to cover a whole range of the kinds of rhetorical sentences. That is the aim of style manuals, some to be mentioned further along. Here, for the most part, we feature "is" sentences.

In his classic textbook on style, William Strunk urged his students, "Write with nouns and verbs, and without adverbs, for they give your writing "toughness and color."[15] As we shall see later, an "is" sentence doesn't have much force or color. The subject of an "is" sentence is often a thing-like noun, something made out of substances, such as foodstuffs. It exists or has existed in space. Second, the verb of a sentence has a "case" that wires the subject in time. "Abraham Lincoln was killed right after the Civil War ended." So many sentences combine an implicit pointing in space and a movement in time. So a descriptive sentence is usually a space-time combination because it links together a noun and a verb, a subject and a predicate. Students will have learned that most sentences in English follow the basic directional baseline of subject, verb, and object or predicate adjective. That serial baseline is the most important following sequence in English. (When you hit a baseball in a game, you must round first base first, but sometimes when writing sentences, you can start at third.) Most students will have worked with nouns, considered as classes of things (called "substantives" by linguists because nouns are usually substantial, made of substances or stuff), and with verbs considered as the actions or mobility of things. This is not to say that nouns are things. As Lord Byron wrote quizzically,

"I do believe,
Though I have found them not, that there may be
Words which are things."[16]

In everyday life, we trust that there is a basic order of things, and we know now that the primary order of things is the first conservation law of balancing. That is why we stress nouns and verbs together as the gist of sentences. They anchor us to the world of things and events, of objects in space and doings in time. Descriptive sentences help us to connect to the real world of our experiences, how we exist, in space and in time. They are linguistic baselines that point to individuals in the real world (*deixis*). This framework of stuff in space and actions in time is also the stuff of strong plain writing, and it can also be seen as a scientific description of material things and energies. In our diagrams, we draw a single system in which the spatial aspects and temporal aspects are seen as vertical and horizontal axes. Notice that we have to know something about a concept of space-time that implies physical connectivity. (See Next Generation Science on cause and effect.)

Again, the point to remember in all this kind of combination into a more creative organization is that any such structure whatsoever is built upon the principle of balance. When we move step by step to more complex structures and aims, we are always depending upon balance as our keystone. When we have understood *how* to balance our thoughts with language, then we ready ourselves to aim toward the *why*.

Sentence Diagrams

Diagramming sentences excited Gertrude Stein in school, and she claimed too that learning how had taught her self-possession:

> I really do not know that anything has ever been more exciting than diagramming sentences. I suppose other things may be more exciting to others when they are at school but to me undoubtedly when I was at school the really completely exciting thing was diagramming sentences and that has been to me ever since the one thing that has been completely exciting and completely completing. I like the feeling, the everlasting feeling of sentences as they diagram themselves. In that way one is completely possessing something and incidentally one's self.[17]

Stanley Fish uses this big assertion as the epilogue to his style manual about sentences. If we were to screen Stein's passage on a smart board, we would certainly notice how carefully she reiterates and modifies her phrasing of sound and sense. Maybe students could explore her growing excitement by the way she repeats words in different contexts. Students may also discuss Stein's idea that when she came to possess the knowledge of how to diagram sentences, she gained emotional self-p   ossession as well. Doesn't that idea also carry over to the skill of learning to make sentences? Here is an important question: Does self-possession come from a "know-how" skill? As we learn a language about our world, are we building in our brains a skill? Does that internal model of the world serve as a confident guide? Students could discuss synonyms for self-possession. A thesaurus could list words that we have already used for emotional balance: composure, equanimity, poise, and calmness. Stronger emotional feelings are self-confidence and self-trust. In the background is one of the most important texts in

American social history, Ralph Waldo Emerson's essay "Self-Reliance," which can be a significant reading assignment for classroom discussion. If you are competent in one skill, and if you trust your own emotional values, maybe you become more self-possessed at large, whether it may be by means of playing soccer or weaving baskets or blankets.

Sentence diagrams have their own logic: Once you have learned the code, you can fit each part of speech into its higher context. Once you have skillfully mastered the code and context, the sentences "seem to diagram themselves." Although Common Core State Standards emphasize the teaching of grammar in primary and middle schools, they do not explicitly support the traditional method of diagramming sentences. Despite Stein's claim, some teachers object that diagramming sentences needlessly complicate the teaching of grammar with yet another logical system, still another code, to be learned by students. However, for many students, especially those who tend to think visually, a diagram is a big help, because a diagram depicts a seeable logic for placing the parts of grammatical sentence into graphic linkages. Diagrams, as patterning structures, are visual icons. In what follows, we are similarly demonstrating a principle of diagramming without urging a method to be followed.

For instance, some linguists prefer to draw tree diagrams in order to show how the inner parts of sentences are linked together.[18] Steven Pinker explains that a tree diagram is like a tree with branches and leaves all interconnected from the top down.[19] He discusses several ways to compose tree diagrams of sentences. Because we are featuring the idea of a sentence that connects a noun and a verb at a central pivot such as "is," we can choose to draw a tree with its tiptop drawn as a verb.

Figure 4.2 shows a sentence seen as a tree diagram, but it now includes a Sender-Receiver direction, and it puts a verb as the pivot: "That brown and white poodle is a strange beauty." Let's think of a verb in terms of information. Just as a fulcrum is the balancing governor of a lever, and just as an equals sign is the governor of an equation, a verb is the active governor of a sentence. A verb "steers" the sentence by directing the reader backward and forward, like a lever, like a tiller. That is why, in our diagram, we feature a verb as the central pivot of a feedback loop. More curious students might question the very use of a tree. Why so? Because a tree grows up from beneath the ground against gravity, it doesn't grow down and out, from top down. We can ask then what would be a more accurate substitute for a tree diagram: a series of cascades, where water falls down in steps? Tree diagrams are extremely useful in other

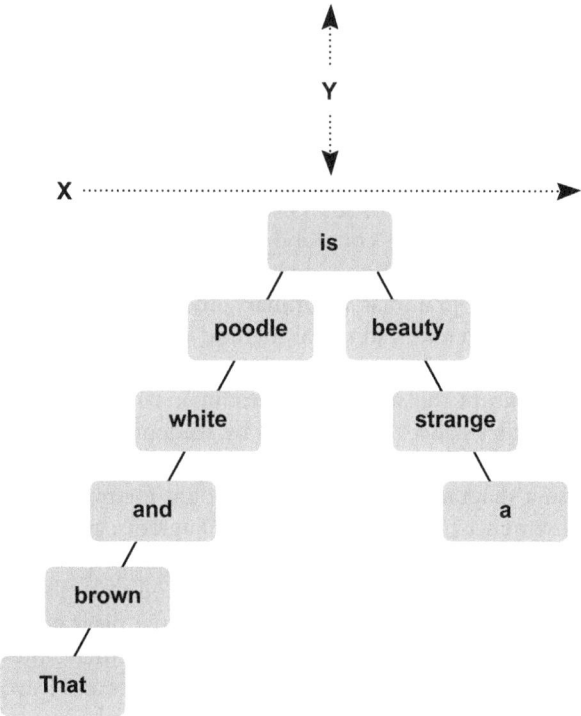

Fig. 4.2 Sentence tree diagram with "is" at apex

kinds of problem solving in the Common Core Curriculum. We can ask students, what are their benefits?

At this point, we stress that to reconstruct things into categories of space and time is what we do with diagrams, not what we do in reality. In the real world of our own experiences, we balance ourselves by feeling our bodies moving in a space-time continuum. When acting, when hammering a nail, or when balancing on a seesaw, we do not think about the categories space and time. As we said, as children, we lived in a world of tacit teaching and learning, where at first we were not taught a grammar, where there were no things called "nouns," where there were no separate actions called "verbs," and where there was no abstract space split from a unit of moving measure called "time." (See also Chap. 3: we can't really perform algebraic operations on physical things in space and time.)

What About "Is"?

The linguist Roman Jakobson cites a preamble to some folk tales. Majorcan storytellers, for instance, begin with a kind of caution: "'Aixo era y no era' (It was and it was not)" (*CS*, 371). Here the "principle of equivalence" serves as a cross-reference to the idea that fiction is both true and untrue. Later, in Chap. 5, about a strange balance in arts and ethics, we explore the idea that fictions can reveal the truth by telling untruths. Truth and fiction may not be pure opposites, not absolute contradictions. Notice that the verb *era* is the past tense of *es*, the Spanish version of "is." So the adage underscores a compounding function: The equalizing verb "is" can make a true assertion about the existence of a thing, and it can also mean "It was not true." Teachers may pause and show how Spanish has two different forms of "to be," *es* and *esta*, which, unlike the English "is," explicitly divide up statements of existence, as opposed to statements about quality.

To review what we said in the Introduction about the two ways of using "is," consider the most personal statement or claim: "I Am!" And: "You are you!" These are fundamental assertions about our existence to be. Sentences like these: "It is true" or "It is no lie," suggest that the description of these assertions relies upon the copula "is." "Is" sentences are fundamental statements; they are important assertions about how we exist as beings. For instance, in his chapter "Truth," Howard Gardner says at the very beginning: "I am committed to telling the truth—otherwise, why should you waste your time reading my words? So let me begin with this simple assertion: Truth is essentially a property of statements, of propositions—two plus two are four." Truth is something you express as a sentence. As he suggests later, although truth must be stated as assertions, not all assertions are true.

When the German philosopher Immanuel Kant puzzled about how to assert truthfully the meaning of existence itself, he thought about its expression in terms of subject and predicate in logic and in grammar. That is a big claim: A subject and predicate in grammar can tell us something about how we exist. Let's recall that the word "predicate" comes from the Latin "to proclaim" or "to declare." Predicate and assertion are synonyms. Kant argued a paradox, that existence is not a predicate. "I" is a substantive! Although arguments about existence are difficult to decipher, they are central to any philosophy of living, so it pays to understand that these questions of subjects and predicates are not trivial.[20] Samuel Taylor Coleridge revised Kant's assertion as a tricky self-referring sentence:

"Existence is its own predicate."[21] Some students may want to play with this as a puzzle; others may treat it seriously as a feedback loop, while others, of course, may say, "So what?" And yet, for Coleridge, the sentence was a "self-affirmation," an assertion of self-possession.

Not all sentences are assertions, however, because many sentences are not really assertions of truth or falsity. Many are utterances that seem to be more like performances or actions or persuasions or conjectures.[22] For instance, "let us reason together." So when we use "is" sentences, we are often making true descriptions about equivalence and balance that characterize scientific and technical writing, as well as statements about living. Assertions also characterize plain, strong writing. Strunk said it loud and clear: "Make definite assertions" (xii). Poets often exploit this kind of stark assertion, as we shall see at the end of this chapter, with Emily Dickinson's poem that begins "The brain is wider than the sky." Is this assertion a fiction, which it is both true and not true?

Another way to clarify "is" sentences is to claim that "is" is a very weak action verb. It is a mere empty copula of drab linkage. For example, a linguist has said the verb "to be" is a "purely grammatical dummy."[23] In a famous little book about art, Ernest Fenollosa said that in William Shakespeare's plays, there are very few instances with "is."[24] Fenollosa argued that sentences should follow the dynamics of nature's energies. He claimed, "All truth has to be expressed in sentences because all truth is the transference of power. The type of sentence in nature is a flash of lightning" (12). If we see a real flash of lightening close by, we know that it is an **index**, a sign that works by a real physical connection between an event and our senses. You do not want to be contacted by lightening. You could interpret the sentence to mean, "Get out from under that tree." Students can discuss Fenollosa's definition of truth and its relation to power. He means that a sentence channels communication in a sequenced direction like a flash of lightening or the flow of a river. A sentence seems to follow an energy channel only because it is carried by an energy wave of a speech sound or a reading module. Although truth may come to us in powerful jolts, it also may trickle into our awareness like a little hint or a hidden clue. So it is more lively to say "A sentence channels communication in a direction" rather than saying, "A sentence is a channel of communication." Similarly, he said that natural phenomena are characterized by "the transference of force from agent to object, so that they "occupy time" (7). "Dad raked leaves" is a sentence that shows the transference of force from sender to receiver in a direction.

You can see how our Sender-Receiver diagram can show a transference of information in a direction in space and in time from an agent to a patient by way of the real physical energy wave of the transporting medium seen as a **contact**. Information is physical. And so too is language, at least in the **contacting** part, as in the sound waves as we hear or in the light waves as we read. So it is more accurate to say that when we read, our brains are applying the energy, not the sentence, as we follow the sequence of the subject-verb-object in its coded direction. (As you read this sentence, for instance, your brains are sending wave-patterned messages along your axons by way of electrical and chemical contacts.) When we say that we supply the energy of speaking, writing, or reading and listening, we also understand that language is another tool invented to make our work easier, where work in this case is ease of communication. So when we compose a sentence, we want to write clearly so that it is easy for a reader to understand, but writing clear sentences is not easy. Many people have said: "Easy writing is vile hard reading."

Fenollosa argued that Shakespeare's sentences follow the directional line of human thought, which matches nature's flow. Why is Shakespeare's language "so immeasurably superior to all others"? "I found that it was his persistent, natural, and magnificent use of hundreds of transitive verbs" (29). But it would be a mistake to say that a sentence is a mirrored reflection of nature's force. Why so? Because we say that though nature may have a direction to its force, like a river's flow, a sentence is aimed at a goal. Although animals, plants, and humans have aims, evolution has no aims, no intentions, no overall plan. But sentences do. They have an aim. In English, the subject of a sentence is usually parked up front, while the predicate drives it on its way as a proclamation. Notice that in writing a sentence, expectation and anticipation are always oriented toward some kind of goal, as expressed by a predicate. A sentence gets you somewhere by weaving together a noun and a verb. "I promise not to lie." In fact, there are no "no's" in nature, but there are plenty of negatives in sentences.

The point to remember is that the writer can achieve a sense of direction and momentum by writing a sentence that includes active transitive verbs. "Mary rides a bike" is actively about her power and her momentum. "Mary slept quietly" is also active even though the sentence implies a peaceful rest. So to say with Fenollossa that a sentence seems to enact force and momentum, we mean that our thinking minds are doing the work as we follow along the linear syntax of the actual order of composition. So a sentence sets up an apparent movement of dynamic, not static, balance. The impression of static balance is a weakness of the verb "is." "Ryan is a boy." "Ryan runs fast."

Equal Measure

How much accuracy lies in the idea that sentences transfer information in sequences like the forces in nature? Is the syntax of the word order in a sentence a kind of mirror that reflects nature? Not really. In the past, some physicists said that nature chooses the most economical path, but that is a misleading idea. Nature does not follow the shortest path of straight and narrow. Nor should sentences all the time. Nature, most now agree, takes a meandering path, which runs back and forth from extremes of massive outpourings of information to tiny trickles. Nature runs to extremes. Nature runs in extremely opposite directions. Nature brings life but also death. Sentences, however, tend to weave extremes together.

Consider this famous sentence about woven extremes, from the Old Testament of the Bible. It begins with an assertion: there is a season for everything, so we should choose the right time for our aims and actions:

1. To every thing there is a season, and a time to every purpose under the heaven:
2. A time to be born, and a time to die; a time to plant, and a time to pluck up that which is planted;
3. A time to kill, and a time to heal; a time to break down, and a time to build up;
4. A time to weep, and a time to laugh; a time to mourn, and a time to dance;
5. A time to cast away stones, and a time to gather stones together; a time to embrace, and a time to refrain from embracing;
6. A time to get, and a time to lose; a time to keep, and a time to cast away;
7. A time to rend, and a time to sew; a time to keep silence, and a time to speak;
8. A time to love, and a time to hate; a time of war, and a time of peace.—*Ecclesiastes* 3:1–8 (King James version)

Notice the writer's following series of opposite values, plus his effort to reconcile them. We should time our own balancing acts to the right moment, as we confront extremes and contradictions in nature and in culture. (See Chap. 5.)

Equal Measure in a Sentence

What then is a balanced measure of information for a good sentence, if any, either pronounced or written? What balancing skill are we aiming for as we take apart and then put together a serviceable sentence? To answer these questions we need to focus sharply on the question: What is a balanced measure of good information within a sentence? As a point of departure, consider this extremely important assertion by Aristotle. He says that in everything that we can divide up, we can choose a greater amount of information, a lesser amount, or what he calls an "equal measure." "The equal measure is a certain kind of mean between excess and deficiency."[25] Here then is another important opposition: excess and deficiency; too much or too little. Notice that we can paraphrase this opening and say information is continuous and divisible. This search for an equal measure between extreme oppositions, sometimes called "The Golden Mean," is Aristotle's main claim about ethics. (See Chap. 5.) To claim an equal measure between our conflicts is easy to say but often hard to achieve. We seek to make a balanced choice to gain our best ends. The writer of *Ecclesiastes* says that you must seek the right time or timing. But can it be applied to sentences?

Can we focus on an equal measure of excess and deficiency in terms of information? For example, as we said in Chap. 3, an equation such as $F = ma$ aims at saying a lot with very few signs. That equation exemplifies the aim to express a maximum amount of information with a minimum number of signs. Although a sentence takes longer to say the same thing, it may tell you something a little bit different about Newton's second law of motion: "The greater the force, the greater the acceleration, but the more massive the object, the smaller the acceleration." Notice the parallel construction of inverse proportion in the sentence. When does a sentence have deficient information within its context? When is one excessive? When does it satisfy our aims? Do we need to find a certain mean between excess and deficiency of information within a sentence and/or a group of sentences? Yes. It turns out that we can use systems thinking to point the way. Let's say this at the outset:

In writing sentences, we usually aim towards a balance of information, combined by subject and predicate, into a middle measure.

We have said that declarative or descriptive sentences are the basic means for saying something like an expression of belief or fact about our existence in space and time. You need the basic combination of subject, copula, and predicate to assert anything to somebody else. You want to be able to assert an idea clearly and simply. But you want to avoid being too short, being deficient, as you simplify. You don't want to say too little with a minimum of words. Strunk always stressed, "Avoid unnecessary words," but he also urged his students not to take shortcuts: "The longest way round is usually the shortest way home, and the one truly reliable shortcut in writing is to choose words that are strong and sure-footed, to carry the reader on his way" (74). Notice how he supports his rule about writing shortcuts with one of the oldest proverbs about real life. (For "proverb" see Common Core "Vocabulary and Strategy" *Flip Chart*, Panel 8.) So you modify a sentence or sentences toward a bit more iteration; that is, you repeat the same idea with a slight difference so as to be understood. You follow up. But as we reiterate, we don't want to be too excessive. Students can work on the verb "to reiterate." This is a process of following up by being redundant, which is to say, saying the same thing in a slightly different way so as to make our ideas clear by varying repetitions, both within a sentence and within several.

Here is a clear and simple nursery rhyme:

Jack Sprat could eat no fat.
His wife could eat no lean.
But betwixt them both,
They licked the platter clean.

This rhyme is all about excess and deficiency, Aristotle's opposites. "Sprat" is an outmoded word that once meant a kind of small herring; and then a small or inconsequential person: skinny. The word was chosen because it rimes with its opposite meaning. The sounds are identical but the meanings are opposite. Good sentences work in a context that balances between lean and fat. Taking advantage of their limitations, Jack and his wife practiced their own version of home economics. Their contradictory eating habits enabled a balancing act. (See Chap. 5 on a "Balanced Food Plate.")

Like home economics, in writing sentences you want economy and speed of expression certainly, like the first two sentences in the rhyme, but you also want a pace and rhythm that turns balance into a more leisurely swing that makes the point in its syntactic slot, like the last sentence in the rhyme. So the rime enacts a middle measure, a golden mean, both in the form of its sentences and in the content of its happy marriage. The structure of the sentences seems to echo the sense. Sense and sentence are near allied. In setting up an opposition between fat and lean, the poem expresses a mini-max proportion. It's funny, odd, and clever.

THE SENTENCE 143

We should discuss with students the differences between the "brevity of expression" in equations (Chap. 3) that characterizes much of the scientific method (Chap. 2), as opposed to the ampler range that characterizes sentences. In this regard, we might discuss not just formulas and equations, but also the various ways we can use codes that are characterized by economy of expression, secret, and otherwise. For instance, in his book on *Information*, von Baeyer tells how Samuel F. B. Morse struggled to invent a set of telegraphic signs to equal letters of the alphabet (112–115). Without knowing it, Morse was on the way toward using a basic principle of information theory: "… the most efficient code assigns short symbols to the common letters, and long symbols to the rare ones" (115). Morse solved his practical problem of saying more with less, when he went into a newspaper office and carefully studied the numbers of letters that were assembled in a printer's box of alphabetical types. The numbers of "e" letters in the box led all the rest because they were used most often in the composition of words and sentences. So he assigned one dot (.) to it, the minimum **code** for the maximum number of uses of "e." The letter "t" got a dash (-). So he not only invented a new code, but also, when he used nothing but dots and dashes, he unintentionally invented the either-or concept that would later become the opposing bits of information theory (117–121). Students may want to discuss the distress signal "S-O-S." It is easy to remember: " …—…" Sailors translated the signal into a sentence that meant, "Save Our ship."[26] Students may want to discuss mnemonics. There are plenty of secret codes that pivot the plot in literature, like Edgar Allen Poe's "The Gold Bug" or the Black Spot in Robert Louis Stevenson's *Treasure Island*.

So then a sentence, or group of sentences, should have equal proportions of not too much, not too little, like Goldilocks' portion of warm porridge. Not too hot, not too cold; it was just right. Aristotle said, "In arithmetical proportion the equal is a mean between the greater and the lesser."[27] So on balance, we seek a right proportion of information in composing sentences, not too fat, not too lean. Here is good advice: "Long sentences are not necessarily wordy, nor are short sentences always concise. A sentence is wordy if it can be tightened without loss of meaning."[28]

Classroom Exercise

For homework, students can find samples of wordy writing in newspapers or on websites. They can revise them on chrome books and bring them to class where teachers can display examples on a smart board. The goal would be to show how an excess of information can lead to diminished understanding. Teachers can supply other awkward examples, for instance, of academic writing, legal writing, scientific writing, or business writing.

Information theory can help put this idea about an economy of expression into a larger context. Any communication depends upon a "choice or selection from a set of alternatives."[29] You choose your own code depending on the context. Information theory is filled with codes of binary oppositions that usually involve choices between opposites. A bit is either a zero (0) or a one (1). For instance, in the effort to write a meaningful sentence, you seek a balance between easily understood words as opposed to clichés. You want to write originally, but not so originally as to be misunderstood. Then too, if a sentence is too predictable, you dismiss it being not worth writing or reading. "So what?" From the reader's point of view, if s/he reads with a certain amount of expectation, following the course of an argument, a completely unexpected turn of thought in the next sentence will be in danger of being rejected. So the less predictable an idea seems to be, the more information it contains. Information is high when expectation is low. Is that the case? You learn most when you least expect it.

Notice that the last couple of sentences are completely balanced in terms of less and more, high and low.

INFORMATION HOVERS IN A SENTENCE

Perhaps the most important idea that we can say about the following sequence of noun, verb, and object is that they let us project forward to a new meaning. The combination of subject and predicate implies a transformation into a meaning on the way. In terms of our Sender-Receiver diagram, when the symbols have been selected from their **code**, and applied in a larger **context**, that selective operation amounts to a transformation of meaning. "Maisie's life is harsh." Furthermore, when the sender writes, and when the reader reads, each is thinking about the new meaning by thinking backward and thinking forward. The transmission and transformation of all meaningful information follows this twofold process of being carried forward while also remembering backward. In terms of our Sender-Receiver diagram in the Introduction, s/he is working by feedback and feed-forward in a process that is somewhat circular. The expression is a "feedback loop." If you will excuse the expression, this cyclical process of thinking in back-and-forth combinations is loopy. In truth, if a sentence carries a very new meaning, it may seem at first to be more than a little odd, even loopy. "They licked the platter clean."

A Sentence Is Like a Moiré Pattern

Let's look at the balance of information in a sentence from another point of view. Let's focus more sharply on the sounds we speak in sentences because the patterns of sounds also contribute to the balanced measure in sentences. When linguists sometimes speak of the sound sense of language, they mean a combination. Let us say that the grammatical series of subject, verb, and object overlies the sound pattern series of phonemes in a spoken sentence. Consider our Sender-Receiver diagram once again. The grammatical choices are parts of the message's **code**, while the phonetic choices are parts of the transmitting **contact by sound waves**. Two different serial patterns of sound and sense are slotted on top of one another in the construction of a spoken sentence. The sounds of the spoken sentence are part of the serial order of energy **contacting**, while the grammatical order is **coded** in the serial order as noun, verb, and predicate. So they are composed together.

Let's think of an analogy taken from visual thinking; when we lay two similar grid patterns on top of one another, we can see a *moiré* pattern of pleasing wavy lines and shapes, which is a kind of third pattern. If you see two wire screens superimposed on top of one another, you see a kind of rippling pattern. If you move a bit, the patterns seem to ripple rhythmically. We need to understand the combined sound sense of a sentence so as to understand its meaning. The meaning of a sentence is its third pattern, an overlay of the contact and the code, of sound and sense. So when we hear a nicely composed sentence, we hear a rhythmic ripple. If you want to test the soundness of your sentence, read it aloud, says Pinker: "Though the rhythm of speech isn't the same as the branching of a tree [diagram], it's related in a systematic way, so if you stumble as you recite a sentence, it may mean you're tripping over on your own treacherous syntax" (115).

When we learn to speak a language as children, we are using intuitively this third pattern all the time because we unify the sound and the sense as we speak. But here we are practicing a skill, which means that we are taking a sentence apart and then putting it back together on a different plane. The different plane is our Sender-Receiver diagram. For example, in ballet practice, we might learn the various steps by performing different positions on a floor with square grids traced on it. (See Chap. 5.) Or we might correct our swing at batting practice by working on our grip on the bat or by attending to our wrists as we finish a swing. When writing sentences, we are heeding the ways that a sentence sounds as well as the way it means. To feature the sound sense of language is also to celebrate rhymed poems.

(See also Chap. 5.) Here, for instance, William Blake writes a rhymed sentence that asserts a judgment:

A robin redbreast in a cage
Puts all heaven in a rage.[30]

You can work on the sound patterns of phonemes (alliterations) that transmit the grammatical patterns. You can also modify the sentence a bit to reveal its repeated grammatical pattern: To put a robin in a cage puts all of heaven in a rage. You can see now that the first part of the sentence features the physical action of putting, even though unexpressed, while the second part transfers the physical act of putting "in a cage" to the rhyming metaphor "in a rage." The full balance of information of the sentence is its overlaid third pattern of sound and sense, like a moiré effect. Even though the couplet is very simple, its balance of information is more accurately speaking a rhythmic combination of sound and sense.

How does a sentence work as the transfer of units of meaning from one side of the verb to the other? The word "transit" in the definition of a "transitive" verb can begin that kind of exercise in transference. So often the reader and writer are thinking with their judgments held in abeyance, their decisions about an assertion hovering up in the air, as each sentence is processed on the way to a completed new meaning. So information often hovers, as a sentence is being written and then read. In Chap. 5, we explore a special kind of artful hovering.

Now we explore the idea that a hovering sentence sometimes employs a special kind of balancing act.

CHIASMUS

Chiasmus is a special style of parallel construction in a sentence. The term is Greek. It means something is marked like a crisscross. The Greek letter *chi* is an x. In Greek, *chi* means "cross." You can formulate the crisscross as the inverse ratios of algebra:

$$\frac{a}{b} = \frac{b}{a}$$

Or you can express it in this way:

$$a : b :: b : a$$

You can see here that a sentence with chiasmus is like an equation of inverse ratios. "The greater the force, the greater the acceleration, but the more massive the object, the smaller the acceleration." It is a mini-max proposition in which the crisscross is like cross multiplying in an equation of fractions. The crisscrossing itself is an act of balancing feedback.

In rhetoric, the balanced sentence is well known to be a powerful style of composition, such as the famous opening of Charles Dickens' novel, *A Tale of Two Cities,* which you might screen on a smart board. Dickens juxtaposes the best of times and the worst of times, the time of hope and the time of despair, the time of wisdom and the time of foolishness.

We can see here the great opposites, all assembled together into a puzzle. This kind of parallel balancing reached its pinnacle in the style of the eighteenth-century English writer Samuel Johnson, who perhaps overdid it, so later stylists sought a more fluidic rhythm in their sentences that still have balance as their feature.

In his chapter "The Sentence," Herbert Read says, "Antithesis operates by a tension or suspense between two ideas; the sentence becomes a balance between equal but opposite forces (42)." Again, the issue is tense opposition, and it is expressed as a suspension between opposite forces. You can see how the metaphor of balanced opposing forces has been transposed from the first conservation law. He uses the phrase "antithetical parallels." *In Chap. 5, we shall explore this idea of a tension of balanced forces as a main definition of the arts.* He cites Samuel Johnson's "a state too high for contempt and too low for envy" (41). It is clear that this kind of crisscross sentence is one that balances extremely opposite ideas and inverted relationships. Can you see too that a crisscross format is a special kind of syntactic slot, a background framework?

To sum up here, we can ask students to invent some balanced sentences in a classroom exercise. A good beginning is to list some of the great opposites and contradictions that we come across everyday and that will confront us all of our lives, as in the opposites in the passage from *Ecclesiastes.* To do a good act or a bad act. To love or to be just. To submit to power or to rebel. To tell the truth or to lie. We seek balance in our lives everyday because we need to make choices between tense opposites that happen to us all the time. And we often feel those opposites as forces or powers acting upon us. Thus, a balanced sentence is one of the most common of styles because it expresses a pair of opposite conflicts and contradictions that we confront all the time. Sometimes a balanced sentence seeks to resolve the conflict, as in Jack and his wife's division of the fat vs.

the lean. Sometimes a balanced sentence merely expresses the oppositions as an abiding tension, a controversial fact of life. Here are two inverted parallels in one chiasmus: "to stop too fearful, and too faint to go" (Oliver Goldsmith, "The Traveler"). Here's another example: "Powerful people take all that they can, and weak folks give up what they must." (See also Chap. 5, a section called "Balance of Power.")

Here Alexander Pope satirizes an enemy in a triplet whose rhymes act like slots and whose up-down imagery of a seesaw everyone knows:

His wit all see-saw, between *that* and *this*,
Now high, now low, now Master up, now Miss,
And he himself one vile antithesis.[31]

When we practice writing a crisscross sentence, we most often use coordinate conjunctions like "and" or "but." So we can review the grammatical definitions of "coordinate." In most dictionaries, the leading definition is "equal in rank." In mathematics, we know that "coordinate geometry" is a study of graphs (Chap. 3). In the study of physiology, "coordination" means a harmonious combination of faculties, muscular and mental, that leads toward a balanced action, such as Rembrandt's sketch of a child learning to walk (Introduction). (See also Chap. 5.) So we can range back and forth over our several methods of inquiry, learning how balance and equality are coordinated.

Before leaving this section, we should note that an extremely persuasive use of balanced sentences is to compose a series of "parallel" phrases in a sentence or in a series of sentences. Pinker calls this kind of construction a "structural parallelism" (124–127). For instance, students can study Abraham Lincoln's "Gettysburg Address:"

Lincoln says twice that we who are gathered here and American citizens at large, that we dedicate ourselves and resolve for a new birth of freedom. And then he employs the now famous recurrent phrases "government of the people, by the people, for the people." We note that it is the reiteration of the phrases in parallel, with only a slight shift of prepositions, which makes for the powerful assertion. Students will also certainly listen to and study Martin Luther King Jr's famous speech, which repeats the sentence "I have a dream" in rising fervor. Students can study that sentence in itself as a liberating exclamation. Both of these examples will be studied in the Common Core Curriculum. So you can see from these two examples that repetition of sound-sense combinations works as a useful redundancy. Read again the passage from *Ecclesiastes*, quoted above. They are not too brief, like a mathematical formula, nor too much like verbal formulas in the crisscross of chiasmus. They **bundle** the same units in **following** sequences. They feature repetition with a difference. We notice too that the following sequences move us forward in the reading, and they seem to impel us to agree, so that we can become free.

To close this section about parallel compositions, we can ask students to write sentences that rhyme. Any pair of words that rhyme are in parallel. As Jakobson says, "Rhyme is only a particular, condensed case of a much more general, we may say, the fundamental problem of poetry, namely parallelism" ("Closing Statement," 368). Is poetry all about parallelism? That is worth study, and we shall in Chap. 5.

We might mistakenly suppose that rhyming is a trivial or an old-fashioned skill. But an eminent mathematician once claimed that he liked the discipline of writing verse because the search for a rhyming word, one with another, often led unintentionally to a new idea. The chance combination of similar sounds can lead to a new sense emerging. You can ask students to write their own couplets. How can a rhyme lead to a new idea? Students can learn that rhyming "breath" with "death" might be too predictable and opposition. And to be more up to date, you can test the idea of rhyming toward a new idea by playing some rap music, in which chanters sometimes improvise lyrics along the way. You can notice that end-stopped rhymes are **matching** demands (in our terms), even while each couplet moves the thoughts forward in a **following** series of sequential ideas. You might even try to start a discussion about the process of thinking that we go through when we read and or write a couplet. To understand the rhyme, we think backward, recollecting the first word by the rhyme of the second, even while we are repeating forward the sense of the idea. A couplet is the very essence of balancing feedback because it combines recollection and anticipation. Isn't that combined process of recollecting and repeating the very model of what we do when we think with language. We feed forward and we feed back. Maybe find some really good rhyming couplets to stretch students' minds.

"Parallel" and Other "Para-" Nouns

"Use common, grade-appropriate Greek and Latin affixes and roots as clues to the meaning of a word..." (*Common Core Flip Chart*, Panel 9, Standard L.5.4b).

Language, like algebra, is a code built upon our awareness of parts of speech that we can turn into recurrent patterns of meanings. To complete this section on parallel patterns, we could ask students to list words that use "para" as a prefix. This is an exercise in etymology and translation. This list could be an exercise in finding *likeness* among similar words that we often use in sentences. For instance, a parallel line in geometry means one kind of equal measure, but in language use, as we have just seen, it means a balanced series of syntactical likeness of repeated phrases. If we were to look up the prefix in a dictionary, we would find that "para-" derives from a Greek term that means "beside, alongside, beyond, closely related." So then our word "para-graph" combines "para," as in "closely related," with "graph," which means writing or to write. So a paragraph means a series of written sentences closely related to one another by recurrent ideas. A paragraph is composed as a higher slot than a sentence, but it is a stylistic slot, not a grammatical slot. When writing a paragraph, you have a lot more latitude than a sentence. Another word from rhetoric is parataxis. (See below.) Another is parenthesis. Here are some more general words that now can be seen as part of a linguistic **context**: paralegal, paramount, paranormal, paranoia, paramour, and paratrooper. So all of these possible choices await in memory as the possible context for the next choice of one of them.

A Prospective View of Narrative

As we compose sentences into paragraphs and then into longer sections, we are always attuned to the narrative that we are building. Here is the Common Core overview about narrative:

> Students' narrative skills continue to grow in [grades 6–8]. The Standards require that students be able to incorporate narrative elements effectively into arguments and informative/explanatory texts. In history/social studies, students must be able to incorporate narrative accounts into their analyses of individuals or events of historical import. In science and technical subjects, students must be able to write precise enough descriptions of the step-by-step procedures they use in their investigations or technical work that others can replicate them and (possibly) reach the same results.[32]

Here is the opening sentence of Herbert Read's chapter on "Narrative" (97). "Narrative is of two kinds, being descriptive either of *events* (what *is taking place*) or of *objects* (what *has taken place*); that is to say, it either *active* or *passive* in character." Notice how nicely balanced is his sentence. Objects tend to be things, and events are actions; that is, they are nouns and verbs. Further,

> ... the writer should convey to the reader the *speed* of events and the *actuality* of objects. Both these effects are best secured by economy of expression: that is to say, the words used to convey the impression should be just sufficient. If there are too many words, the action is clogged, the actuality blurred. If too few, the impression is not conveyed in its completeness; the outlines are vague. In either case there is a lack of visual clarity.

You can see that the aim in the construction of sentences is to achieve an equal measure between too many words and too few, an economy of expression.

When children first learn longer strings of language, they often tell stories by connecting independent clauses and simply by using coordinating conjunctions like "and" or "but." Telling a narrative is a series of "and then, and then, and then." At first, children don't learn to make up sentences that contain qualifying words of superordination or subordination, which introduce compound clauses. This "and then" style is sometimes called "telegraphic," but you may need to describe what a telegraph is. (Think Morse code.) As Ernst Cassirer says, the language of children is everywhere "paratactic."[33] You can do exercises in writing paratactic sentences. They tend to be lists of objects in space, of things, and often they just list sequences of "and then." Nevertheless, the additive style has its uses.

As we close this chapter about sentences, we should stress that the composition of sentences is not the be-all and end-all of good writing. Just as you can't derive the rules of sentence construction from the rules for the construction of words out of phonemes and morphemes, so you can't derive the arts of composing paragraphs and longer periods from the rules of sentence construction (Fig. 4.1): "The Greek grammarians and rhetoricians saw the touchstone of style in the development of the period, in which clauses do not run along in an indeterminate sequence, but support one another, like stones in an ["interlocked"] arch" (310). In passing, we notice how Cassirer transferred an idea from architecture and used it as a metaphor for longer periods. And we can also focus on the curved keystone at the center of the arch as another instance of a middle measure. For instance, students will be taught the style of writing an argument that uses comparison and contrast as a way of reasonably setting forth a series of ideas that moves toward a balanced conclusion.

To summarize here, maybe the most important thing we can say about learning to write sentences is this: As we express ourselves, sentences let us express forecasts about our own possible future actions. When we write narratives with sentences, we are always forecasting. We read forecasting sentences all the time; for instance, we hear or read a weather forecast like this: "A north-easterly flow of air will bring rain and snow to the Atlantic seashore states." Another may warn about road closings. "The New York State Thruway between Buffalo and Albany will be closed until further notice." So we make predictions about daily actions based upon what we know or guess about coming events, based on what we remember about past events. We do this kind of forecasting all the time, everyday. Often a guess is quickly intuitive. But sometimes if a coming event seems unpredictable, or not immediately predictable, we need to say explicitly, "Now what do I do next?" Especially if we seem to be caught between two conflicting events, we pause, in between.

This kind of internal conflict is so familiar as not to need much analysis: Shall I go outside and play, or do I stay inside and do homework? A parent will surely put it in a following sequence, "First one, and then the other." She assumes, obviously, that doing homework first will lead to a more capable daughter or son. But if you stop and say to yourself on your own, "First I do this and then I do that," then you will have made a sentence that is self-expressive. You have moved from your revolting predicament toward a self-encouraging judgment about yourself. You have begun a kind of inner dialogue that presumes you are moving toward a slightly newer self just a little bit later on. By means of a self-referring sentence, you may be able to forecast your future self. What do we mean by an inner dialogue? Here is what Plato says: "Well, thinking and discourse [speech] are the same thing, except that which we call thinking is, precisely, the inward dialogue carried on by the mind with itself without spoken sound" (*Sophist*, 263e). What an important idea this is. A sentence can let you say to yourself, "Where am I heading?" or "I am on the way." You are not moving just from fifth grade to sixth; instead you are expressing your inner self. When you have a little talk with yourself, in an inner dialog, you may be moving toward that other person you hope to become. "What shall I be?" Sentences let us express our own Being, as we think about and hope for our future lives. By means of the verb "to be," we think about how we exist and even why we exist ("To be" is the infinitive for "is."). We do this kind of feedback and feed-forward mostly with sentences. You are both your own sender and a receiver, an actor and a patient, at the same time. In this kind of writing, you seem to take possession of your actions. Isn't that what Stein's self-possession means? You can write yourself a journal. You can write a kind of fiction called an "interior monolog." You can write yourself a poem. You can have pleasant surprises in this kind of work as you move toward a new sense of self-accomplishment: "Onward!"

You might think that this is too much of a claim to make about sentences, that they help us to judge and to act. Yet no less a philosopher than Immanuel Kant makes that claim about language and predication. In his study of symbolic forms, Ernst Cassirer summarizes Kant's definition of judging as a linking of a subject and a predicate in order to compose a completely meaningful idea:

> For Kant, judgment meant the "unity of action" by which the predicate is referred to the subject and linked with it to form a whole meaning, to form the unity of an objectively subsisting and objectively constructed relationship. And it is in this intellectual unity of action which finds its linguistic representation and counterpart in the use of the copula.[34]

That is a difficult passage, but it is worth study because it is a big claim about sentences. When we construct a balancing relationship between subject and predicate, then we can compose an objectively existing unified action. How so? With this unity of action, we express a meaningful judgment. Though difficult, it is hard to find a bigger claim than this about the importance of writing sentences. A copula completes the symbolic unity.

Sentences let us move forward in our imaginations and judgments. First, we slowly learn grammar and the slots of syntax. They are readymade following patterns. They are "how to do it" exercises. They are first given to us as we learn them all put together by our folks in their speech. A 5-year-old child said to me recently, "What are consequences?" Somebody else had just said, "You have to face the consequences." Then later our teachers give them to us as rules: the parts of speech, how the conjunctions work, subject-verb agreement, where the clauses go. These rules of grammar are hand-me-downs, but when we struggle to say something new, we turn those old clothes into fresh garments. We move from "how" questions to "why" questions. But our intent is not just a fresh or fashionable style, though that may be important. We may want to move a reader by appealing to emotions, or we may want to appeal to her reason. They are different kinds of tasks, and they are taught as kinds of rhetoric.

But when we speak or write for ourselves in sentences, as when we write in a journal, or when we write a lyric poem about ourselves, then we are using our minds to become slightly changed persons. In pointing toward our possible future selves in our changes over time, we possess ourselves; we find equipoise that our skills serve our purposes. Every time a child says, "Let me do it," she is learning a skill to move onward.

"Know Yourself"

Gertrude Stein said that she learned self-possession from diagramming sentences. Can we learn to become more self-possessed by using language to think about ourselves with sentences? I can draw a portrait of myself in order to see myself, or I can dance to express myself. As we have said, one of the most important functions of language is that it is self-referring. I can use a sentence to think about myself. All along in this chapter, we have been using sentences to talk about sentences. But implicitly, we have also been using sentences to make self-references about our own existing. The sentence "I am" uses a form of the copula "is" as a judgment about my existence. It lets me proclaim, "I exist." "Know thyself" is perhaps the oldest Greek proverb. To know myself, to have self-knowledge, means that we want to learn how to understand ourselves. Self-correction by self-reference is a method of balancing feedback. Another related phrase is "self-regulation." Also, in his discussion of educational feedback, mentioned in the Introduction, Perkins uses the phrase "self-assessment" (84–85). (Self-assessment is a tried and true method of the Common Core Curriculum.) Sometimes too we can know something about ourselves by "standing outside" and trying to see us as others see us. Do other folks see us on the outside as "objects," at first at least? Other people don't know our inner dialogs, our thought processes, out feelings, our emotions, or our inner lives, unless we tell them in some format. They often see me as an exterior person with a label attached, "teacher" or "student," a label attached to a body who lives in the real world, who moves around, has shape, and occupies space. He exists. From this outside standpoint, we are seen as parts of the world of objects and events in space and time. Sometimes it helps to try to see ourselves as an eighth grader among others. And then sometimes we can look within and say, in so many words, "I know I am growing, but what kind of person do I want to become?" I can keep a journal about my feelings, or I can write a lyric poem about myself. Emily Dickinson wrote a lyric that goes, "This is my letter to the world that never wrote to me." By means of an inner dialog of self-questioning and self-answering, we become self-possessed, balanced.

The idea that language can both refer to itself as an existing thing and that it can also refer to itself as language is tricky: "This sentence no verb." That is an example by Dennis Hofstadter, and he wrote a book about these kinds of self-referential identity games called *I Am a Strange Loop*.[35] When we say "I," we seem to mean both our physical selves and also our ways of thinking and feeling; so, under the cover of "I," we flip back and forth in feedback loops of self-reference and assessment. These are two different points of view, and they often involve telling stories about ourselves, both about our past and about our possible futures, as seen from the first-person point of view and the third-person point of view. Literature helps us see ourselves as we read and think about others. Literature allows us to become self-referential. We can see ourselves in the characters of stories and novels. We can see ourselves as Tom Sawyer or Becky Thatcher. We can see ourselves, at a remove, as characters struggle through their own polarizing conflicts that make up a plot. For example, in Esther Forbes' *Johnny Tremain*, the main character, a promising silversmith, seems to be heading down a path of self- destruction after his hand has been maimed. As the narrative continues, we follow with sympathy his growing self-awareness and eventual self-rescue.[36]

CLASSROOM EXERCISE: EMILY DICKINSON'S POEM ABOUT THE BRAIN

To conclude this chapter, let's study a poem, which begins "The Brain is wider than the sky." We can display the whole poem on a smart board. Its three quatrains are composed as three "is" sentences. Speaking starkly in terms of our Sender-Receiver diagram, we know that the embodied brain serves as the ultimate sender-receiver of our messages sent to and fro. It receives inputs from the outer world and it converts them into sent symbolic messages. It feeds backward and forward. As we learn things, we are building in our brains a model of the ways we tacitly predict that the world works. Put too crudely maybe, the brain is our means-ends converter. But we recall that the thesis of embodied knowledge suggests that there is no real split between body and mind: "The Brain—is wider than the Sky."[37]

Although the poem begins with an "is" sentence, we know that the sentence is untrue. It calmly asserts a strange absurdity. How can a brain be wider than the sky? Dickinson describes the extent of the massive brain's containment of even more far-reaching mental activity. But as we shall see, her assertion is not just a little oppositional paradox blown out of all proportion. In the next stanza, the poet continues to play off the rhetorical trope of synecdoche, the substitution of the container for the thing contained, which is a spatial trope: "The brain is deeper than the sea." Another absurdity, how does she justify it?

The last stanza begins: "The Brain is just the weight of God." If you can heft, balance, and measure the massive brain and God (the law of the fulcrum), the difference will be the difference between the pronounced measure of the sound and the sound itself. What is the weight of the sound sense of language? Dickinson searches around, with her rangy skills of rhyme and syntax, to find the right analogy "in" the vastness of her own brain. Here the balanced mechanics of the brain's weight, measured against God's, slips away into the metaphorical weight and measure of testing for the sound sense of the right word. What is the difference between the pronunciation of a syllable and the sound that carries its message? We could continue to study the balancing act of the poem itself, its metrics, its phonemes and morphemes, and its rhetorical use of the balanced sentence. (See again Fig. 4.1.) Here we are simply underscoring her use of balance and the paradox that, though brain exists in a material universe, the mind's mental acts called "thinking" exist nowhere in space. Well, does thinking exist only in one dimension?

In each stanza, each of her sentence structures follows the basic grammatical principle that the subject designates something that has weight and occupies space, while the predicate points to an un-thing-ly concept or attribute, an "Idea." This kind of "is" sentence is the very stuff of scientific or descriptive writing, as we have seen. Scientific writing, textbook writing, has no personality, no voice, no self-attending style. It is composed of rational information. But we can say too that poetry is beyond reason, beyond rationality. A poem can assert a creative mystery.

And poetry must also be a voice that sets a mood. So Dickinson speaks with this very formal mood of logical assertion so as to assert an illogical paradox, even a slightly outrageous paradox that is very like a riddle. It is not information she is exchanging, but a playful insight. She is not diagramming a brain; she is creating her Idea of one. She hefts the brain's weight against the weightiness of God. God is perhaps the ultimate universal concept, the last predicate. You just can't balance them like that, can you? This lyric tells us, in no uncertain terms, how a poet sees the brain as the modeler of the world, of poetry. But what she may be alleging about the relations between the brain as a material thing and the great universals is something else again. That is for each of us to decide. As we shall consider in the next chapter, art is often very strange.

Notes

1. See David Lewis-Williams, *The Mind in the Cave: Consciousness and the Origins of Art* (London: Thames & Hudson, 2002), 271–277.
2. Alexander Marshack, *The Roots of Civilization: The Cognitive Beginnings of Man's First Art, Symbol and Notation* (New York: McGraw Hill Book Company, 1972), 21–32. Also, online: http://sservi.nasa.gov/articles/oldest-lunar-calendars/.
3. See Jerome Bruner, *The Process of Education* (Cambridge, Mass: Harvard University Press, 1960, 1982), "Readiness for Learning," 34.
4. Ferdinand de Saussure, *Course in General Linguistics*, trans. Wade Baskin (New York: McGraw-Hill Book Company), 1966) 67.
5. See Douglas Hofstadter and Emmanuel Sander, *Surfaces and Essences: Analogy as the Fuel and Fire of Thinking* (New York: Basic Books, 2013), 69–71.
6. Anthony Burgess, *Enderby Outside* (1968). Quoted by Stanley Eugene Fish, *How to Write a Sentence and How to Read One* (New York: Harper Collins Publishers 2011), 2. Fish cites a number of web sites about nifty sentences.
7. Herbert Read, *English Prose Style* (Boston: Beacon Press, 1970), 33.
8. See http://www.corestandards.org/ELA-Literacy/L/language-progressive-skills/. See also CC Flip Chart, Panel 9, Standard (L5.3a): "Expand, combine, reduce sentences for meaning...."
9. See Morton W. Bloomfield, "The Syncategorematic in Poetry: From Semantics to Syntactics," in *To Honor Roman Jakobson: Essays on the Occasion of His Seventieth Birthday* (The Hague, Mouton, 1967), 309–317.
10. A useful website reproduces Dickinson's original handwritten versions, with her own corrections: *Emily Dickinson Digital Archive*, Amherst College: http://www.edickinson.org/editions/1/image_sets/240388.
11. See Walter Jackson Bate's chapter "Negative Capability," in *John Keats* (Cambridge, Mass., Harvard University Press, 1963), on stationing as a kind of dynamic poise, 246.
12. Roman Jakobson, "Verbal Communication," collected in *Communication* (San Francisco: Scientific American, 1972), 44.
13. *Plato: The Collected Dialogues*, eds. Edith Hamilton and Huntington Cairns (Princeton, NJ: Princeton University Press, 1963). See *The Sophist*, 262 d).

14. See this online entry for knitting: https://en.wikipedia.org/wiki/Knitting.
15. William Strunk, Jr., *The Elements of Style*, 2nd rvsd. ed., Introduction by E. B. White (New York: The Macmillan Company, 1972), 65.
16. *The Project Gutenberg EBook of Childe Harold's Pilgrimage, by Lord Byron*. Free download at: gutenberg.org, Canto 3, 114.
17. Quoted by Fish, 160. In her book on diagramming sentences, Kitty Burns Florey also quotes this passage, *Sister Bernadette's Barking Dog* (New York: 2006 Harvest Books). See also "Sentence Diagrams," *Wikipedia* online.
18. For discussion plus many exercises about tree diagrams, see Koenraad Kuiper and W. Scott Allan, *An Introduction to English Language: Word, Sound, Sentence*, 2nd ed. (Palgrave Macmillan, 2004), "The Structure of Simple Sentences," Chapter 7.
19. See Steven Pinker, *The Sense of Style: The Thinking Person's Guide to Writing in the 21st Century* (New York: Viking: 2014). 78–79, 88–89.
20. For an overview of in the question of being or existence in modern philosophy, beginning with Kant, see *Stanford Encyclopedia of Philosophy* online: http://plato.stanford.edu/entries/existence/.
21. Samuel Taylor Coleridge, Essay XI, *The Friend*. See Google Books online.
22. J. L. Austin drew this distinction *in How to Do Things With Words* (Cambridge, Mass: Harvard University Press, 1962).
23. John Lyons, *Introduction to Theoretical Linguistics* (Cambridge: Cambridge University Press, 1968), 322–323.
24. Ernest Fenollosa, *The Chinese Written Character as a Medium for Poetry*, ed. Ezra Pound, 29.
25. Aristotle, *Nichomachean Ethics*, trans. Joe Sachs (Newburyport, Mass.: Focus Publishing, 2002), p. 208.
26. https://en.wikipedia.org/wiki/SOS.
27. *The Ethics of Aristotle*, trans. J. A. K. Thomson (New York: Penguin, 1959), 129.
28. Diana Hacker and Nancy Sommers, *A Pocket Style Manual*, 6th ed. (Boston: Bedford/St. Martins, nd), 2.
29. See Lyons, *Theoretical Linguistics* 89–91. See also Kahneman, *Thinking, Fast and Slow*, on memorable sentences, 29–61.
30. William Blake, "Auguries of Innocence," online The Poetry Foundation: http://www.poetryfoundation.org/poem/172906.
31. "An Epistle to Dr. Arbuthnot" *The Complete Poems of Alexander Pope*. Gutenberg.org.
32. See commoncore.org; narrative.
33. Ernst Cassirer, *Philosophy of Symbolic Forms*, trans. Ralph Manheim (New Haven: Yale University Press, 1953), volume 1, Chapter 5, "Forms of Pure

Relations," 310. See also Fish, on parataxis as a style of rhetoric, and Chapter 6 "The Additive Style."
34. Immanuel Kant maintained that the meaning of objective judgment depended on the linguistic formulation together of a subject and predicate. See Ernst Cassirer, *The Philosophy of Symbolic Forms*, trans. Ralph Manheim (New Haven: Yale University Press, 1953), I, 213–214.
35. Douglas Hofstadter, *I Am a Strange Loop* (New York: Basic Books, 2007). See especially Fish, Chapter 10 "Sentences That Are About Themselves (Aren't They All)?"
36. Esther Forbes, *Johnny Tremain* (New York: HMH Books for Young Readers, reprint 2011). Find a Common Core study guide at .http://www.centerforlearning.org/PDF/standards/johnny-tremain-common-core-standards-4983.pdf.
37. The psychologist Gerald Edelman made this poem more famous when he used it for the title for *Wider Than the Sky: The Phenomenal Gift of Consciousness* (New Haven: Yale University Press, 2004).

CHAPTER 5

Seeking a Middle Measure

Throughout their years of schooling, students learn these three methods of composition because we know that these are practical skills that will serve students in their futures. And throughout this book, we have focused on these compositional skills as methods of taking things apart and then of recombining them back together again into a balance. Now, in this chapter, we broaden the idea of balance to include balancing-up as an essential element in seeking a middle measure in larger social and cultural issues. In short, this chapter is about finding a middle measure among cultural issues. So we broaden the practice of balancing as a set of skills in levering or writing or computing toward a kind of learning that is associated with a middle measure, and that is an ability called "practical reason" or "practical wisdom," as we shall see. How do we use those practical skills of composition and apply them as ways of taking things apart and then recombining them into *new* creations for their own needs? In this chapter, then we feature the artistic and cultural aspects of the "Language Arts" section of the Common Core Curriculum.

CULTURAL STRIFE AND THE "ETERNAL CONFLICT OF OPPOSITES"

By the time students have reached middle school, they will have needed to learn that we live in a culture of polarizing conflicts and contradictions, tension, strife, and stress. In the streets, in families, and even in schools, strife seems all around. Although strife and stress seem to pervade much of our lives nowadays, they are not new feelings. So we start again with some history. From ancient times, people have composed themselves into protective societies because many believed that the whole world, even the cosmos itself, was thought to be an "eternal conflict of opposites."[1] Understanding and regulating those antagonisms, some thought, was "the root principle of existence." Is it also for our students' existence?

To support this huge claim about regulating eternal conflicts, Johan Huizinga quoted the ancient Greek thinker Heraclitus who said, "strife is the father of all things," but he also said that this kind of strife can be naturally balanced, our large theme. For instance, in one of his preserved fragments, Heraclitus said, "The unity of things lies beneath the surface; it depends upon a balanced reaction between opposites."[2] Heraclitus said that a balancing between opposites causes a reaction, which makes for change, a good result. So he says we should look for unity beneath the surface of things, and that unity demands a balanced reaction between opposites. In the last three chapters, we have found this kind of reaction in balancing feedback, and we have focused on the unity of a pivot, an equals signs, and the word "is."

We might shrug off Heraclitus as an outmoded ancient thinker, but recall what Bronowksi said about the search for unity in the sciences, quoted in the Introduction: "All science is the search for unity in hidden likenesses. Here is a way to think about creative discovery in the arts and sciences: We should seek the underlying unity of things by looking for a tense balancing act in a composition. So in this concluding chapter, let's focus on balancing as a middle measure that can help to unify the arts, the sciences, and ethics.

Here is a good summary of Heraclitus's thinking: "The total balance of the cosmos can only be maintained if change in one direction eventually leads to change in the other, that is, if there is unending strife between opposites" (*PS*, 193). Change is a good thing, isn't it? Balance is a good thing, isn't it? Balanced change comes about because of the eternal strife between opposites. We shall test this idea here.

Heraclitus also said that an underlying and often hidden unity between opposite forces was stronger than an easily apparent connection, so he often spoke in paradoxes to make us think. Here is one of his adages, which is almost like a riddle: "The world is back-stretched, like the bow and the lyre" (*PS*, 192). Students could discuss this saying. What does it mean that the world seems back-stretched? Is the whole world counterbalanced by tension? What is the likeness between a bow and a lyre? You can make war with a bow and arrow, but also you can make music on a stringed instrument. How may a stress or tension of counterstretched strings create both the twang of a war bow and the harmonies of sweet music? Is each instrument somewhat like a lever, just as the bent-back pole of a pole vaulter gives him leverage? Does Heraclitus' strange adage imply that all of nature, the cosmos itself, is always in stressful or tensed counterbalancing? What measuring skills do you need to do both, what ratios of music, what feelings of muscular resistance? Is there an underlying relationship between play and war, like checkers, chess, or videogames? Is stress itself also a feeling of tense balance? Is strife more of a physical word, while stress is more of a psychological word? What are some other likely synonyms? Tension? What hidden unity, and what logic, gathers together into a new concept these two familiar instruments? We notice too that Heraclitus composes his sentence with a simile "like...," which itself features an unapparent connection, like a little riddle, or an unapparent ratio, which we must seek for ourselves. We spoke extensively about likeness in the Introduction. Notice that a feeling of tension is information that is communicated in a **contact** channel as an **index**, a physical sign of a real connection interrelating a sign, brain, and object.

At this point, a Sender-Receiver diagram can help to make his sentence clearer (See Fig. 5.1).

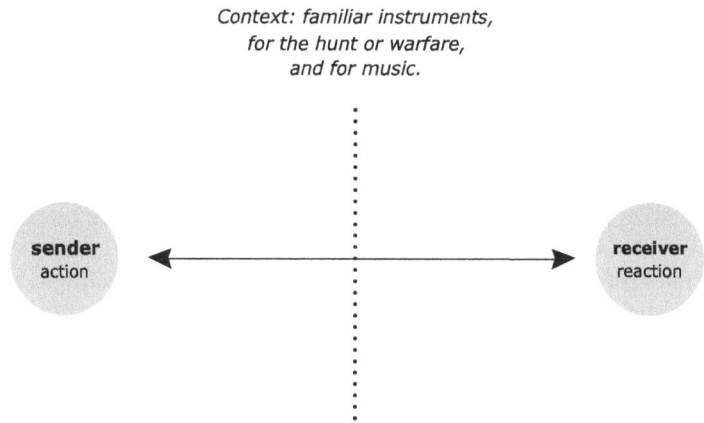

Fig. 5.1 Bow and the Lyre
The two instruments are back-stretched, bent back, so they are held in tension, ready to act. So the cosmos is held in tension. If it is cosmic, it is universal. So this adage exposes a universal principle of physical form.

The editors of Heraclitus' fragments explain what "counter-stretched" means for them: "tending equally in opposite directions. A tension in one direction automatically produces an equivalent tension in the other; if not, the system collapses" (*PS*, 193). Does this explanation seem very modern, like Newton's third law of motion, discussed at the end of Chap. 2? "For every action there is an equal and opposite reaction." Newton's assertive sentence is now seen as a universal law of motion, so familiar as to seem a truism, self-evident as Lincoln apparently said. Students can discuss this assumption: *The very principle of balancing feedback, at least in the physical world, relies upon Newton's third law of moving things*: for every action there is an equal and opposite reacting motion. For students this is a law worth memorizing.

But where do we find the middle measure in a force of action and equal reaction? In this chapter, we shall find out that the middle point is also a pivoting point, the point between turn and return. Finding that in-between point, as we have seen, involves once again learning a skill and a method. In ethics, we shall see, the method is called "practical reason" or practical wisdom. And in the arts and sciences of discovery, we shall call that method "combinatory play," the ability to combine things into a new creation. And what we do in school, we shall call "serious play." Now we discuss these three closely related methods of composing things.

Schooling Is Serious Play

How does play enter? The fundamental polarization of opposite forces and things apparently calls for us to seek, find, and regulate an underlying balance that unifies oppositions. Turning now to Huizinga, he shows that an essential way that many cultures seek to regulate these oppositions and antagonisms is to set aside a ritualized playground of some sort, and to dramatize and test these conflicts within a safety zone. He thinks that culture truly begins with the regulation of organized play as the best way to corral strife. His big claim is that play is the origin of culture. Recall that this chapter features middle measures in culture. Playing is not trivial. It is wonderfully important. As we shall, he called this kind of distancing playground a "magic circle." Playing a game on a set-aside arena seems to offset strife and stress, not by repressing them, but by reenacting them in a safe place. Throughout this chapter, we shall celebrate a principle of creative play, often composed as a middle measure between opposites.

Ever since Plato celebrated "serious play" in his *Laws*, people have devoted themselves to this kind of unifying action. Plato thought too that schooling can be considered serious play. For Plato the Greek word *skhole* meant "leisure," and his extension of it as a place of leisurely but serious play is the origin of our word "school."[3] So a school may be seen as a place set aside from the world of strife where we can seriously play out these oppositions and see how we can balance them for a better future. That is our aim.

Sender and Receiver Play in a Magic Circle

In the "Introduction" and in "The Fulcrum," we began with a seesaw in a playground. Let's start with what we know about real playgrounds. They are places set aside from the rest of our lives. We usually play in a space that has been created especially. We play on soccer fields, baseball diamonds, and football stadiums. We play board games like chess or checkers that serve as the playing fields. According to Huizinga, when we play we usually do so in a so-called "magic circle." This circle is a circumscribed arena that has been set aside from the real world in a certain space and within a time set for the performance. Think of several kinds of playing fields that have chalk lines for their limits. Nowadays the phrase helps to describe a virtual reality that characterizes the player in a video game.[4]

It's useful to discuss the idea that this kind of magic circle is part of the **code and context** of the playground, because it too is a framework, a background that helps to shape the action, like delineated squares on a chess board that constrains certain limited kinds of moves, the **codes**, for instance, that allow a bishop to move only along diagonally situated squares or a rook to move only vertically and horizontally on the playground.

Now consider a playground like a tennis court or a volleyball court or a badminton court. You can imagine the net that divides the players as a vertical line or an axis in our Sender-Receiver diagram. You can also consider the play itself as a form of strife between two opposing forces. Huizinga says that sometimes play can be seen as a kind of ritualized warfare that abstracts actual war into an acceptable alternative on a playing field. Students may want to discuss the archer in *The Hunger Games*, who is forced to play a deadly game of killing other players within a hemmed-in forest set aside for the action. Is this killing playful? Students may want to discuss the tension between primitive archery, her bow and arrow, and sophisticated explosives that govern the games. We are beginning to define play as a kind of strife or tension that has been displaced into a magical realm all its own, with a special set of rules, of codes that show it is not a warfare of "every man for himself." Playing tennis or in badminton, when we volley back and forth in a long series of nifty strokes, we feel exhilarated by the balancing feedback. When we watch great players in a prolonged tennis volley, we admire the artistry and grace of the players, even above the eventual outcome of one winner. So we can see how play can become creative play. We can see too how play can become an art form, because they are both based upon the feeling of aestheticized strife or tension.

We began this chapter with Heraclitus's assertion, "strife is the father of all things," but now we are saying that creative play displaces hurtful strife into an alternative space and time, a magic circle separated from the real world but one that is freer and happier, at least during the interval we are playing within its code. We are still struggling for available energy, but now the effortful stress feels good, as we play well. Obviously not all games are net games, and not all games are played within a three-dimensional (3-D) space. Consider that games like chess, checkers, and Monopoly are set aside on a small symbolic space, a flat plain, in which little tokens are moved around. Recall that you can play chess or checkers on your computer, upon a two-dimensional (2-D) grid, where you can play against your computer. If you know the rules of chess, you can walk into the middle of a game and see who is winning by the arrangement of figures on the board. Where does the middle measure come in? The fun of the game is to play against an opponent who is as talented as you are. You hope to be well matched, because an inexperienced opponent is just not as much fun. Or if you play chess against your computer, you know that the computer has been programmed to respond to your amateurish moves with a feedback system that will beat you every time. Is that a contest between equal and opposite forces? In play, you want a balanced opposition. In one of Rex Stout's novels, his brilliant detective, Nero Wolf, asks a visitor if he plays chess. When the visitor says that he would like to play a game, Wolf leans back in his easy chair, closes his eyes, and says, "Pawn to the Queen 4." How can his opponent compete with the implication that Wolf can hold the whole sequence of moves on an imaginary board in his visual memory? Is this serious play, or is it a bluff? His visitor predicts to himself in an inner dialog: "I have no chance to win against this guy."

We should discuss as well with students that not all play is a game of opponents. Along the way, we can point out different kinds of creative or free play, unrestricted by opposition, but still with a little bit of tension.

And even when we are playing freely, even when by ourselves, during those moments we are playing in a magic place, a symbolic space, maybe even a sacred space, that is ours for the nonce. Even the most modest play space in a backyard or garden or public park can become a magic space that a child may set aside for imaginary play. In the following sections, we shall see how serious play continues to be important.

Practical Reason

Often this kind of serious play includes a practical wisdom that is part of the rules of the game. Can we learn a kind of "practical reason," Aristotle's phrase for using a middle measure, by playing? When we are playing, are we also learning a practical skill?

Because strife and stress seem to characterize the world at large, surely they also influence our own inner worlds, our emotions, and reasons. We are told that we should compose a balance between our pleasures and our pains, our unruly urges and our reasonable judgments. As we shall see, many scientists say our brains have a built-in structure that allows us to "balance" or "coordinate" reasonable judgments as opposed to our urges or passions. For instance, the function of the brain's neo-cortex is: ... "the maintenance of the proper balance between action and restraint, and the capacity to perform actions for which the reward is delayed."[5] (See here how a scientist uses balance as a metaphor.)

Classroom Exercise for Finding Practical Reason

Students can bring to class examples from daily newspapers or online news sources that show this kind of balanced reasonableness. Here, for example, is the leading sentence, a topic sentence, from a column by a distinguished journalist, David Brooks: "As individuals we all try to build on our strengths and work on our weaknesses, and it's probably a good idea to balance these two activities."[6] Teachers can provide examples, both contemporary and historical.

We learn to pause, to take stock, and to look ahead. We learn to reason about our pleasures versus our pains. We learn to delay an immediate gratification and to postpone it for a better pleasure in our futures. We learn to regulate ourselves and to adjust to influences from outer conflicts and contradictions. Practical reason has always been the temperamental counterbalance to the stress of unbridled passions. We seek inner composure.

Here we say that the middle measure lies with the equipoise that makes the choice, not a mean condition between good and bad. We learn that leaning toward the right choice is not easy. Above all, for Aristotle, one chooses the good as an end, which he calls the mean: "The balanced choice that precisely achieves its end" (Sachs, *NE*, 208). In this context, our desire for a good end goes before the means of achieving that end. But he also cautioned that this is easy to say but hard to do. We need to learn practical reason that leads to a good act. In a recent work, Barry Schwartz and Stephen Sharpe argue that we all need a practical wisdom in solving the conflicts and quandaries of our everyday world.[7] We must choose between conflicting rules and principles all the time: "We're always trying to find the right balance. Aristotle called this balance the 'mean'" (29). Sometimes this balanced stance is called a "Golden Mean." So now we see explicitly how practical reason, balancing, and a middle measure all go together. A reasonable person weaves together opposing points of view, desires, and wishes for her own good choosing. Aristotle says too that this seeking our own good end leads to happiness. If we act ethically in search of our own best goal in life, we shall be happy. This active search for own best goals is the value of practical reason.[8]

Because we try to compose ourselves, we study these three forms of balanced inquiry, which help to show how. We shall take up some of these balancing issues of everyday stress along the way. We balance these opposing tensions, and we seek a hidden unity by means of the arts, with play, and by ethics. Indeed, the arts, many games, and most ethical dilemmas have stress built-in as an oppositional tension. In Chap. 2, we said that a tense harmony of opposing forces or energies would be a basic definition of composed beauty in Chap. 5. By way of a middle measure, we move toward a fuller understanding.

So far we have seen that the skills in composing the balanced fulcrum, the balanced equation, and the balanced sentence are fundamental tools of reasonable problem solving. We have also seen that without skills in these three forms of composition, we can't understand our own meaning very well, nor can we tell much of importance to anyone else. With these practical skills, we learn how to explain ourselves to another by demonstration. They are everyday, real-world skills about working in the world. In Chap. 4, we also began to show, via the self-referring sentence, that the mastery of these skills can lead to a mental state of reasonable balance, self-possession, as we learn how to think, act, and play in the world. To continue now, a good word for this state of rational composure amid stress is "equipoise," another *equi* word. A good feature of this word is "poise," which does not mean static balance but instead a kind of readiness for a right action, either way, with equity, as we look forward. As with all goods, equipoise is something learned and earned. It is a calm state of mind that is achieved amid the strife of contradictions, of social and physical conflicts.

You are calmly poised between action and restraint, on the verge of a good decision, ready and willing, but sometimes reluctant. This poise in the real world, this standing ready to act, is similar to the physics of potential energy. We remember that, in science, potential energy is just a momentary pause, on the verge of a change, for energy is always on the move, always in transit, always channeling in a circuit. We remember the pendulum at the peak of its swing, poised to provide the stored energy for the force of kinetic energy. Or recall the image of a pole-vaulter at the top of his leap, who has just used all the bent-back energy of the pole to propel himself up and over the bar. We remember that when we are on the verge of taking a step in the world, we are getting ready to swing into precarious balance. For our arms and legs rotate and swing into action just like a pendulum does, or just like a pole-vaulter at the peak of his jump propelled by his sprung-back pole. Dynamic balancing acts happen all the time, whenever and wherever we meet some kind of resistance. When we jump or walk, we resist gravity by swinging with and against it. (Recall James Gray's passage at the end of Chap. 2, about Newton's action-reaction law and how animals propel themselves by the resistance of their environment.) Wherever a person or a people encounter resistance in a world, or harsh contradictions, or political oppositions, they push back and pull away, in a natural counterthrust.

BALANCE OF POWER

What is the social context for the middle measure of ethical virtues? By the time they have come to primary school, most children will have experienced plenty of psychological stress and strife in their lives. So we need to teach ethics in the Common Core Curriculum.[9] Family stresses, neighborhood conflicts, even the anxieties of the schoolyard, such as bullying, have divided students' lives. Amid all these tense contradictions, youngsters need to be able to find equanimity. They need to learn calm rational and emotional equipoise. They need to learn not so much that the teacher says, "Calm yourself," but rather, "I need to calm myself," as we saw in Chap. 4. The root *equi* in the word "equanimity" is another one of those figurative balance words, this time having to do with one's search for a more tranquil temperament.

The idea of contradicting balances is often applied as a figure of speech where no actual mass is being measured and where there is no real equivalence. An important exercise for students is to discuss the three forms of government in the U.S. Constitution under the concept of "checks and balances." Students learn that this structure of balances was designed to check against the too powerful growth of one form of government over the others. A mixed form of government traditionally speaking—democracy, aristocracy, monarchy—also checks against the eventual deterioration of one form of government into its worst semblance: anarchy, oligarchy, and tyranny.

Students can also be introduced to the international version of checks and balances, the concept of "the balance of power," in which a government seems always to help the weaker against the stronger country. They can discuss this sentence: "The enemy of my enemy is my friend." Is this distrustful awareness based on the basic principle about war? The Greek historian Thucydides said, "the powerful exact what they can, and the weak grant what they must." Notice that this also a balanced sentence: "Of the gods we believe and of men we know that, by a law of their nature, whatever they can rule they will. ...."[10] We can rephrase this as a modern balanced sentence. All these examples cope with contradictions and tense oppositions in society. In the Common Core Curriculum for New York State, Engage New York, there is a section on the United Nations' International Declaration of Human Rights, to be studied in the fifth grade.[11] How do principles of equity and counterbalance offset what is sometimes called "real politic"? In what follows, we discuss the idea that the aim of law is to establish the equity of laws and rights.

In his book on ethics, Aristotle himself extended the idea of contradicting balances with metaphors that do not use quantities of things, but rather opposing mental issues, such as a balance between the search for pleasure and the avoidance of pain. In fact, Aristotle took the idea of the middle measure, the mean, from contemporary treatises of medicine, which saw health as a symmetry between opposing elements in the body of the hot, the cold, the wet, and the dry.[12] The ethics of the middle measure in thinking and acting came from the ethics of a healthy body.

A Balanced Food Plate, "An Ethics of the Body"

Balance and stability in the pursuit of health are *homely* principles, perhaps among the first principles of our "earth household," the translation of "eco" and "ology," where *oikos* is Greek for "household."[13] Students can discuss the phrase "home economics" as a synonym for ecology. In Chap. 2, we discussed the nursery rhyme about Jack Sprat and his wife. One loved fat and one loved lean, and neither could abide the other kind of food, but between them both they licked the platter clean. Theirs is one solution to a balanced food plate, but is it a healthy opposition? In physiology, "energy balance" is defined as "the relation of the amount of utilizable energy taken into the body to that which is employed for internal work, external work, and the growth and repair of tissues."[14] As we shall see, this description of energy balance is a summary of the conservation law of energy. Students can learn that the intake of energy in the forms of nutrients in our bodies must be *balanced* by the outflow of wastes.[15]

Our bodies are always at work in self-repair, in self-regulation, taking energy from outside and removing wastes from within. This balancing act of bodily self-regulation, of balancing feedback, is the first premise of physiology. In Next Generation Life Sciences (LS1.D), the analysis is put in terms of "Information Processing":

> Animals have body parts that capture and convey different kinds of information needed for growth and survival. Animals respond to these inputs with behaviors that help them survive. Plants also respond to some external inputs. (1-LS1-1).

Throughout this study, we have said that bodily awareness of balance as an abiding measure comes from the first conservation law that matter and energy must balance up in any of their conversions. Now we can say that the principle holds for organic inputs and outputs as well as for inorganic transactions in physics. To demonstrate this assertion, Feynman mentions that the first person to really express this conservation principle as a law was not a physicist but rather a physician.[16] His name was Julius Robert Mayer, and he experimented with the photosynthesis of light by plants, and also with heat generated by rats as they ate food. He called this balance a conservation law. So a balanced food plate, at its most basic level of the conservation law, must be physiologically true.

Recall that throughout this study, we have said that a skill is a process of taking something apart, like Feynman's mechanical toy, and then putting it back together again. When we study the ways that plants and animals take in energy from the environment, take it apart for use, then reassemble it, and then evacuate it, we understand that we are following energy patterns of transferring and converting things into new compositions.

As David Suzuki said in *The Sacred Balance* about the processing of food, "Our bodies are wonderfully adapted to obtain the nutrition we need. Like the creation of the soil, feeding is a matter of taking things apart in order to put other things together."[17] All organic systems organize energy by this process of mobilization, of taking things apart and putting them back together for another use.

For Aristotle apparently, a healthy diet, comprising the mean, was an "ethics of the body" (Jaeger, 417). So we correct our eating by means of a process of balancing feedback; that is, physiological self-correction. Can this ethics of the body carry over to an ethics in the community?

Eating and digesting the right foods can become one of most familiar forms of energy use. In a number of interactive classroom exercises with formulas and equations, students can ask, "What exactly is the meaning of "a balanced food plate?" Students can draw diagrams of the several divisions of food groups on a food plate, as they are recommended by the U. S. Department of Agriculture?[18]

Although students need to know the basic food groups, some skeptics might argue that a big cheeseburger and a milkshake fill all the requirements for a balanced meal. There you have meat, cheese, lettuce, tomato, and dairy. So a balanced meal is not necessarily a healthy meal. In order to get a better understanding of what you eat, how do you compute portions of food groups by weights and ratios or percentages? What are calories? What is the average number of calories best consumed over three meals? You can design exercises that feature the movements of foods by weights: How many ounces or cups do you want to eat for each food grouping a day? How do you convert ounces into grams, measures that are most often featured on food labels? How do you convert grams to calories? What does it mean that the food groups are often divided like this, so that the total *equals* 100%?

> fruit and vegetables:33%
> bread rice potatoes pasta:33%
> milk and dairy foods:15%
> meat fish eggs beans:12%
> foods and drinks high in fat and/or sugar:7%[19]

We can see that our analysis of this question must include all three of our methods of inquiry, physical and physiological balances, equations, and sentences.

How do students learn to adjust to the fact that some families do not eat meat? For instance, if your family does not eat beef, how do you correct for a lack of iron in a daily diet? If other families do not drink milk or eat cheese, how do they make up the balance? Different ethnic groups have different food plates.

The aim of a balanced food plate is obvious: to maintain our health. Put another way, we measure good health by feeling good, which is an ethics of the body. When we feel really bad, we go to a doctor who has various instruments that may help detect an inner disorder. Maintaining a constancy of good health inside our bodies is done by a part of our nervous system, which is called "autonomous." A body self-regulates, by itself, without our attending to it. It regulates inner organs such as stomach, kidneys, and heart. Unless we become doctors or physiologists, many of us won't even understand the workings of the "autonomic nervous system" (ANS). Nevertheless, its job is to maintain an inner *homeostasis* of our bodies.[20] This kind of inner balancing act is a different kind of system from the central nervous system (CNS), which processes information into the brain and controls our external bodily movements as balancing acts. They are different "systems," yet both depend upon the principle of balancing feedback. Students may want to discuss how these model systems of homeostatic health differ and agree in terms of the meanings of balanced self-regulation. Later on in this chapter, we attend to the idea of an inner dialogue, mentioned in the last chapter, where we consciously self-regulate by asking questions within our own minds about our own actions and others.

More advanced middle-school students may learn that what is waste to one kind of animal is nutrient to another. For instance, when students learn about photosynthesis in a science class, they learn that as a plant draws in sunlight as a nutrient, it exerts oxygen. From the plant's point of view, oxygen is waste, but it is life to us. Is this kind of oppositional use of energy just like the cooperation of Jack Sprat and his wife? Some biologists see this kind of energy exchange as a form of cooperative co-development in evolution. See Next Generation Science Standards for sections about ecosystems and evolution.

BALANCING THE BOOKS

Here is another real-world example. Balancing is always a counterbalancing of shifting weights and energies in space and time. You walk by swinging arms and legs against the imbalance of falling. On the seesaw, you can shift your position along the board to compensate for too much weight across the fulcrum. Recall this point from Chap. 2: Counterbalancing can be seen as an exchange of energy-mass across or around the pivot of a fulcrum.

Balancing feedback is an act and measure of exchanging or interchanging information equally, from one arm of a fulcrum to the other.

As we saw in the definition above, energy is involved with a definition of work. It takes work to propel a swing on the playground. Work-exchange from one part of a diagram to another is a central part of energy balance. What does this sentence mean? "There is no free lunch." Once students see that energy exchange involves work, they can see how other commonplace problems may be solved. For instance, this design model of balancing arms for middle-schoolers can be extended to arithmetic and algebraic exercises in balancing a checkbook, or other basic budgets in home economics. How much money does an average family spend on food in a week? Some families give their children allowances of money each week. There are websites for these learning kinds of calculation.

Supply and Demand

Historical background: One of the earliest uses of balancing feedback was Adam Smith's use of a metaphor to show how markets are apparently self-regulating. He called this principle of self-correction "the invisible hand."[21] Isn't this metaphor like Heraclitus's paradox about an unapparent unity? His metaphor of a guiding hand substituted for a word that had not yet been coined: feedback. His principle of a market's automatic self-correction became the famous promise of a free market economy. Here is a current definition from a business dictionary:

> Effect of an action returned (fed back) to oppose the very action that caused it. Balancing-feedback has a correcting or stabilizing effect on the system, and it reduces the difference (variance) between where the system is (the current status) and where it should be (the target value, or objective). For example, demand and supply in an economy work on each other to reach a stable (equilibrium) state through the feedback of information about price and availability. If supply is known to be greater than demand, price falls. Low price forces suppliers to pull out of the market, causing shortage that results in increase in price. High price attracts more supplies than there is demand ... and so on until a rough parity is achieved.[22]

Students can discuss how or how often, and whether or whether not, stable equilibrium is achieved in this free-market model, this invisible hand. Can students discuss this balancing act as an inverse ratio, as in Chap. 4? As another instance, by the sixth grade, most students will have been introduced to some of the cycling principles in ecosystems. Where is the invisible hand of self-regulation? By the eighth grade, most students will have been introduced to the natural cycles of respiration by the mutual dependency of plants and animals upon a carbon and carbon dioxide cycle. Industrial cycles are governed by carbon and carbon monoxide interactions. In that context, teachers may decide to discuss proposals for reducing carbon and methane emissions. What is the large-scale proposal called a "carbon tax?" Is that tax a free-market principle? What are the incentives and detractions in terms of supply and demand? How far does a carbon tax serve to balance the books? We can ask students to name our businesses and industries that are devoted to the extraction of energy from the environment: agriculture, oil, coal, copper, forests, water. Where can we replenish in order to try to balance the books? What is renewable energy?

All life forms must participate in the struggle for available energy. That is a true assertion about life. Life is a struggle and it can lead to strife and stress in our work. "He shall have but a penny a day...." But we try to address this kind of inequity with fair and just business practices. We try to share.

JUSTICE

To start, here is a basic assertion, expressed in a sentence: *Without a fairly equal exchange of goods, a just society is impossible.* To begin to test this, you can introduce the word "equity," as the basis of both goods and rights. Equity, inequity, equivalence, equilibrium, equipoise—all are family **likenesses** that are not quite synonyms. They all derive from the Latin *aequus*. Seen in terms of the Sender-Receiver diagram, these words are all parts of a **context** of possible choices awaiting use. Seen in terms of social justice, many of the issues of domestic governance require laws for the equal or proportional distribution of wealth by taxes and by poverty laws that help the needy. What is a fair share? Notice in passing that this kind of questioning and answering with students is a kind of serious play.

The idea that in nature there is an equivalent balancing exchange among opposite things is very old in the Greek tradition. For instance, Heraclitus also said that fire is the ever-living energy of the world: "All things are an equal exchange for fire and fire for all things, as goods are for gold and gold for goods" (*The Presocratics*, 198). Notice the balanced sentence in his description of equal exchange. When he groups together fire, gold, and goods, he lets us see that they can be unified by forms of information exchange. But notice that the exchange of gold for goods or the exchange of fire for things requires a hidden ratio, as in $a=b$. Another measure is assumed to make for the equivalence.

In this view, change and exchange between apparently extreme opposites seem to make for the balanced adjustments of all things. How is this idea like and unlike the conservation law of balanced energy? Is energy the basic format of information exchange? Although we do not preset fire as a basic premise of energy exchange, we do recognize the burning energy of the sun as the source of most energy on earth. (When studying the Periodic Table of Elements, students will learn that the sun's hydrogen collides and creates helium as its source of energy.) Students may also discuss how, in Heraclitus's simile, the exchange of fire and things transfers to the exchange of money and goods.

In economics then there is a close relation between the exchange of energy and the exchange of money. According to Sachs, Aristotle coined the word *energeia*, and throughout the *Nicomachean Ethics*, he used the word in association with "work" as a kind of energy exchange.

Here is Aristotle's challenge about the composition of citizens in a city, expressed in a sentence about the exchange of money as a principle of equity. Can money serve as an equalizer between contradictory goods and evils? Money is the measure in his idea of a democracy. A "city stays together by paying things back proportionately, since people seek to pay back evil, and if they cannot, that seems to be slavery, or to pay back good, and if they cannot do that, exchange does not happen, and they stay together by means of exchange" (Sachs, *NE*, 88). Proportionate exchanges, he says, keep us together as a community. Here is Aristotle on the measurable exchange of currency (gold for things) which, for him, keeps the community together: "Hence, all things ought to be valued in currency, for in this way there will always be exchange, and if this, then also a shared community. So the currency, like the unit of measure, equalizes things by making them commensurable, for there would be no community if there were not exchange, and no exchange if there were not equality, and no equality if there were not commensurability."(Sachs, *NE*, 90.) This is a big claim: that the contradictory claims of a community are kept together by an equal exchange of money! Here the back-and-forth exchange of money is like a kind of visible hand of balancing feedback between the claims of monetary equity and civil equality. In this point of view, money is the measurable ratio that makes possible the formula $a = b$. For Aristotle, the very existence of social equality derives from equitable exchange. "Commensurable" is a dense word that means having the same measure, or in this case, proportionate accountability. (See the similar use of "parity" in the quotation above about the invisible hand.) Exchange, equality, and commensurability are supposed to go together. We can ask students how in their experiences money itself is a commonplace symbol of equivalence.

Does this kind of balancing feedback hold true in our communities? For instance, we can discuss the justice of a small claims court. A judge can settle a small claim by deciding to split the difference of a disagreement between two parties. Or a fine may be imposed. Here home economics becomes community economics. Isn't this kind of equitable exchange of money another kind of middle measure, where currency keeps us accountable?

Aristotle's reasoning is that the city, and the currency exchange that keeps them together, is the ethical basis of justice. For "justice is a certain kind of mean condition, but not in the same way that the other virtues are, but because it is concerned with a certain mean quantity, while injustice is concerned with extreme quantities" (Sachs, *NE*, 90). It is easier to understand Aristotle's logic once we know that the words justice and judge in Greek derive from *dika* "in half," so a judge is a "divider." "In arithmetical proportion the equal is a mean between the greater and the lesser."[23] *Because justice is a kind of dividing compromise, a split compensation of half and half, it is not the best of virtues*, as we shall see below.

In pursuit of truth, goodness and beauty, Aristotle says over and over, we should seek the mean because we are ourselves "compound" creatures. All of us are mixed and often divided compositions, just like our three forms of inquiry. So we should seek a mean between anger and an emotional state that is too slow to anger. So here the mean is, for him, "gentleness between extremes." As for truth, "one who is at the mean is a truthful person and let the mean condition be called truthfulness; pretence in the direction of exaggeration is called bragging and the one who has it is a braggart, while pretence in the direction of understatement is irony and the one who has it is ironic" (Sachs, *NE*, 32). For Aristotle, the mean condition is always praiseworthy, while the extremes are to be blamed.

Who can doubt that as our students grow up in larger communities of town, city, and state, that questions of economic justice will loom large? Home economics, environmental economics, business economics, and political economics will urge themselves upon our attention. Who can doubt that we need to introduce these questions of balancing equity to students? We might ask students whether a just distribution of goods in a community is good enough to solve inequities of goods in our communities.

When you think back upon all your remembrances about how we ought to act, and when you decide upon the basis of your experiences, some say that your process of thinking back is a certain kind of reflection about a just act. In one of the most influential books about justice, this process has been called "reflective equilibrium."[24] Here one tries to balance among variously held beliefs by a process of reasoning back and forth among them. This stance is another version of self-reflection and self-correction, that is, of balancing feedback back and forth. As we said in the last chapter, when we need to ask these questions about our best ends, then we often compose them as self-referring sentences.

Taking a Stand

Justice, according to Aristotle, is not the best of virtues, for some virtues are not really quantifiable, like friendship or morality or happiness, or truth. *Justice is not the highest good.* If justice is not the highest good, then neither is exchange an ultimate good. At this point, we could ask students about the ethics of balancing exchange. Although many kinds of exchange are a basic necessity in life, as we take in and excrete different forms of energy, it is not necessarily always a good, is it? For instance, consider once again that famous passage from "The Declaration of Independence," discussed in Chap. 3. In the movie, Abraham Lincoln interpreted "self-evident" in a certain way. "We hold these truths to be self-evident, that all men are created equal, that they are endowed by their Creator with certain unalienable Rights, that among these are Life, Liberty and the pursuit of Happiness." The phrase "inalienable right" is not really self-evident to most people, especially to middle-school children. However, when they learn that "to alienate" means to transfer or to exchange, and that inalienable means non-exchangeable or non-transferable, it becomes clearer. In the context of freedom, Jefferson means that you have a right not to have your freedom transferred or exchanged for slavery. It is an inalienable choice, and it is your own. So if you are forced to give up one of these rights, like the freedom of speech, you may feel alienated. Maybe you feel that you are treated unequally, unfairly; then you may feel like an alien in your own country. Children often feel alienated from their own communities, and runaway children are extreme examples. You can discuss any number of books and films about this theme of being a misfit, an outcast, a stranger in your home room.

Freedom then is an inalienable or non-exchangeable right. Immanuel Kant celebrated freedom, and he explained it in this way:

> In the realm of ends everything has either price or dignity. Whatever has price is exchangeable by another thing; it can be replaced by something else. Whatever, on the other hand, is above all price, and therefore admits of no equivalence has a dignity.... Thus morality and humanity, as capable of it, has dignity.[25]

This passage is a bit hard to understand, but it is worth our close attention. Each of us has the right to choose our own ways of life, our own ends, our own purposes. This is what he meant about freedom as the basis of individual action and an ethical society. But Kant says that in talking about ends, our higher goals, our true aims, we must choose between price or dignity. That is a big either-or choice. If we choose to live in the world where time is money or where everything has a price, or an "equivalence," then we must place an exchange value on each thing in terms of its price. But to stand in dignity as the cornerstone of our lives, we make choices that have no equivalents. Most of us must live in the world of social exchanges because we must have a job and its wages in order for us to live in a community. We must exchange goods for gold and gold for goods. We hope that justice prevails in our community of exchanges. The basis of economics is the exchange of goods, a mutual transfer of one for another. Isn't a job almost always a tradeoff? Where and how do we take a social stand that is above all price? We can ask ourselves if we know people who have dignity, either in their own lives or in history or in literature. Isn't dignity also a stance of self-possession? Most would agree that Lincoln had dignity. Martin Luther King? Woody Guthrie? Eleanor Roosevelt?

When we think of dignified people, we often think of older folks who have achieved renown. They seem to have poise, composure. But children can have dignity too. "I'll take my stand, right here and now." "Don't mess with me." We know that some children have self-possession. There are lots of stories that feature these hard choices. For in a fiction, if there is no conflict, there is no plot. Aren't there a number of books in fiction on

Common Core Curriculum lists that feature this kind of hard choice? Can a very young child like Scout Finch in *To Kill a Mockingbird* have dignity? What about her father, the honorable lawyer? At what cost dignity? When Mark Twain's Huck Finn decides not to expose Jim, a slave who wants to escape to freedom, he feels ashamed and guilty for betraying the law of his own community that he grew up with, the law of slavery, but we as readers think he is honorable, even noble, for Huck chooses to make loyalty to a friend more important than sending Jim back into slavery. Because he refuses, Huck chooses to make himself feel alien in his own community. In guilt and some anguish, Huck believes he is a no-good traitor to his upbringing, but we think he is above price. Can a scapegrace boy have dignity? He has taken a stand.

A good synonym for a dignified stand is "uprightness." It is tacitly an embodied word that implies that we can stand straight and tall, like Hans Christian Anderson's "The Steadfast Tin Soldier." When I say to myself calmly, "I'll take my stand here," then maybe I can't find a middle measure between right or wrong. "I'll not retreat; I'll take up another's fight or plight." These are declarations of independence.

The Golden Rule

Many students will agree that we sometimes make decisions to help others without needing to be paid and without needing to be asked. Many people do good deeds often, even without asking to be noticed. You take out to the street an old neighbor's garbage, without being told or without being seen. Yours is an invisible hand of kindness. Much of the world's wisdom literature agrees with this adage: do to another person what you would like others to do to you. "It has been said that the golden rule comprehends all the requirements of morality in a single formula."[26] Here we go again, trying to balance up an equation. Like algebra, what you do for one side of an equation, you must do for the other side. Is the Golden Rule about treating others as equals? How does the Golden Rule of morality apply? For instance, the golden rule of equations says you must perform on one side of an equation what you do on another side. That seems like the old morality of exacting an eye for the loss of an eye, of extracting a tooth for the loss of a tooth. "An eye for an eye, a tooth for a tooth." What kind of equity is that? At the very least, it warns we should not make the punishment exceed the crime.

So we come to understand that the Golden Rule of morality is not about justice. It is not about Aristotle's "mean" condition of just exchange in a community. It is a decision based upon charity and dignity. So it cannot be a rule that one must do. It is about trying to put yourself in the place of another.[27] More than an act of reason, it is an act of imagination. Do we need to be imaginative in order to do good? Yes. Imagination is the means to a good end. To put myself in the place of another, I want to undergo a reversal of roles. (There are lots of plots in narratives that turn on a reversal of roles.) I need to stop thinking of another as an object, and I need to think of her as like me, a subject. Students can discuss the word "empathy." Is it the same as "sympathy"? Notice that this kind of back and forth-ness between oneself and another is the basic act of feedback in two-sided dialog. In the dialog, you are the agent and another is the patient. But instead of being an agent, or sender, of an action, we imagine ourselves as the patient, or receiver, of an act. The moral assumes that if you are capable of action, you may put yourself in the position of one who is in need of care, whether it is poverty or ill health. It is important to see that this kind of situation is not the busy world of social exchange. Instead, you reach into your world of memories and experiences, with your own "reflective equilibrium," and you say to yourself in so many words, "In my own inner world of experiences, I would act as if the whole world were based upon this kind of caring. I know that much of the real world does not think and act in this way, but I myself can act as if I lived in a world of caring." Here I stand in my own invisible world of caring and sharing. You can create a possible world of your own imagining. Maybe in order to achieve your own good ends, you need to imagine the results of your actions on others. If you look around among your schoolmates, you know already that some kids "march to their own drum." They seem to be self-possessed. They are ready to act, according to their own inner laws of habit, belief, religion, and school.

But what is my own drum beat? What is my own song of belief about right or wrong? In the last chapter, we mentioned that the way we think is like an inner questioning, a kind of dialogue of inner speech. The stories of many cultures feature a kind of inner guide that is doing the questioning. In our culture that inner guide is often called our inner "genius." Guides and false guides are central to most quest myths and to lots of stories. For example, in Walt Disney's *Pinocchio*, Jiminy Cricket, Pinocchio's guide, sings a little song that says, "Give a little whistle, and always let your conscience be your guide." We might ask students, "Why give a whistle?" Another example is Frank Baum's *The Wizard of Oz*, in which each of Dorothy's three guides is also searching for his own inner genius. Still another example is J. R. R. Tolkien's *The Hobbit*, in which Bilbo gets misled by a false guide. Gollum's leading characteristic is his bedeviled dialogue with himself about "My Precious!" In these stories and fables, we learn about the self- questioning of the main characters, and so we may learn something about our own inner guides as we make balanced choices.

Classroom Exercise: "Stone Soup"

Consider the very familiar folk tale "Stone Soup" as an example of how a guide uses his imagination to put himself in another's shoes, in order to achieve a very practical end. We can tell the story in class in order to try to figure out a moral. The guide has practical wisdom. He is quick witted and ready to act. As he and his squad approach a village at nightfall, hungry and tired, he anticipates, he predicts, that the villagers will be suspicious. So he picks up an ordinary stone by the roadside and persuades the villagers that it is a magical stone. Then he weaves a lie. But was his action good or bad? Does the story imply that sometimes we need to be tricked into being cooperative? Does it mean that it is better for the villagers to distribute and circulate food than to stockpile it? We can examine more closely the magic stone, because here is the essence of fiction. Although it is a familiar plot, its moral is ambiguous. We like to be enchanted with stories, but has the guide misused the villagers with a deceptive story? The guide transforms an ordinary stone by taking it out of context and removing it to a world of make-believe. The guide reframes an inert object by lifting it up from the ground and making it into a magical transformer of food energy. It is not golden like Gollum's precious magic ring. There is something everyday about it. Can students think of other everyday objects that seem to have been given magical power? What about Dumbo's feather that seems to give him the power to fly? Where is the magic? "Stone Soup" has several possible uses as a moral about cooperation. Is the stone like Aristotle's money, which serves as a medium of equity in a democratic society? It is not like the equal ratio of gold exchanged for goods in Heraclitus's account. It is more basic. Much like the zero-place in an abacus, the stone means nothing in itself. But moved around, it can amount to a lot. The fable, like much art, though familiar, is still very strange.

To conclude this section, consider that Ralph Waldo Emerson also saw justice as a balancing measure. And he points to all three of our forms of inquiry. In his essay "Compensation," he said, "The world looks like a multiplication-table, or a mathematical equation, which, turn it as you will, balances itself." The complete essay would be a good reading assignment for a classroom discussion of reasonable balancing acts. For instance, have the villagers in "Stone Soup" been compensated? If we think so, then haven't we learned something about how to use practical wisdom?

Howard Gardner asks whether truth, beauty, and goodness are merely ancient virtues, classical, but inapplicable for us today. If students use equivalent balance as their abiding model of reasoning and imagining, perhaps the rest will follow, at least some of the time.

Arts of Balancing

A balanced stance of tension between opposing forces often characterizes art forms. Teachers may screen some examples, such as the Greek sculptor Myron's statue of a discus thrower, whose body is twisted and stooped yet balanced, ready to whirl and to throw.

To begin, here is a passage from John Dewey's *Art as Experience* in which he defines artistic rhythm as if it were a composite of rhythmic change of opposing energy in a natural system:

> A gas that evenly saturates a container, a torrential flood sweeping away all resistance, a stagnant pond, an unbroken waste of sand, and a monotonous roar are wholes without rhythm. A pond moving in ripples, forked lightning, the waving of branches in the wind, the beating of a bird's wing, the whorl of sepals and changing shadows of clouds on a meadow, are simple natural rhythms.* [See below] There must be energies resisting each other. Each gains intensity for a certain period, but thereby compresses some opposed energy until the latter can overcome the other, which has been relaxing itself as it extends. Then the operation is reversed, not necessarily in equal periods of time but in some ratio that is felt as orderly. Resistance accumulates energy; it institutes conservation until release and expansion ensue. There is, at the moment of reversal, an interval, a pause, a rest, by which the interaction of opposed energies is defined as and rendered perceptible. The pause is a balance or symmetry of antagonistic forces. Such is the generic schema of rhythmic change save that the statement fails to take account of minor coincident changes of expansion and contraction that are going on in every phase and aspect of an organized whole, and of the fact that the successive waves and pulses are themselves cumulative with respect to final consummation.* The fact that we designate it a "whorl" indicates that we are subconsciously aware of the tension of energies involved [Dewey's footnote].[28]

"The pause is a balance or symmetry of antagonistic forces." As we shall see, this kind of pause-and-swing in a balanced tension of antagonistic forces characterizes a lot of rhythmic art.[29] The discus thrower is poised, ready to whirl his body. Communication may be said to occur here, when we pause at an interval, perhaps having encountered some resistance, on the verge of an action.

So when we speak of a middle measure in this cultureal chapter and at large, we do not mean a static balance but rather a moving proportion of energy flow that has a feeling of stressful swing at an interval.

Please recall the diagram of weights rotating on a balance scale like a seesaw (Fig. 2.3). Much dynamic balancing in the real world is usually expressed as a whirl or whorl or swirl or arc. Even a balance scale, like that of Ma'at's (Introduction) which might look static, will have a sliding scale for the adjustment or weights on the move to seek the middle measure. In art and in ethics, we understand that conditions always change, so the measures must adjust to the circumstances, even while we hold our poise.

At the outset of this chapter, we discussed the ancient awareness that the cosmos itself was composed and unified from great forces of nature working together in opposition. So the composition of art forms was a way to understand these complementary forces.

Like the ancients, we too look for the patterned unities that may underlie the discord between opposing forces. Or as Alexander Pope put it in balanced couplets,

> Not *Chaos* like together crush'd and bruis'd,
> But as the world, harmoniously confus'd:
> Where order in variety we see,
> And where, tho' all things differ, all agree.
> – "Windsor-Forest," lines 12–16

These two couplets sum up the ancient aesthetic principle of *concordia discors*, that of finding concord in discord, and vice versa, in a world of opposing forces. In the couplet, "to agree" means something very like "to equate." The aesthetic pleasure of proportional balancing of like and unlike components enters into the design of any compositional pattern. However, we know that balanced proportion is not the be-all and end-all of structure in the arts. That is what *concordia discors* means. You need some discord to go along with a concord. You need some imbalance to recognize the need for balance. You want some strange disruption to make a plot. Maybe you want a lot of disproportion in your definition of beauty. But you still need to find the right proportion that balances up the parts. In this chapter, we call this right proportion a "middle measure."

In Chap. 2, we featured 3-D balancing levers that can be transformed into larger mechanical tools. In Chap. 3, we suggested that algebraic equations and formulas exist primarily as iconic patterns that balance on a 2-D plane. And in Chap. 4, we showed how the sentence is composed in a following sequence that is primarily one-dimensional (1-D). Now we can stress an important dimensional point about the arts in general. It is clear that the so-called plastic arts exist in 3-D space. Painting, sculpture, architecture—all exist statically in space, so many artists try to compensate, Emerson's word, to balance static spatial objects with a semblance of movement. In this way, artists may make spatial objects seem to move, and they may invoke the illusion of time passing as well. In contrast to the plastic arts, music and literature unfold during the times of their performances, so an artist may compensate in order to render linear sequences into a shapely pattern that feels spatial. There is genre called "shaped verse," which renders poems into significant shapes, such as George Herbert's angel wings, or "concrete" poetry. And yet all literature is shaped with repetitive patterns in one guise or another. All artful writing builds patterns by unapparent redundancy, as in Gertrude Stein's passage about diagramming sentences. Literature exists primarily as the unfolding of a 1-D narrative sequence, and a poem takes shape by means of its recurrent patterns of parallel constructions, as seen in Chap. 2. Every "parallel construction" gives shape to a temporal flow. In what follows, we discuss this kind of compensatory balancing of space and time.

We have also seen that the starting point for an understanding about stress or tension between opposing forces in the physical world is the balancing-up principle of the conservation of energy, which Einstein said was a principle of "balance."

So let's begin with a physical play between opposing forces of form, matter, and movement, as in the arts of 3-D movement in theater, dance, and kinetic sculpture. Let's say that in these arts, we find enacted a balanced stress or tension of opposing forces, and let's say too that the stress or tension, back-stretched like the bow and lyre, is an act of creative play that is not necessarily resolved into one thing or another.

Classroom Exercise: "Snap the Whip"

What about Plato's sense of serious play, with a school as the magic space? Consider this schoolyard playground. One of the most famous images in the history of American art is Winslow Homer's *Snap the Whip*.[30] All of these art forms are easily brought up on a smart board and on students' chrome books. Some have celebrated the painting as a picture of childhood innocence, with a one-room schoolhouse in the background. Here is an example of a 2-D painting in which embodied movement is stressed. If this magic circle is a playground, it is not delineated as such. Here the magic circle is the rotational game described by its swinging players. At the center of a string of boys, the biggest boy is pivoting his feet around a rotational fulcrum, and he is pulling inward with all his might. While he is pivoting slowly, the rest of the boys are running faster and faster as they are being pulled farther outward. At the end of the following sequence, one little boy has already fallen while another boy is toppling, hovering, in imbalance, for he is about to fall because he can't keep up the pace. *Snap the Whip* shows the opposing physical forces of centripetal and centrifugal force. As the radius of the rotating circle increases, the pace and the momentum accelerate. (See Chap. 2.) Here is a remarkable depiction of opposing forces in art, and it is technically accurate. Although the dynamics depict a childhood game, the image of balancing centripetal and centrifugal forces can also explain the large movements of a moon and planets. (See Bunn, *NLC*, 21–25.) Here too viewers can watch at a distance, the pleasures of vertigo, mentioned in Chap. 2. As Roger Callois says, in games of vertigo, we feel a "delightful panic": "Every child well knows that by whirling rapidly he reaches a centrifugal state of flight from which he regains bodily stability and clarity of perception only with difficulty." It is not by chance that the boy at the end is the smallest, for the trick is to whirl him off his feet into flight and fall. We see him hovering (forever), suspended in imbalance. Teachers may also want to juxtapose Homer's painting called *Left and Right*, in which two ducks have been shot, and they are seen hovering in air in opposite whirl patterns. Here the sport of killing ducks has been converted into an art form. But is there an ethical slant, as we notice that the flare of the gun shot seems to be aimed directly at the viewer?

How can a middle measure apply equally in general to ethics and arts, as Weyl was quoted in the Introduction? Here is a very traditional example of someone poised in a middle measure between opposing ethical movements, this time in a painting by Jan Vermeer, *Woman Holding a Balance*.[31] Students can discuss how art and ethics come together here in a balancing action. The woman is measuring her jewels. The online discussion stresses this moral: We should live a "balanced life," between earthly and spiritual aims, between a life of material possessions and a life symbolized by the background painting of the Last Judgment. If you screen this painting in a classroom, and study it more closely, the theme of balanced judgment is reinforced by the painting's balanced composition. The woman's embodied poise is a good example of "reflective equilibrium." Here is another analysis of the painting that describes a similar set of oppositions: "The scales, which are empty, are ready to be weighted. The painting divides at the crossbar into upper and lower halves of equal weight. Will the lady choose a higher center of gravity or a lower?[The lady] is pregnant and pregnancy is the metaphor for her suspension. Will the scale tip toward vanity or humility? Her fate, as we say, hangs in the balance."[32] We can see here how a static painting can intimate movement. We can also note that the corner of the picture frame, which brings together the vertical and horizontal axes of the whole designed composition, seems to brace her hand and elbow up. The background painting of Jesus on the cross, a sacred space, provides an implicit but important context for the issue of moral judgment in her room. It is a sort of frame within a frame, like a play within a play, where the background shapes the theme as a compositional **context**. You could diagram the vertical and horizontal lines on an x-y axis of a Sender-Receiver diagram. They are like chalk lines on a playing field. So the metaphor of suspended judgment between vanity and humility, and impending choice, is built into the whole structure. The crisscrossing vertical and horizontal lines center the issue in a really perceived **middle measure**. The aesthetic design bolsters the moral issue. She is ready to act, but how?

Poised in a stance of suspended judgment, or suspended imagination, hovering between opposing forces, is the way that a lot of art ends. In many art works, we are left to do the balancing ourselves. Pausing to look at a painting, we may choose to interpret it, or not. We may look at it and pass on, or we may look into or through it, and turn back into ourselves. So the painting may allow a turn toward self-reference, like Homer's flash of a gunshot, which may be seen as pointing to ourselves. When we choose to interpret it for ourselves, we take our own stand. We do this kind of balancing between our urges and our judgments all the time. It is all about choices. Every middle-school student can understand the cartoon picture of a child with a little angel perched at one ear, and a little demon perched and whispering into the other.

Middle-school students may also have been introduced to the basics of the central nervous system, that the frontal parts of the brain's neocortex govern our judgments, our rational plans, and our learned restraints that check the unruly passions of our sub-cortex. As Oliver Sachs says in a recent analysis of an artist and the artistic process: "There is normally a beautiful balance, a delicate mutuality, between the frontal lobes and the subcortical parts of the brain that mediate perception and feeling, and this allows a consciousness that is free-ranging, playful, and creative."[33] That is a significant sentence about creativity. He describes a beautiful mental balance between parts of the brain that govern feeling and perceptions, and neocortical parts that govern rational thinking. If we can find that embodied balance, if we can mutually coordinate our mental states, we too may learn to play creatively. So the brain is a coordinator, but isn't the word "balance" a metaphor?

Within Sachs's creative context, let's reconsider how we might widen the definition of a magic circle so as to include the scene that Vermeer has created for his balancing woman. The room seems to be her own place, at least a place where she occasionally worships alone. Isn't she living within a magic circle of her own making? Are we included, or are we just looking on? Now the circle is not just a play area for a game; instead she is living within her own private inner sanctum, her own private little sacred space. How will she guide her pleasures? So now we can pose a question for ourselves: If it is true that lots of people create a private hideaway for themselves, especially children, is it also true that as we build up in our minds an educational model for our futures, isn't this learning model itself a kind of magic circle that we live within as we carry onward? Isn't this learned model our basis for making choices, for taking stands, large and small? When we learn something, are we building in our brains a model of future use? If you have found a magic garden, don't you always carry it with you, in your imagination, even though you may decide later that magic is suspect in the real world? When we are learning to make ethical and artistic choices, we are building in our brains a model of the ways that we shall act in the world. That mental model works like a magic circle.

For instance, here is another example of an artwork that represents a sort of magical balancing between bodily feeling and reflective reasoning, this time of ballerinas practicing ballet steps. They are practicing the **code** of their calling. They are building in their brains an interior model of the magic circle of dance. The French artist, Edgar Degas', painted a number of pictures of ballerinas rehearsing in the dance studio, a magic circle set aside from the real world, in which the steps were diagrammed on the floor in lines, grids, and corner points. Here he was not after the magical apparition of dance, its lovely rhythms and pirouettes, but rather the effortful practice beforehand of learning the steps in following sequences, all in preparation for an eventual performance. For instance, in one such painting, *The Rehearsal*, the ballerinas seem slightly awkward as they stretch to make their legs and feet fit the chalked positions they are to successively reach.[34] In the more famous painting at the Metropolitan Museum of Art, New York, *The Rehearsal Onstage*, the girls, the teacher, and the onlookers, all seem especially awkward. Degas' painting analyzes the ways that the abstract grids, faintly drawn on the floor, force the dancer into a felt background space. Here we see the actual physical stress on arms and legs that underlies the eventual magic of the later performance. Degas represents the push and pull of bodily sentience. In this painting, the whole scene is sun-lit by extremely high, floor-to-ceiling windows, with long geometrically divided window panes, and arched panes at the tops rounding them off, that remind of the angles and arcs of solar geometry. It is another tacit but important background **context** that helps to shape the background framework. The solar energy and the chalked symmetric grids relate to one another, like the line, shadow, and angle of the early geometers mentioned in Chap. 3. We can refer back to Vermeer's painting and think about the slant of sun that lightens the woman. Is it both natural and supernatural?

Once the girls have mastered rehearsals, and their analyses have become rote, and when the chalk lines have finally been erased, then it seems as if the dance itself appeals to the apparition of a magic power, a secret law, driving the rhythmic sequences, intervals, and patterns. The ballerinas are learning how to build in their minds a good model of their future roles. These learned stances and steps taken are like the "slots of syntax" in Chap. 4. You fit into them and then you move out on your own. They have learned practical reason by practicing certain skilled steps. They are getting ready to act in their futures. Here we can see the bodily mechanics, and we know the purpose. *The Rehearsal* is a sustained critical analysis, in which the creative work is pointedly decomposed into its abstract, geometrical slots of composition, and then recomposed, combined, and enacted later, on another plane entirely. Their painfully learned skills of balancing feedback will be transformed into an effortless and graceful art of the dance.

So sometimes in art, the magic circle is reinforced by self-reference back to its own so-called laws of composition. This painting is "so meta-, so self-referential." Rehearse this movement as a skill by breaking it down into its components. They decompose and recompose it. The ballerinas are self-correcting along the way. They are practicing the center of balance for each stance. They are building in their brains a model of their future actions. Each move of a ballerina is part of a highly ritualized **code**, which is practiced in a magic circle, in this case a grid, which as **context**, constrains or shapes each move in a certain way. When the audience watches a ballet, it does not see the grids, for they have been erased. But the background grids, like the chalk lines on playing fields, still serve the dancers as a kind of invisible hand that helps them self-correct their rhythmic movements.

In life forms, self-reference is a kind of self-repair or a turn-back gauge that combines retrospection and anticipation in order to retain homeostasis. When you are working on a skill, you take all the pieces apart, you study them as parts of a whole, and then you recombine them, just as Feynman said about taking apart a toy. In the painting, Degas is representing the mastering of a skill by rationally rehearsing over and over the parts which anticipate the magic of the enacted dance. Study this, over and over, putting your symmetric arms and legs through their paces. Is this also a kind of "reflective equilibrium?" Ordinarily we in the audience pay attention to the magic of the dance, but here we are asked to pay attention to the hard workout within the magic circle.

So the painting looks back in retrospection upon the painfully learned skills that go into the future performance of that number. Recollecting and anticipating, the dancers enact a graceful semblance of balancing feedback and feed forward. When all the self-conscious rehearsing is done, the rhythmic re-enactment of the dance seems hardly to depend upon the momentary fulcrum of the earth itself, for it has been erased by the magical rhythms of arms and legs in symmetrical movements. What we may admire in the grace of animals, their fitness of dynamic balance within their niches, arts like the dance would re-enact.

You can begin to solve many compositional problems by looking for their center of balance.

All training camps, whether for tennis or football or soccer or ballet, take apart the moves and then put them back together again. You figure out the "how-to-it" of a composition, and then you move onward to a "why-to-do-it" point of view. At first you feel awkward, but then you move toward self-confident grace. Skill in a composition leads to balanced self-possession, in Gertrude Stein's sense, quoted in the last chapter.

But now we can take this idea of a learned skill in composition a step further. The dancers are learning how to perform a kind of dance, a ballet. In rehearsals, they are practicing toward a future, feeding back and feeding forward.[35] Their newly possessed skill, their self-possession, leads to a creative skill. Once they have learned the basic skills, they can begin to interpret the mysteries of dance. Their bodily and mental coordination leads to a feeling of beautiful harmony of rhythmic movements. They laboriously learn the routines, so they are freer to dance beyond the fundamentals. From technical skill comes artistic interpretation. From rote comes art.

Classroom Exercise: Mobiles

Making mobile sculptures is an excellent classroom exercise in creative play.[36] Many middle-school students will have made a hanging mobile sculpture whose parts balance from an arm of a central fulcrum, while the whole composite sways in the wind. As a child puts together a mobile, she learns quickly to arrange and bend the parts into an artful balance. She learns how to position the struts and wires so that they don't appear too prominently. The arrangements can seem almost magical because the mechanical parts are almost invisible. So she masters the mechanics of the mobile even while suppressing the slotted wires of syntax in favor of the semantics. If she is making a fish mobile, she may use a clear filament, maybe even a piece of fishing line, so the fish appear to be floating in an invisible medium, not hanging.

Notice that in beginning to compose a mobile, you start with a strut and a string. You are beginning with the basic parts of balance scale, and you need to work tacitly with principles of levers (Chap. 2) as you add more struts and strings.

Alexander Calder virtually invented this medium of mobile suspension, and his whimsical, even lyrical, compositions became so popular that many museums hang them at the entrances or stairwells of exhibition halls.[37] Although the 3-D invention was his own, the ancient model was surely the beams and cords of a suspended balance scale.

The mechanics of physical suspension lead to an artistic balancing action. His mobiles are wonderful instances of dynamic balancing acts in which all the parts seem to move in a strange equilibrium. They move back and forth and round about because they sway in invisible air currents that seem to create their own magic space.

For instance, according to the philosopher Jean-Paul Sartre, Calder's mobiles are not like works of sculpture, which seek to "imbue something immobile with movement." Instead a mobile "captures movement rather than suggests it."[38] That is his opening thought. Here is his concluding conjecture:

> In short, although Calder has no desire to imitate anything, his one aim is to create chords and cadences of unknown movements—his mobiles are at once lyrical inventions, technical almost mathematical combinations, and the perceptible symbol of Nature: great elusive Nature, squandering pollen and abruptly causing a thousand butterflies to take wing and never revealing whether she is the blind concatenation of causes and effects or the gradual unfolding, however retarded, disconcerted and thwarted, of an Idea (81).

Sartre's rare poetic sentence is a little bit difficult, but it is worth study for what he says about nature and its relation to art. The mobiles exhibit strange motions, like the uplift of butterflies or like a galaxy of starlings, lyrics, and cadences of unknown movements, chords stirring with and against the wind. Wind is the invisible hand that bestirs the balanced movements back and forth. Wind is a force that we can feel but cannot see. We can ask students to think about what it is that nature is never quite revealing: whether nature is just a blind concatenation of physical forces in strife, an inorganic chaos of atoms bumping together in a hazardous series of causes and effects, or whether nature may be evolving, slowly and hesitantly, toward an organic Idea, as if it had an aim. That aim toward an Idea is certainly not Charles Darwin's definition of evolution, for in his view nature has no larger intention like that. But organisms take aim, like butterflies that take off according to their own inner laws of butterfly cognition. So Sartre's composition of a "whether" sentence is a strange kind of evolution-forward toward some unfathomed Idea, a "whither" concept. Calder's mobiles may be explained as technical and mathematical compositions, or as lyric expressions of an idea that is not quite evident. You can see here that, for Sartre, Calder's mobiles are more about the expression of a poised pattern of opposing forces in art and perhaps in nature. Artists often evince the great questions without trying to answer them. Is it enough to pose the question in equipoise? Although both Vermeer's painting and Calder's mobile feature suspension, and though neither Vermeer nor Sartre arrive at a hard and fast conclusion, one moves toward an art and ethics of imagination or judgment, while the other moves toward the free form of natural play of physical movements. Both end in a stance of suspended judgment.

If Calder's elegant mobiles seem technically simple, even childishly playful at times, in their balance and symmetry, a more threatening mix of technological and biomechanical wings, fins, and struts in fantastical mobility would be Lee Bontecou's marvels of playful composition.[39] These too are suspended mobile symmetries of strange and grotesque creatures made up of odd composites of string, glue, and tacks. The balanced creatures seem at once both beautiful and ugly works of art. What are they? You can compare these creatures to Calder's. It's always interesting to ask students about their feelings as they experience works of art. For instance, Vermeer's woman with a balance scale seems poised in quiet and solitary calmness. Calder's mobiles seem playful as balance and sway in a breeze. Bontecou's mobiles look distorted and perhaps filled with struggle.

COMBINATORY PLAY

Classroom Exercise: Little Girl Skipping Rope

Few artists have played more strangely with everyday objects than Pablo Picasso. For example, his witty *Bull's Head* can be seen as an equation. As one art critic put it: "bicycle saddle plus handle-bars equals a bull's head."[40] We discussed "The Aesthetic Equation" in the Introduction, and here is another kind of expressed equation in which we see how the balance and symmetry of a playful machine can be imaginatively transformed back into an animal's symmetrical shape. Here we have a kind of reversed prosthetics. Because the bilaterally symmetric handlebars of a machine ultimately derive from the bilaterally symmetric arms and legs of a rider, Picasso inverts the norm. He has combined two different objects into a playful and hitherto invisible unity. Another of his witty fusions, just as famous, is his *Baboon and Young*, in which he combined and fused together two of his son's toy automobiles to make a head and torso. Here are examples of combinatory play that seriously make art strange. Isn't all art slightly strange?

What about his skipping girl? Most children have tried skipping a rope, so most should recognize that something strange is happening in Picasso's sculpture, because nothing is really happening at all. The girl is inert, and so the feeling is all wrong. If you can skip a rope, you remember the skill of swinging the rope, rotating it faster and faster, with your arms and body increasing the whorling momentum of the rope into a heady rhythm. Why is that snake there? Some students will certainly remember the rhymes that kids used to sing while skipping. There is a snake mentioned in one version, both in French and English; maybe that is why there is a snake at the bottom of this piece. Here the sculpture depends on an awkward static balance. The twisted rope should not really support a skipping girl, but the requirements of sculpture demand a strut. Look at her shoes. Aren't they on the wrong feet? The girl's body is symmetrical but awkward. There is no sense of embodied rhythm or grace. Although many artists will try to incorporate movement into a spatial medium such as sculpture, here Picasso seems to stress her inertness. She just hangs there. At first, Picasso composed the sculpture assembled from commonplace things from around his studio: a willow (osier) basket, a cake mold, wood, pottery, plaster. The combination looks helter-skelter. He attached wires horizontally from the rope to her legs. You can ask students how that connection might violate the principle of skipping. His use of found objects makes for a kind of "found art," a matching or combination of unapparent similarities, likenesses, where you are allowed to guess at the artist's aims.

Here is a final example of a strangely balanced form of plastic art, also timely for classroom discussion. But there is almost no playfulness in it. Henry Moore's large sculpture *Nuclear Energy* is a troubling example of a strangely balanced art form. There are plenty of mages online to study. In late 1973, a committee of faculty members at the University of Chicago asked Moore whether he would like to propose a design that would commemorate the 25th anniversary of the first successful generation of a nuclear chain reaction. The sculpture would be placed near the original site of the experiment, a campus squash court. It is now part of a public park. As one committee member wrote, the piece would be "a monument to man's triumphs, charged with high hope and profound fear, just as every triumphant breakthrough has always been."[41] Students can consider the oppositions of hope and fear, triumph and what? How are they balanced in the image?

By the time that Moore was offered this opportunity, he and every other thinking person had come to realize the frightful complexity of this new age of atomic power. How could he symbolize a balance between peaceful and warring ends, like the bow and the lyre? Is there a reasonable balance for nuclear energy? How could Moore represent within a symbolic form the opposite consequences in the nuclear transformations of atomic energy? In this country, we have large plants powered by nuclear energy, and we have large stockpiles of nuclear warheads. As Moore explained his artistic process to the committee, he had been working on a small maquette that might work. When he later showed the committee a larger working model, "they liked my idea because the top of it is like some large mushroom or a kind of mushroom cloud. Also it has a kind of head shape like the top of the skull but down below is more an architectural cathedral. One might think of the lower part of it being a protective form constructed for human beings and the top being more like the idea of the destructive side of the atom. So between the two it might express to people in a symbolic way the whole event."[42] Although we might discern the combination of destructive and constructive oppositions as we study his sculpture, it does not seem to be a nicely balanced piece of work. Instead of a calm cathedral-like support, the whole may seem ominous to some students. Does it seem to evoke the feeling of struggle? Was he able to contain those oppositions in the figure of a skull, a dome, and a cathedral?

A Stance of Art

We learn from these examples that artistic facts are not the same as truthful facts. Archibald MacLeish, in "Ars Poetica," expresses an equivalence:

> ... a poem is equal to, not true,...
> a poem, should not mean, but be.[43]

As Majorcan storytellers would sometimes begin: "'Aixo era y no era' (It was and it was not)." We have seen that more often than not, works of art express opposing patterns of forces that seem poised to tell us something other than themselves, but they do not. We are left with suspended judgment, but we can get a glimpse, make a guess. We can take our own stand or not. Here is a passage by the Argentine storyteller Jorge Luis Borges:

> Music, states of happiness, mythology, faces molded by time, certain twilights and certain places—all these are trying to tell us something, or have told us something we should not have missed, or are about to tell us something; that imminence of a revelation that is not yet produced is, perhaps, the aesthetic reality.[44]

We can ask students how it feels to have a revelation blocked. Is it stressful to be on the verge of an insight that is not yet revealed? Have we missed the point of the telling? What does "imminence" mean? Is it a kind of foreshadowing? How does foreshadowing work in stories? Can a student give an example of an imminent experience? What about one that has been blocked? Have we just experienced a hint, an intimation of a truth, a conjecture, the glimmer of an Idea? Are art forms like many sentences, and like living itself, always suspended, on the way toward an insight? Even when we successfully catch a fleeting idea, that success may lead us onward toward another challenge and response. Maybe that is what compositional thinking is all about, moving and combining toward the completion of one idea and glimpsing another just ahead. As we think we solve one problem, are we always given another? Is there never closure? Where is the calm poise? Is that too much like the classroom for fun?

We have said along the way that art forms are a form of serious play that seems to evince a balanced tension that often feels like stress. The stress is usually a feeling of irresolution, as in the too famous ending of John Keats's "Ode on a Grecian Urn":

> Beauty is truth, truth beauty,—that is all
> Ye know on earth, and all ye need to know.[45]

At this point, you might say, "Oh no, not another balanced assertion." But here the assertion is not rational information; it is equal to the truth. We are poised in act of suspended judgment, on the verge of an aesthetic fact. Another of Keats's lyrics, "On First Looking Into Chapman's Homer," ends with the wonderful phrase, "a wild surmise." In his chapter "Beauty," Gardner argues that truth and beauty are "fundamentally different."

Balanced Calmness

In the Introduction, we discussed Margaret Atwood's summary of moral balancing, and she named related concepts in different cultures. Since she starts with Tao or the Way, let's consider Chuang Tzu's commentary about the central pivot of Taoism. In Thomas Merton's rendition, Chuang Tzu taught that one must understand the "complementarity" of opposite values.[46] "Complementarity" is a big word for a now-familiar concept about oppositions. Here again is another rendition of a balance of opposite forces:

Hence he sees that on both sides of every argument there is both right and wrong. He also sees that in the end they are reducible to the same thing, once they are related to the pivot of Taoism. When the wise man grasps this pivot, he is in the center of the circle, and there he stands while "Yes" and "No" pursue one another around the circumference (*TWC*, 44).

So we see here another version of the ancient principle of oppositions with which we opened this chapter. We know now that it is not just an ancient principle of wisdom literature. For it is also practical wisdom, as we have seen, to seek the rotating pivot, the fulcrum, the center of balance, the tipping point on a seesaw of oppositions. Each of the great existing values must reverse course and go over into its opposite, somewhat like Dewey's energy cycle but more like the pivot on a fulcrum or a wheel and axle (Chap. 2). What Merton means about opposing values is that we soon learn that too much of a good thing can go over into its opposite and can become a bad thing. If we eat too much candy or ice cream, we can get sick and sickened. Adults who drink too much alcohol, smoke cigarettes, or take drugs for pleasure can become so habituated that the pleasure is gone and has become an anxious and horrid necessity. We can work out other examples with students, in order to show that values can shift over into their complements. Goodness and badness can "pivot" and go over into their opposites. And you can define "complements" in a different sense than "compliments."

Taoism and Confucianism may be seen as the great complements of a Chinese way of life, but, as Merton shows, each of the great ways incorporated aspects of the other (*TWC*, 20–23). Most students will know the visual image of a rotating *yin-yang* emblem, if only seen as tattoos. These values remain central to Chinese ways of thinking, and Chinese culture will surely loom large in our students' futures.

When Ezra Pound edited and selectively translated some works of Confucius, he entitled a main section "The Unwobbling Pivot."[47] With that phrase, Pound translated the Chinese *Chung Yung*, and Pound says that it incorporates all of Confucius's comparatively rare discussions of metaphysics (*C*, 96). Here Pound translates from an ancient commentator's Preface:

The word *chung* signifies what is bent neither
to one side nor to the other. The word *yung*

signifies what is unchanging. What exists plumb in the middle is the just process in the universe and that which never wavers or wobbles is the calm principle operant in its mode of action (C, 97).

He says, here is how we find equipoise or calmness. And we notice that calmness is like potential energy an operant for action. We don't wobble like a faulty wheel and axle. Lin Yutang describes the calligraphic strokes of the pictograph for *chung*: It is simply a kind of square or rectangle, with each side slightly puckered inward, and with a vertical stroke, the main vertical "axis," running through the middle of the square. So the visual representation signifies the meaning of *chung*, and it is "middle."[48] So the phrase signifies a universal metaphysics for the awareness of a moving balanced form that serves at the same time as a middle way for the regulation of one's calm moral action. The Golden Mean is not just a static *Ebenmass*. It is a calmness and balance, plumb at the center of a smoothly rotating wheel. To act with integrity is to integrate one's active life into the unwobbling hub of the large cosmological order. As Confucius said, in Lin Yutang's translation, "The life of the moral man is an exemplification of the universal moral order (*chung yung*, usually translated as 'the Mean')."[49] Real wheels do wobble, however, and the great globe itself wobbles as it tilts off-angled from its true poles of rotation, and humans do depart from the Golden Mean. Life forms swerve, wobble, and squeak, but sometimes they dance and sing with grace. So to solve any compositional problem, we start to look for its center of balance or imbalance. In this short survey, we see that in ancient history, a middle measure was thought to be a way of life, not just thinking.

In their short book about aesthetics, C. K. Ogden and I. A. Richards discuss a number of definitions of beauty, but they use the principle of *Chung Yung* as their leading principle for balancing opposed forces, our definition for art. For them, Confucius's moral principle also exhibits a foundational principle of beauty that they call "equilibrium."[50] We have already seen that "reflective equilibrium" is a good description for rational judgment, for practical reasons. Now it serves as an aesthetic stance. They begin with a drawn image of the two calligraphic symbols of *Chung Yung*. Now you can see that Yutang's description above is precise. The visual icons deftly and beautifully represent the meaning in the shapes of their strokes. You can discuss calligraphy with students as an art form. The icons themselves indicate the larger pattern. How is calligraphy like algebra?

Here is part of their opening translation: "Having no leanings is called Chung. By Chung is denoted Equilibrium; Yung is the fixed principle regulating everything under heaven" (13). If you think of our model of balancing feedback as a self-regulating principle, then it sounds like Chung Yung. What this means is that the "balancing up" of scientific laws is as old as wisdom literature.

They claim that this feeling of equilibrium as we experience a beautiful work is often "fugitive and evanescent in the extreme...." With no other comment, they quote one of William Wordsworth's strangest passages, taken from a great poem about his own growing up. The boy is blowing through cupped hands, whistling happily at owls, and listening to their hooting back:

> And when there came a pause
> Of silence such as baffled his best skill:
> Then sometimes, in that silence, while he hung
> Listening, a gentle shock of mild surprise
> Has carried far into his heart the voice
> Mountain torrents; or the visible scene
> Would enter unawares into his mind
> With all its solemn imagery, its rocks,
> Its woods, and that uncertain heaven received
> Into the bosom of the steady lake.[51]

Let students discuss the strange interval, the instant of balanced hovering that occurs both in the scene and in the sentences, and in the boy's mind as he hung listening, suspended, and waiting. Is this an example of an intimation, an imminence? How is it that the heaven is uncertain? Ogden and Richards call this balanced union of different, often opposing, feelings and emotions a "synaesthesis, which achieves equilibrium (Chap. 14, 72–73). Here too we are poised on the verge of an imminent discovery. Has Wordsworth's boy, while he hung listening, experienced an intimation of a truth by way of a baffled "Idea," which the poet has expressed without revealing it? The troubling image of the boy suspended, like a mobile, becomes the meaning of his experience.

In these examples we see how studying the arts and sciences lets us build in our brains a model of the world that we may choose to live in— Dickinson's world or Vermeer's, Confucian or Taoist. This internal model that we have learned is our own sort of magic garden, our own magic circle, in which we live imaginatively with our genius. As we interact in the world, we may use our own model of a world in which to take a stand, self-possessed and calm.

As we conclude this section about art, let us suppose that any creative act—whether a sentence in a poem, or a Calder mobile, or a machine invention like the Wright brothers' airplane—is an assemblage of parts recomposed into a new whole of opposed energies. A creative act may be seen as a playful struggle for available energies that takes place in a magical space and time. So the making of any tool or machine or a sentence or a magic stone is an act of displacement where a combination of parts amounts to a new transformation. You could say too that the transformation is a metamorphosis, like the myth of the sculptor Pygmalion, who fell in love with the statue he was creating, and his wish was so strong that the cold marble turned into a warm living girl.

"Combinatory Play" as Serious Play in Science

Late in life, as he thought about his own methods of problem solving and discovery, Albert Einstein said that his creative work was based upon visual and muscular thinking, but not really upon the use of words. His thinking is what we know as embodied thinking:

> The words of the language, as they are written or spoken, do not seem to play any role in my mechanisms of thought. The psychical entities which seem to serve as elements in thought are certain signs and more or less clear images which can be "voluntarily" reproduced and combined. But taken from a psychological standpoint, this combinatory play seems to be the essential feature in productive thought—before there is any connection with logical construction in word or other kinds of signs which can be communicated to others. The above-mentioned elements are, in my case, of visual and some muscular type. Conventional words, or other signs have to be sought for laboriously only in a secondary stage, when the mentioned associative play is sufficiently established and can be reproduced at will.[52]

Einstein used his own mode of embodied thinking with which to discover. The phrase "associative play" should let us recall the several kinds of "likeness" that we have considered here and there: matching, following, cause, and effect, as the basic ways of associating ideas together. We have seen how these ways of matching and following serve us in our everyday thinking about combinations, as well as more difficult kinds of problem solving, as well as in creative play. And we have isolated a muscular sign of feeling as an index and a visual sign as an icon. He calls his method of creative discovery a kind of "combinatory play," as if his most sustained and abstruse thinking were made up of a play of visual, kinesthetic, and muscular combinations. Einstein was describing the play of his inner genius. Holton says that Einstein rarely discovered with words, but always with pictures, and he thought of his method as imaginative play. His way of multidimensional thinking features a compound of 3-D and 2-D modeling, with the use of 1-D sentences as a secondary reframing for sending a communication to others. His combinatory play exhibits a cloverleaf of inquiry.

Here is a famous example of combinatory play in science, Dmitri Mendeleev's construction of the Periodic Table of Elements. It too is an example of very serious play, and it too features multidimensional thinking. Although many students may not study the Periodic Table until high school, they will have learned how to balance some chemical reactions of elements and compounds. (See "Balancing Acts" in Chap. 2.) His discovery can serve as a sustained example of combining all three of our methods of inquiry, because we can find him using physical balancing, visual thinking with formulas, and verbal thinking. Mendeleev was looking for family likenesses within the elements. Eventually he found a common structure for the atoms of the known elements by writing each element on a separate piece of paper, like an index card. This can be done as classroom exercise in middle school or in high school.[53] Then he arranged them into a grid, as you might lay out a game of solitaire. He would sort and shuffle them in different patterns, moving them around in different combinations, just as you do with a deck of playing cards. He shuffled them and sorted them in vertical columns and horizontal rows so that he could match them up vertically and link them together horizontally in following sequences.

His friends called this sorting and rearranging slips of paper his game of "Patience" (Bronowski, *AM*, 324). Let's pause for a moment and consider the analogy of a card game. A card game is, like algebra, chiefly a pursuit of iconic patterns. In a small way, every card game also exemplifies Einstein's "combinatory play." In almost every card game, after the deck has been shuffled into disorder, players begin to combine and sort their own cards into their own orderly patterns: We bundle them into matching likenesses of two or three equivalent numbers or suits, and/or we can also group our cards into following sequences (see cardinal and ordinal numbers, Chap. 3). As we combine, we build up patterns of information, against the chaos of chance shuffling. In terms of our Sender-Receiver diagram, the rules of the card game are its **code**, whatever it is—Patience, Hearts, Old Maids, Bridge, Poker—while the framing background is its **context**, that is, the other players' group of cards, either laid out on the table or hidden in their hands, the whole set. "Combinatory play," that is what we do as we are composing with a lever, an equation, and a sentence.

Mendeleev was trying to figure out the rules of the combinatory laws that governed the periodic order of atomic elements. He was patiently playing a game of his own invention, ready to act, but willing to wait. In Chap. 2, we discussed Bronowski's idea about splitting and fusing the atom with a wedge-like probe. Mendeleev was splitting up and recombining the atomic elements in order to find what Bronowski calls their "family likenesses" (*AM*, 322). Taking them apart and then putting them back together again, he was seeking their hidden unity. What are the family likenesses in Moore's sculpture of atomic energy? Mendeleev was searching for the secret **code** of atomic weights by arranging them into a **context** of rows and columns. He was composing a new kind of magic circle, except that the circle was a grid. Eventually, Mendeleev constructed a grid of columns and rows, with the elements arranged in horizontal rows of increasing atomic numbers, a *following* sequence. And he stacked the elements into vertical columns of bundles or groups of family relationships, a process of *matching*. He would study an element at the crisscross of rows and columns. He was searching for patterns of resemblance by matching and following the elements, seen as index cards. So his discovery of a *periodic* pattern was based on his construction of a sort of x-y grid, where the numbers and symbols served as hypothetical equivalents of their masses. Mendeleev presumed a principle of orderly equivalence for the atomic elements. The increasing weights in the order of the elements were evidence of an orderly system. The periodicity of his array later provided a visual clue about the periodic *evolution* of the elements, one after the other in increasing atomic weights, from hydrogen to helium, and so on: "Matter itself evolves [in a following sequence]" (Bronowski, *AM*, 344). Is that sentence not an astonishing assertion? How does helium come out of hydrogen? In a classroom discussion, students can focus on the energy of the sun.

Mendeleev also saw that there were gaps in his grid of chemical elements. So he left a space in his model where he predicted that a new element would later be discovered. He saw that gaps in the rows meant the hidden existence of as-yet undiscovered elements. What an imminence that is:

In science we do not simply march along in a linear progression of known instances to unknown ones. Rather, we work as in a crossword puzzle, scanning two separate progressions for the points at which they intersect: that is where the unknown instances should lie in hiding. Mendeleev scanned the progression of atomic weights in the columns, and the family likenesses in the rows, to pinpoint the missing elements at their intersections (*AM,* 326).

The intersection is another example of crosshair thinking, a central point of periodic order. Here then in this example of scientific discovery is a creative breakthrough in Perkins's sense, of combinatory play. Mendeleyev had built a model of the world of elements, and with it he could scan back and forward, and predict a future discovery by way of a blank slot in the syntax.

Combinatory play is a kind of creative problem solving that often joins two apparently unlike domains and puts them together into a new unity, like a crossword puzzle and a model of scientific discovery. "Eureka!" as Archimedes apparently shouted. He joined together his experience of settling into a bathtub and watching the volume of water displace an amount equal to his weight, so he applied that framework to the density of metal with an equal volume of water in order to solve his problem of a golden crown. In *Archimedes' Bathtub,* Perkins also uses the term "reframing" as one of his components for breakthrough thinking (51–56).

Patient Problem Solving

The patient solution of any composition requires sustained attention that goes with an acquired skill, like a game of Patience. As we are on the way toward solving this kind of compositional problem, our minds are full of intense attention. Since we are intent on solving the problem, we may be somewhat tense, even though patient, maybe even a little bit stressed, as we play any close game. As we seek we hover attentively. We are suspended, maybe pausing momentarily in a stance of "wild surmise." This intense attentive state of mind characterizes most creative discovery seen as a higher order of play. We can see too that this mental state of being on the verge of discovery, in which we search for clues, test out hunches, and seek good and satisfying answers, is very much like many art forms which leave us ever on the verge, like a bird perched on a branch and about to take wing. Students may be willing to compare Coleridge's phrase "a willing suspension of disbelief," which describes a reader's state of mind when reading fictions, with Mendeleev's patient suspension of knowledge as he patiently tests a belief.

Is this kind of combinatory play also a way that Emily Dickinson made the poem "The brain is wider than the sky"? However, unlike Einstein's claim about his secondary use of language, she does it with language, with three assertive sentences, and she transforms a grammatical linkage of subject and predicate into a wonderful claim about the brain's mental power, its creativity. For her, this kind of imaginative association seems to be a kind of combinatory play with language. Let's compare and contrast brain and sky. In each sentence, she combines two very dissimilar elements, and she joins them into a unity. She makes big claims, with her own hyperbolic logic, and she does it freely, with no fear of contradiction, no fear of winning or losing a game, nor any stress about getting a low grade in school. Here at the end, consider again the poem's mood. It is not excited, not ecstatic about an imminent discovery. It is a completed composition, and her tone is one of calm composure, of a middle measure, perhaps even of playful patience. A poem, an art work, a scientific experiment and discovery, each in its own way is a certain kind of magic circle, with its own strange codes and contexts of combinatory play.

Notes

1. Johan Huizinga, *Homo Ludens: The Play Element in Culture* (Boston: Routledge and Kegan Paul, 1949), 116. Hereafter cited as *HL*. Available online: http://art.yale.edu/file_columns/0000/1474/homo_ludens_johan_huizinga_routledge_1949_.pdf.
2. *The Presocratic Philosophers: A Critical Study with a Selection of Texts*, eds. G. S. Kirk, J. E. Raven, M. Schofield (London: Cambridge University Press, 2nd edition, 1983), 192. Hereafter cited as *PS*.
3. See Pierre Bourdieu, *Practical Reason: On the Theory of Action* (Stanford, Cal.: Stanford University Press, 1998), 128.
4. See http://en.wikipedia.org/wiki/Magic_Circle_(virtual_worlds).
5. J. Z. Young, *An Introduction to the Study of Man* (New York: Oxford University Press, 1971), 487.
6. David Brooks, "Where America Is Working," *The New York Times* (June 3, 2016), Section A, 21.
7. Barry Schwartz and Stephen Sharpe, *Practical Wisdom: The Right Way to Do the Right Thing* (New York: Riverhead Books, 2010).
8. For the most inclusive analysis of this argument about practical wisdom or reason, see *Aristotle on Practical Wisdom: Nichomachean Ethics VI*, trans.

C. D. C. Reeve (Cambridge, Mass: Harvard University Press, 2013), "Introduction."
9. See Gardner, throughout his book *Truth, Beauty, Goodness*. Also, see this online site for an ethical common core: http://www.wholechildeducation.org/blog/the-ethical-core-of-common-core.
10. This passage is translated by William James in his *The Moral Equivalent of War*, as quoted by Edward O. Wilson, *The Social Conquest of Earth* (New York: Liveright Publishing Corporation, 2012), 73.
11. See https://www.engageny.org/resource/grade-5-ela-module-1.
12. This transference from medicine is studied by Werner Jaeger, *Aristotle: Fundamentals of the History of His Development*, 2nd ed., trans. Richard Robinson (Oxford: Clarendon Press, 1948), 44 n.
13. For a brief description of ecology in the context of systems theory, see Capra and Luisi, *The Systems View of Life*, 66–67.
14. See online, *McGraw Hill Science and Technology Dictionary*. http://www.accessscience.com/search?q=energy+balance
15. For a careful analysis see "Common Core Standards Matrix for the Nutrition Competencies K-6": http://projecteat.acoe.org/sites/default/files/Common%20Core%20Standards%20Matrix%20for%20the%20Nutrition%20Competencies.pdf.
16. Feynman, *CPL*, 72–73. See also my *NLC*, 298–300.
17. David Suzuki, *The Sacred Balance: Rediscovering Our Place In Nature* (Vancouver: Greystone Books, 1997), 93.
18. See http://www.choosemyplate.gov/. Also http://www.fns.usda.gov/sites/default/files/sump_level3.pdf
19. See http://wiki.answers.com/Q/What_are_the_percentages_for_the_eat_well_plate.
20. See "Neuroscience for Kids" on ANS: https://faculty.washington.edu/chudler/auto.html. For a recent description of the ANS and homeostatic health, see Oliver Sachs, "A General Feeling of Disorder," *New York Review of Books* vol LXII, no. 7, April 23, 2015.
21. Adam Smith, *The Wealth of Nations* (New York: Modern Library, 1937), Book IV, Chapter II, 423.
22. Definition of "balancing feedback" from Business Dictionary. http://www.businessdictionary.com/definition/balancing-feedback.html#ixzz3WXrDk3dF.
23. *The Ethics of Aristotle*, trans. J. A. K. Thomson (New York: Penguin, 1959), 129.
24. See the entry "Reflective Equilibrium," *Stanford Encyclopedia of Philosophy* online. Also see http://plato.stanford.edu/entries/reflective-equilibrium/ about John Rawls' phrase introduced in *A Theory of Justice* (Cambridge, Mass. 1971, 1999).

25. Immanuel Kant, *Grundlegund der Metaphysik der Sitten*. Section II, Werke, IV, 293 ed. Ernst Cassirer. Quoted, translated, and celebrated by Cassirer in his *The Myth of the State*(New York: Doubleday Anchor Books, 1955), 295.
26. See *Internet Encyclopedia of Philosophy* http://www.iep.utm.edu/goldrule/. See especially Gardner's chapter "Goodness" for his large argument that we need to reframe the very concept of goodness in our time.
27. This act of putting oneself in another's shoes is hard to do. See Paul Ricoeur, *Oneself as Another*, trans. Kathleen Blamey (Chicago: The University of Chicago Press, 1992).
28. John Dewey, *Art As Experience* (New York: Capricorn Books, 1958), 155.
29. See Rudolf Arnheim's chapter "Dynamics" where he discusses tension in the arts as an expression of deformation, in *Art and Visual Perception: A Psychology of the Creative Eye, The New Version* (Berkeley: University of California Press, 1974. His idea of dynamics is a counter principle to "Balance," the chapter that opens this book.
30. See the image and a description in the Metropolitan Museum of Art online catalog:http://www.metmuseum.org/collection/the-collection-online/search/11140.
31. Jan Vermeer, *Woman Holding a Balance*, National Gallery of Art: http://www.nga.gov/content/ngaweb/Collection/art.
32. See Martin Pops, *Vermeer: Consciousness and the Chamber of Being* (Ann Arbor: UMI Research Press, 1984), 41.
33. Oliver Sachs, "The Catastrophe, Spalding Gray's Brain Injury," *The New Yorker* April 27, 2015, 28.
34. In the Fogg Art Museum, Harvard University, Cambridge, Mass. Online: http://www.harvardartmuseums.org/collections/object/303496?position=1. See an exhibition catalog, prepared by Linda Muehlig, *Degas and the Dance* (Smith College Museum of Art, 1979). This catalog reproduces a number of Degas's graphite sketches that show the dancer's body blocked out, and shaped for transfer.
35. For the large issue of preparing student for their futures, see David N. Perkins, *Future Wise: Educating Our children for Changing World* (San Francisco, CA: Jossey-Bass, 2014).
36. Here is a web site for children, sponsored by the National Gallery of Art, that features Calder's compositions: http://www.nga.gov/content/ngaweb/education/teachers/lessons-activities/counting-art/calder.html.
37. See The Calder Foundation: http://www.calder.org/.
38. Jean-Paul Sartre, "The Mobiles of Calder," in *Essays in Aesthetics*, trans. Wade Baskin (New York: The Citadel Press, 1963), 78.
39. *Lee Bontecou, A Retrospective of Sculpture and Drawings, 1958–2000*, eds. Elizabeth Smith and Robert Storr (New York: Abrams, 2004). See MOMA online: http://www.moma.org/visit/calendar/exhibitions/1051.

40. See Roland Penrose, *The Sculpture of Picasso*, (New York: The Museum of Modern Art, 1967), 29. See also MOMa's exhibition at "Picasso Sculpture." moma.org.
41. Quoted by Henry J. Seldis, *Henry Moore in America* (New York: Praeger, 1973), 128.
42. *Henry Moore, Sculpture, With Comments by the Artist*, ed. David Mitchinson (New York: Rizzoli, 1981), 178.
43. Archibald MacLeish, "Ars Poetica," http://www.poetryfoundation.org/poetrymagazine/poem/6371.
44. Jorge Borges, "The Wall and the Books" in *Other Inquisitions*, trans. Ruth L. C. Simms(Austin, 1964), p. 5.
45. John Keats, "Ode on a Grecian Urn, The Poetry Foundation: http://www.poetryfoundation.org/poem/173742. In his chapter "Beauty" Gardner argues that truth and beauty are "fundamentally different."
46. Thomas Merton, *The Way of Chuang Tzu* (New York: New Directions, 1965), 30. Hereafter *TWC*.
47. Ezra Pound, *Confucius: The Great Digest, The Unwobbling Pivot, The Analects* (New York: New Directions), 1951. Hereafter *C*.
48. Lin Yutang, *My Country and My People* (New York: John Day, 1935), 315.
49. *The Wisdom of Confucius*, ed. and trans. Lin Yutang (New York: Random House, 1943), 72.
50. C. K. Ogden and I. A. Richards, *The Foundations of Aesthetics* (New York: International Publishers, 1925).
51. William Wordsworth, "There Was A Boy," http://www.poetryfoundation.org/poem/174827.
52. Quoted by Gerald Holton, "On Trying to Understand Scientific Genius," *Thematic Origins of Scientific Thought: Kepler to Einstein* (Cambridge: Harvard University Press, 1973), 368–369.
53. Here is an online lesson plan that begins with students writing an element on a slip of paper: http://www.discoveryeducation.com/teachers/free-lesson-plans/elements-of-chemistry-the-periodic-table.cfm.

BIBLIOGRAPHY

American Museum of Natural History. *Dancing Leg Calipers*. http://americanhistory.si.edu/collections/search/object/nmah_904332.
Archimedes Home Page. http://www.math.nyu.edu/~crorres/Archimedes/Lever/LeverLaw.html.
Aristotle. 2002. *Nichomachean Ethics*. Trans. Joe Sachs. Newburyport: Focus Publishing.
Aristotle on Practical Wisdom: Nichomachean Ethics VI. 2013. Trans. C.D.C. Reeve. Cambridge, MA: Harvard University Press.
Arnheim, Rudolf. 1974. *Art and Visual Perception: A Psychology of the Creative Eye, The New Version*. Berkeley: University of California Press.
Atwood, Margaret. 2008. *Payback: Debt and the Shadow Side of Wealth*. Toronto: Anansi.
Austin, J.L. 1962. *How to Do Things With Words*. Cambridge, MA: Harvard University Press.
Balancing Act—Force, Torque, Rotation. http://phet.colorado.edu/en/simulation/balancing-act
Basic Machines. 1994. US Navy Training Manual 121199. Washington, DC.
Bate, Walter Jackson. 1963. *John Keats*. Cambridge, MA: Harvard University Press.
Bateson, Gregory. 1979. *Mind and Nature: A Necessary Unity*. New York: E. P. Dutton.

Benveniste, Emile. 1971. *Problems in General Linguistics*. Trans. Mary Elizabeth Meek. Coral Gables: University of Miami Press.
Berlinski, David. 2013. *The King of Infinite Space: Euclid and His Elements*. New York: Basic Books.
Bertalanffy, Ludwig von. 1968. *General System Theory: Foundations, Development, Applications*. New York: George Braziller.
Bloomfield, Morton W. 1967. The Syncategorematic in Poetry: From Semantics to Syntactics. In *To Honor Roman Jakobson: Essays on the Occasion of His Seventieth Birthday*, 309–317. The Hague: Mouton.
Borges, Jorge Luis. 1964. The Wall and the Books. In *Other Inquisitions*. Trans. Ruth L.C. Simms. Austin: University of Texas Press.
Bourdieu, Pierre. 1998. *Practical Reason: On the Theory of Action*. Stanford: Stanford University Press.
Bridgman, P.W. 1937. *Dimensional Analysis*. revised ed. New Haven: Yale University Press.
British Museum. *Map of the World*. http://www.britishmuseum.org/explore/highlights/highlight_objects/me/m/map_of_the_world.aspx.
Bronowski, Jacob. 1973. *The Ascent of Man*. Boston: Little Brown and Company.
———. 1978. *A Sense of the Future: Essays in Natural Philosophy*. Cambridge, MA: M.I.T. Press.
Brooks, David. 2016. Where America Is Working. *The New York Times*, June 3, Section A, 21.
Bruner, Jerome. 1960, 1982. *The Process of Education*. Cambridge, MA: Harvard University Press.
Bunn, James H. 1981. *The Dimensionality of Signs, Tools and Models: An Introduction*. Bloomington: Indiana University Press.
———. 1991. A Semiotic Model of Conjecture. In *On Semiotic Modeling*, ed. Myrdene Anderson and Floyd Merrill, 405–428. Berlin: De Gruyter.
———. 2002. *Wave Forms: A Natural Syntax for Rhythmic Language*. Palo Alto: Stanford University Press.
———. 2014. *The Natural Law of Cycles: Governing the Mobile Symmetries of Animals and Machines*. New Brunswick: Transaction Publishers.
Business Dictionary. Balancing Feedback. http://www.businessdictionary.com/definition/balancing-feedback.html#ixzz3WXrDk3dF.
Callois, Roger. 1961. *Man, Play, and Games*. Trans. Meyer Barash. New York: Free Press of Glencoe, Inc.
The Calder Foundation. http://www.calder.org/.
Capra, Fritjof, and Pier Luigi Luisi. 2012. *The Systems View of Life: A Unifying Vision*. New York: Cambridge University Press.
Carey, Susan. 2009. *The Origin of Concepts*. New York: Oxford University Press.
Cassirer, Ernst. 1953. *Philosophy of Symbolic Forms*, vol. 1. Trans. Ralph Manheim. New Haven: Yale University Press.

———. 1955. *The Myth of the State*. New York: Doubleday Anchor Books.
The Catholic World Report. Spielberg's *Lincoln*. http://www.catholicworldreport.com/Item/1822/spielbergs_ilincolni_politics_as_mathematics.
Choose My Plate. http://www.choosemyplate.gov/. Also http://www.fns.usda.gov/sites/default/files/sump_level3.pdf.
Coleridge, Samuel Taylor. *The Friend: A Series of Essays*. Google Books. books-google.com.
Common Core Curriculum for New York State, Engage New York. International Charter of Human Rights. https://www.engageny.org/resource/grade-5-ela-module-1.
Common Core Curriculum Standards. English Language Arts: Literacy/ Language. http://www.corestandards.org/ELA-Literacy/L/language-progressive-skills/.
Common Core Curriculum Standards. Math. http://www.corestandards.org/Math/Content/3/OA/B/5/.
Common Core Standards and Strategies Flip Chart. Vocabulary and Strategies. Panel 8. Mentoring Minds.
Common Core Standards Matrix for the Nutrition Competencies K-6: http://projecteat.acoe.org/sites/default/files/Common%20Core%20Standards%20Matrix%20for%20the%20Nutrition%20Competencies.pdf.
Crease, Robert P. 2008. *The Great Equations: Breakthroughs in Science from Pythagoras to Heisenberg*. New York: W. W. Norton.
Davis, Philip J., and Reuben Hersh. 1981. *The Mathematical Experience*. Boston: Birkhauser.
Dewey, John. 1958. *Art As Experience*. New York: Capricorn Books.
Diggins, Julia E. 1965. *String, Straightedge, and Shadow: The Story of Geometry*. New York: The Viking Press.
Dijksterhuis, E.J. 1956. *Archimedes*. Trans. C. Dikshoon. Copenhagen: Ejnar Munksgaard.
Discovery Education. *Elements of Chemistry, The Periodic Table*. http://www.discoveryeducation.com/teachers/free-lesson-plans/elements-of-chemistry-the-periodic-table.cfm.
Edelman, Gerald. 2004. *Wider Than the Sky: The Phenomenal Gift of Consciousness*. New Haven: Yale University Press.
Einstein, Albert. 1967. "E = MC^{2}" in *Out of My Later Years*. Totowa: Littlefield Adams.
Einstein, Albert, and Leon Infeld. 1938. *The Evolution of Physics: The Growth of Ideas from Early Concepts to Relativity and Quanta*. Ed. C.P. Snow. Cambridge: Cambridge University Press.
———. 1967. Physics and Reality. In *Out of My Later Years*. Totowa: Littlefield, Adams & Co.
Embodied Learning Blends Movement, Computer Interaction. 2016. *Education Week*, May 26. http://www.edweek.org/ew/articles/2012/10/10/07embody.h32.html.

Emily Dickinson Digital Archive. Amherst College. http://www.edickinson.org/editions/1/image_sets/240388.
Engage New York. *Astronomy.* https://www.engageny.org/resource/grade-1-ela-domain-6-astronomy.
Evans, Arthur. 1935. *The Palace of Minos: A Comparative Account.* Vol. 4. New York: Cambridge University Press (online edition 2013).
The Ethics of Aristotle. 1959. Trans. J.A.K. Thomson. New York: Penguin.
Fenollosa, Ernest. 1919. *The Chinese Written Character as a Medium for Poetry.* Ed. Ezra Pound. London: Instigations.
Fermor, Patrick Lee. 1986. *Between the Woods and the Water.* London: John Murray Ltd.
Feynman, Richard. 1963. *Lectures on Physics.* Vol. 1. New York: Addison-Wesley.
———. 1965. *The Character of Physical Law.* Cambridge, MA: The M.I.T. Press.
———. 1999. What Is Science? In *The Pleasure of Finding Things Out,* ed. Jeffrey Robins. New York: MJF Books.
Fish, Stanley Eugene. 2011. *How to Write a Sentence and How to Read One.* New York: Harper Collins Publishers.
Florey, Kitty Burns. 2006. *Sister Bernadette's Barking Dog.* New York: Harvest Books.
Fogg Art Museum, Harvard University. *Jan Vermeer.* http://www.harvardartmuseums.org/collections/object/303496?position=1.
Forbes, Esther. 2011. *Johnny Tremain.* New York: HMH Books for Young Readers (reprint).
Fuson, Karen C. 2013. *Math Expressions: Common Core.* Vol. 2. New York: Houghton Mifflin Harcourt.
Gardner, Howard. 2012. *Truth, Beauty, and Goodness Reframed: Educating for the Virtues in the Twenty First Century.* New York: Basic Books.
Gleick, James. 2011. *The Information: A History, A Theory, A Flood.* New York: Pantheon Books.
Gray, James. 1968. *Animal Locomotion.* New York: W. W. Norton & Company.
Hacker, Diana and Nancy Sommers. n.d. *A Pocket Style Manual,* 6th ed. Boston: Bedford/St. Martins.
Hanson, Norwood. 1969. *Perception and Discovery: An Introduction to Scientific Inquiry,* ed. Willard C. Humphries. San Francisco: Freeman, Cooper & Company.
Hofstadter, Douglas. 2007. *I Am a Strange Loop.* New York: Basic Books.
Hofstadter, Douglas, and Emmanuel Sander. 2013. *Surfaces and Essences: Analogy as the Fuel and Fire of Thinking.* New York: Basic Books.
Hogben, Lancelot. 1968. *Mathematics for the Million.* New York: Norton.
Holton, Gerald. 1973. *Thematic Origins of Scientific Thought: Kepler to Einstein.* Cambridge: Harvard University Press.

Huizinga, Johan. 1949. *Homo Ludens: The Play Element in Culture.* Boston: Routledge and Kegan Paul. Available online: http://art.yale.edu/file_columns/0000/1474/homo_ludens_johan_huizinga_routledge_1949_.pdf.
Idaho Public Television. *Simple Machines.* http://idahoptv.org/sciencetrek/topics/simple_machines/facts.cfm.
Internet Encyclopedia of Philosophy. The Golden Rule. http://www.iep.utm.edu/goldrule/.
Isler, Martin. 2002. *Sticks, Stones, and Shadows: Building the Great Pyramids.* Norman: University of Oklahoma Press.
Jaeger, Werner. 1948. *Aristotle: Fundamentals of the History of His Development,* 2nd edn. Trans. Richard Robinson. Oxford: Clarendon Press.
Jakobson, Roman. 1960. Closing Statement: Linguistics and Poetics. In *Style in Language,* ed. Thomas Sebeok. Cambridge, MA: M.I.T Press.
———. 1972. Verbal Communication. In *Communication,* 44–53. San Francisco: Scientific American.
James, William. 1890. Association. In *The Principles of Psychology,* vol. 1, Chapter XIV. New York: Henry Holt and Company.
Jefferson Labs. *It's Elemental; Balancing Acts.* http://education.jlab.org/elementbalancing/index.ht
Johnny Tremain. Common Core Study Guide. http://www.centerforlearning.org/PDF/standards/johnny-tremain-common-core-standards-4983.pdf.
Joseph, Sister Miriam. 2002. *The Trivium: Logic, Grammar, and Rhetoric: Understanding the Nature and Function of Language,* ed. Marguerite McGlinn. Philadelphia: Paul Dry Books.
Kahneman, Daniel. 2011. *Thinking, Fast and Slow.* New York: Farrar, Straus and Giroux.
Keats, John. *Ode on a Grecian Urn, The Poetry Foundation.* http://www.poetryfoundation.org/poem/173742.
Kline, Morris. 1972. *Mathematical Thought From Ancient to Modern Times.* New York: Oxford University Press.
Koestler, Arthur. 1964. *The Act of Creation.* New York: Dell.
Kricher, John A. 2009. *The Balance of Nature: Ecology's Enduring Myth.* Princeton: Princeton University Press.
Kuiper, Koenrad, and W. Scott Allan. 2004. *An Introduction to English Language: Word, Sound, Sentence.* 2nd ed. Basingstoke: Palgrave Macmillan.
Lakoff, George, and Mark Johnson. 1999. *Philosophy in the Flesh: The Embodied Mind and Its Challenge to Western Thought.* New York: Basic Books.
Lee Bontecou, A Retrospective of Sculpture and Drawings, 1958–2000, ed. Elizabeth Smith and Robert Storr. New York: Abrams, 2004.
Lewis-Williams, David. 2002. *The Mind in the Cave: Consciousness and the Origins of Art.* London: Thames & Hudson.

Lujan, Michael L. 2012. *Common Core Standards and Strategies Flip Chart, Grade 5.* Tyler: Mentoring Minds.
Lyons, John. 1969. *Introduction to Theoretical Linguistics.* Cambridge: Cambridge University Press.
Manning, Brenda H. 1991. *Cognitive Self Instruction for Classroom Processes.* Albany: State University of New York Press.
Mark, Johnson. 2007. *The Meaning of the Body: Aesthetics of Human Understanding.* Chicago: The University of Chicago Press.
Marshack, Alexander. 1972. *The Roots of Civilization: The Cognitive Beginnings of Man's First Art, Symbol and Notation.* New York: McGraw Hill Book Company. Online: http://sservi.nasa.gov/articles/oldest-lunar-calendars/.
Mathematical Association of America. Frank J. Swetz. *Mathematical Treasures: Mesopotamian Accounting Tokens.* http://www.maa.org/press/periodicals/convergence/mathematical-treasure-mesopotamian-accounting-tokens.
McGraw Hill Science and Technology Dictionary. Energy Balance. https://books.google.com/books/about/McGraw_Hill_dictionary_of_scientific_and.html?id=9t83ABfTBvQC.
McGraw Hill Science and Technology Dictionary. Energy Balance. http://www.accessscience.com/search?q=energy+balance.
Menninger, Karl. 1969. *Number Words and Number Symbols: A Cultural History of Numbers.* Trans. Paul Broneer. Cambridge: The M.I.T Press.
Merton, Thomas. 1966. *The Way of Chuang Tzu.* New York: New Directions.
The Metropolitan Museum of Art. *Snap the Whip.* http://www.metmuseum.org/collection/the-collection-online/search/11140.
MOMA. *Lee Bontecou.* http://www.moma.org/visit/calendar/exhibitions/1051
———. *Picasso Sculpture.* moma.org.
Moore, Henry. 1981. *Sculpture, With Comments by the Artist,* ed. David Mitchinson. New York: Rizzoli.
Morrison, Philip. 1965. The Modularity of Knowing. In *Module, Proportion, Rhythm, Symmetry,* ed. Gyorgy Kepes. New York: George Braziller.
Muehlig, Linda. 1979. *Degas and the Dance.* Northampton: Smith College Museum of Art.
NASA. *Airplane Flight.* https://www.grc.nasa.gov/www/K-12/airplane/newton.html
———. *Air Pressure.* http://kids.earth.nasa.gov/archive/air_pressure/barometer.html
———. *Balance of Forces.* https://www.grc.nasa.gov/www/k-12/WindTunnel/Activities/balance_of_forces.html
———. *The Lever.* http://www.ohio.edu/people/williar4/html/haped/nasa/simpmach/lever.htm
The National Gallery of Art. *Alexander Calder.* http://www.nga.gov/content/ngaweb/education/teachers/lessons-activities/counting-art/calder.html.

———. *Woman Holding a Balance.* http://www.nga.gov/content/ngaweb/Collection/art.
Neuroscience for Kids. ANS. https://faculty.washington.edu/chudler/auto.html
New York State Education Department. *Elementary Science Core Curriculum, Grades K—4.* http://www.p12.nysed.gov/ciai/mst/pub/elecoresci.pdf.
Next Generation Science Standards For States, By States. NGSS Release. April, 2013.
Ogden, C.K., and I.A. Richards. 1925. *The Foundations of Aesthetics.* New York: International Publishers.
Peirce, Charles Saunders. 1955. Logic as Semiotic: The Theory of Signs. In *Philosophical Writings of Peirce*, ed. Justus Buchler. New York: Dover Publications.
Penrose, Roland. 1967. *The Sculpture of Picasso.* New York: The Museum of Modern Art.
Perkins, David N. 2000. *Archimedes' Bathtub: The Art and Logic of Breakthrough Thinking.* New York: W. W. Norton & Company.
———. 2009. *Making Learning Whole: How Seven Principles of Teaching Can Transform Education.* New York: Jossey-Bass.
———. 2014. *Future Wise: Educating Our children for Changing World.* San Francisco: Jossey-Bass.
Peterson, Ivars. 2006. From Counting to Writing. *Science News*, March 8. https://www.sciencenews.org/article/counting-writing
Pettigrew, J. Bell. 1908. *Design in Nature.* New York: Longman.
Piaget, Jean. 1970. *Structuralism.* Trans. Chaninah Maschler. New York: Basic Books.
Piaget, Jean, and Barbara Inhelder. 1967. *The Child's Conception of Space.* Trans. F.J. Langdon and J.L. Lunzer. New York: W. W. Norton & Company.
Pinker, Steven. 2014. *The Sense of Style: The Thinking Person's Guide to Writing in the 21st Century.* New York: Viking.
Plato: The Collected Dialogues, ed. Edith Hamilton and Huntington Cairns. Princeton: Princeton University Press, 1963.
The Poetry Foundation. Archibald MacLeish. *Ars Poetica.* http://www.poetryfoundation.org/poetrymagazine/poem/6371.
———. William Blake. *Auguries of Innocence.* http://www.poetryfoundation.org/poem/172906.
———. William Wordsworth. *There Was A Boy.* http://www.poetryfoundation.org/poem/174827.
Polanyi, Michael. 1969. The Logic of Tacit Inference. In *Knowing and Being: Essays by Michael Polanyi*, ed. Marjorie Grene. Chicago: The University of Chicago Press.
Polanyi, Michael, and Harry Prosch. 1975. *Meaning.* Chicago: The University of Chicago Press.

Pops, Martin. 1984. *Vermeer: Consciousness and the Chamber of Being*. Ann Arbor: UMI Research Press.
Pound, Ezra. 1951. *Confucius: The Great Digest, The Unwobbling Pivot, The Analects*. New York: New Directions.
The Presocratic Philosophers: A Critical Study with a Selection of Texts, ed. G.S. Kirk, J.E. Raven, and M. Schofield. London: Cambridge University Press, 2nd edn., 1983.
Project Gutenberg. *The Complete Poems of Alexander Pope*. gutenberg.org.
The Project Gutenberg EBook of Childe Harold's Pilgrimage, by Lord Byron. gutenberg.org, Canto 3, 114.
Rawls, John. 1971, 1999. *A Theory of Justice*. Cambridge, MA: Harvard University Press.
Read, Herbert. 1970. *English Prose Style*. Boston: Beacon Press.
Ricoeur, Paul. 1975. *The Rule of Metaphor: Multidisciplinary Studies of the Creation of Meaning*. Trans. Robert Czerny. Toronto: University of Toronto Press.
———. 1992. *Oneself as Another*. Trans. Kathleen Blamey. Chicago: The University of Chicago Press.
Russell, Bertrand. 1958. *The ABC of Relativity*. New York: Signet Science Library.
Sachs, Oliver. 2015a. A General Feeling of Disorder. *New York Review of Books* LXII(7), April 23.
———. 2015b. The Catastrophe, Spalding Gray's Brain Injury. *The New Yorker*, April 27, 28.
Sartre, Jean-Paul. 1963. The Mobiles of Calder. In *Essays in Aesthetics*. Trans. Wade Baskin. New York: The Citadel Press.
Saussure, Ferdinand de. *Course in General Linguistics*. Trans. Wade Baskin. New York: McGraw-Hill Book Company.
Schmandt-Besserat, Denise. *From Reckoning to Writing*. http://en.finaly.org/index.php/Reckoning_before_writing.
———. 1996. *How Writing Came About*. Austin: University of Texas Press.
———. 2006. *The History of Counting*. New York: Morrow Junior Books.
School Physics. http://www.schoolphysics.co.uk/age11-14/Mechanics/Statics/text/Balancing_/index.html.
———.   http://www.pbslearningmedia.org/resource/hew06.sci.phys.maf.rollercoaster/energy-in-a-roller-coaster-ride/.
Schwartz, Barry, and Stephen Sharpe. 2010. *Practical Wisdom: The Right Way to Do the Right Thing*. New York: Riverhead Books.
Science A–Z. Focus Books Teaching Tips. *Let's Ride a Bike*. https://www.sciencea-z.com/main/UnitResource/unit/52/physical-science/grades-3-4/machines.
Seife, Charles. 2000. *Zero: The Biography of a Dangerous Idea*. New York: Viking.
Seldis, Henry J. 1973. *Henry Moore in America*. New York: Praeger.
Smith, Adam. 1937. *The Wealth of Nations*. New York: Modern Library.

Spielberg, Steven. *Lincoln*. Wikipedia. http://en.wikipedia.org/wiki/Lincoln_.
Stanford Encyclopedia of Philosophy online. Existence. http://plato.stanford.edu/entries/existence/.
Stanford Encyclopedia of Philosophy online. Reflective Equilibrium. http://plato.stanford.edu/entries/reflective-equilibrium/.
Stein, Gertrude. 1935. *Lectures in America*. New York: Random House.
Stewart, Ian. 2007. *Why Beauty Is Truth: A History of Symmetry*. New York: Basic Books.
Stroud, K.A. 2001. *Engineering Mathematics*. 5th ed. New York: Industrial Press, Inc.
Strunk, William Jr. 1972. *The Elements of Style*. 2nd revised ed. New York: The Macmillan Company.
Suzuki, David. 1997. *The Sacred Balance: Rediscovering Our Place In Nature*. Vancouver: Greystone Books.
Teach Engineering. Seesaw Activity. https://www.teachengineering.org/activities/view/nyu_seesaw_activity1.
Teresi, Dick. 2002. *Lost Discoveries: The Ancient Roots of Modern Science—from the Babylonians to the Maya*. New York: Simon & Schuster.
Trefil, James, and Robert M. Hazen. 1995. *The Sciences: An Integrated Approach*. New York: John Wiley & Sons.
Tulley, Gever, and Julie Spiegler. 2011. *50 Dangerous Things (You Should Let Your Children Do)*. New York: New American Library.
van Rijn, Rembrandt. *Child Being Taught to Walk* ca. 1656. http://www.royalacademy.org.uk/ra-magazine/from-the-archive-life-drawing,1905,AR.html.
Vitruvius. n.d. *The Ten Books on Architecture*. Trans. Morris Hicky Morgan. New York: Dover Publications.
Von Baeyer, Hans Christian. Einstein at the Ex. In *The Fermi Solution*.
———. 1993. The Aesthetic Equation. In *The Fermi Solution: Essays on Science*. New York: Random House.
———. 2004. *Information: The New Language of Science*. Cambridge: Harvard University Press.
The Waters Foundation. *Systems Thinking in Schools*. watersfoundation.org.
Wechsler, Lawrence. 2005. Vanishing Point: David Hockney's Long and Winding Road. *Harper's*, June, 47–55.
Weisstein, Eric W. *Inversely Proportional*. MathWorld—A Wolfram Web Resource. http://mathworld.wolfram.com/InverselyProportional.html
Weyl, Herman. 1952. *Symmetry*. Princeton: Princeton University Press.
Whitehead, Alfred North. 1947. Mathematics and the Good. In *Essays in Science and Philosophy*. New York: Philosophical Library, Inc.
Whole Child Education. *The Ethical Core of Common Core*. http://www.wholechildeducation.org/blog/the-ethical-core-of-common-core.
Wikipedia. *Crane*. https://en.wikipedia.org/wiki/Crane_(machine).

———. *Egypt*. http://upload.wikimedia.org/wikipedia/commons/7/75/Egypt_dauingevekten.jpg.
———. *Equals Sign*. https://en.wikipedia.org/wiki/Equals_sign.
———. *Magic Circle*. http://en.wikipedia.org/wiki/Magic_Circle_(virtual_worlds)
———. *Plumb Bob*. https://en.wikipedia.org/wiki/Plumb_bob.
Wilder, Raymond A. 1981. *Mathematics as a Cultural System*. New York: Pergamon Press.
Wilson, Edward O. 2012. *The Social Conquest of Earth*. New York: Liveright Publishing Corporation.
The Wisdom of Confucius, ed. and trans. Lin Yutang. New York: Random House, 1943.
Wright Brothers History. http://www.wright brothers.org/History_Wing/Wright_Story/Inventing_the_Airplane/Warped_Experiment/Warped_Experiment.htm.
Young, J.Z. *An Introduction to the Study of Man*. New York: Oxford University Press.
Yutang, Lin. 1935. *My Country and My People*. New York: John Day.

Index

A
abacus, 111
"The Aesthetic Equation." *See* von Baeyer, Hans Christian
air and buoyancy, 74
algebra, 17, 103–9
  pattern of signs inheres in a formula, 128
American Museum of Natural History
  "dancing calipers," 54
antithesis, in a balanced sentence, 147
Archimedes
  and center of gravity, 15
  law of lever (*see* seesaw)
Aristotle
  arithmetical proportion, 143
  "equal measure," 141
  on justice, 177
  on middle measure and practical reason, 167, 168, 170, 172, 176–8, 181, 182
  money and community, 176
  money and democracy, 176
  practical reason and happiness, 168
  relation between energy and work, 176
  three laws of thought, 108
association of ideas
  history of, 25
Atwood, Margaret, 196
  on ancient balancing, 20, 196

B
balance
  brain's mental balancing, 188
  center of, 9
  of energy, physiology, 171
  and German *Bilanz,* 36
  and symmetry, 48
balancing
  cognitive, 5
  as common core, 1
  as counter-balancing, 4
  dynamic, appears as a whorl, 184
  feedback, as negative feedback, 12
  moment, definition, 52
  moral, 196

balancing the books, 173
Bateson, Gregory
  self regulating machines (*see* evolution)
Baum, Frank
  The Wizard of Oz, 182
beauty, not truth, 196
Berlinski, David
  on Euclid, 102
bicycle
  composition of, 59
  formula for riding, 59
bionics, 56
Blake, William, 146
Bloomfield, Morton, 129
boat, as model of opposing forces, 72
bodies, human, and self-repair, 171
body, ethics of, 170
Bontecou, Lee, 193
Borges, Jorge Luis, 195
bow the bow and the lyre, 162
Boyle, Robert
  air pressure, 74
Boyle's law, 115
Bronowski, Jacob, 27–8, 28, 30, 53, 62, 63, 79n16, 80n26, 91, 100, 201, 202. *See also* tongs
  grain-like structure of an atom (*see* wedge)
  and Pythagorean theorem, 91
Brooks, David, 167
Bruner, Jerome, 123

C
Calder, Alexander, 191
calendars, lunar, 120
calipers, as tongs, 54
Callois, Roger, 61, 186
calories, 172
carbon emissions, tax, 175

Cassirer, Ernst, 151, 153
children's language as paratactic, 151
cause and effect
  a method of linking ideas by causation (*see* association of ideas)
cave wall, first cyber space, 121
checks and balances, 170
chiasmus, 115, 146–9
  Greek for, 146
childhood, early
  beginnings of linguistic equivalence, 122–4
children
  alienated, 179
  and dignity, 179
Chromebook, 7
Chuang Tzu, 196
Chung Yung, in the middle, 197
cloverleaf
  of compositional thinking, 1
code
  information theory, 8
Cognitive Learning, 12
Coleridge, Samuel Taylor, 28, 138
  "a willing suspension of disbelief," 203
combinatory play, 164, 201, 203, 204
  Einstein's method of discovery, 200
Common Core Curriculum
  Technological and Scientific Subjects, 5–6
communication, and resistance, 184
compass
  rose, 96
  seen as tongs, 54
composition
  middle of a (*see* middle measure)
computer programming, 9
concordia discors, 184
Confucianism, 197

conservation laws
  in balancing (*see* balancing)
contact
  in information theory, 9, 10
context
  as background framework for
    signs, 121
  in information theory, 9
counter-balancing, and energy
    exchange, 174
counting
  as accounting in ancient Middle
    East, 85
couplet, and balancing feedback, 149
crane and pulley, 60
creative play, 164
cybernetics, 11
cybernos
  helmsman, 11
cycle, carbon and carbon dioxide, 175

D
Darwin, Charles
  Wallace, Alfred Russell, 71
Degas, Edgar
  The Rehearsal, 188
deixis, Latin for "pointing," 122
de Saussure, Ferdinand, 124
Descartes, Rene
  Cartesian grid, 97
  phenomena of nature, 98
Dewey, John, 183
diagrams, tree. *See* Pinker, Steven
Dickens, Charles, 147
Dickinson, Emily
  "The Brain is wider than the
    sky," 155
  "Shall I take thee....," 130
  "This is my letter to the
    world," 154
Diggins, Julia
  Thales and Great Pyramid, 101

dignity
  beyond price, 179
  inalienable. *See* Kant, Immanuel

E
Ebenmass
  in German "well-balanced," 19–20
Ecclesiastes, 140
ecology, 171
economy, free market
  balancing feedback, 174
Einstein, Albert. *See also* conservation
  laws
  fatal error of Euclid's geometry, 107
embodied knowledge, 7
  and measure of gravity, 91
embodied learning, 31n9
  as 3-D thinking, 37
embodied mind, 7
Emerson, Ralph Waldo, 182
  "Self Reliance," 135
energy
  exchange of, 176
  exchanges must balance, 15
  and machines, 37
  resistance, 183
energy balance, 49
  underlies symbolic equivalence, 290
energy, conservation of
  energy balance, 171
  organic exchanges, 171
equals sign, 6, 98
equation(s), 6
  balancing, 83
  golden rule of, 180
  inverse, and most/least principle, 84
equilibrium
  law of, 58
  as principle of beauty, 198
  reflective, 178 (*see also* justice)
equipoise, 169
equivalence, verbal, 122

Euclid, 16, 99, 102, 104, 108
  Elements, 102
"Eureka!"
  Archimedes, 203
Eureka moment, 29

F
feedback
  balancing, 5
  in information theory, 11
  positive, 12
feed forward
  in information theory, 11
Fenollosa, Ernest, 138
Feynman, Richard, 15, 35, 171
  atomic hypothesis, 63
Feynman, scientists must use English, 64
fiction, both true and untrue, 137
fishing rod, third-class lever, 52
Fish, Stanley, 134
flock and field numbers, 88
following
  sentence (*see* association of ideas)
  sequential method of combining ideas (*see* association of ideas)
food plate, balanced, 170
Forbes, Esther
  Johnny Tremain, 155
foreshadowing, fiction, 196
Fuson, Karen C., 98

G
games, board, 69
game, video
  magic circle, 165
Gardner, Howard, 183, 196
  on truth, beauty, ethics, 20, 183, 196
geometry
  algebra and x-y grid, 97

Gleick, James, 7
evolution and information, 71
Golden Mean, 141
  practical reason, 168
  the golden rule, 180
Golden Rule of Algebra, 17, 180–2
Golden Rule of morality, 17, 181
Goldsmith, Oliver, 148
Gollum, as false guide, 182
government, mixed form of, 170
governor, fly-ball
  metaphor for evolution
grammar, rules, 124–7
gravity, center of
  as center of symmetry, 48
  and center of the earth, 48
Gray, James. *See* animal propulsion
guides, and false guides, in imagination, 181
gull, 57

H
Hamlet, and meta-theater, 127
Hanson, Norwood
  on mathematical proof, 105
Heraclitus, 162, 164, 166, 174–6, 182
Herbert, George, 185
Hockney, David, 2
Hofstadter, Dennis, 155
Hogben, Lancelot, 42
  flock and (*see* flock and field numbers)
  importance of abacus, 111
  numbering and time, 121
homeostasis
  in biology, 13
Homer, Winslow
  "Left andRight," 186
  "Snap the Whjip," 186
hovering
  stationing, 130, 186, 187

Huckleberry Finn, 180
Huizinga, Johan, 164. See also magic circle
Hume, David. See association of ideas
The Hunger Games, 165

I
icon
  as 2-D sign, 23
  and Paleolithic drawing, 120
imagination, 181
index
  as 3-D sign, 22, 37
information
  exchange of, 14
  includes code and context, 10
  is surprise, 11
information, balance of
  combination of sound and sense, 126
information theory, 7, 144
is, 6, 133, 136–9

J
Jack Sprat, 142
Jakobson, Roman, 137
Jefferson, Thomas
  inalienable right, 178
  self-evident principles, 101
Jiminy Cricket, as guide, 181
Johan Huizinga, 162, 164, 165
Johnson, Samuel, 147
judge, in Greek, a divider, 177
judgment, suspended, 187
justice, 175
justice, not the best of virtues, 177
  Aristtotle, 178

K
Kahneman, Daniel
  law of least effort, 77

Kant, Immanuel, 137, 153
  on freedom, 179
Keats, John
  "Ode on a Grecian Urn," 196
King, Martin Luther
  "I have a dream," 148
Kline, Morris, 98
"Know Yourself," 154

L
Latin, 1
law of buoyancy
  Archimedes, 73
lever(s), 6
  definition, 50
  first-class, 51
  parts of, 51
  third-class, 51
  work against gravity, 39
Lincoln, Abraham
  "the Gettysburg Address," 148
  and self-evident principle of equivalence, 101
Locke, John. See association of ideas
Lord Byron, 133

M
Ma-at
  Egyptian term, 20, 46
MacLeish, Archibald
  "Ars Poetica," 195
magic circle, 164
matching
  a method of combining ideas (*see* association of ideas)
matter, conservation of. See energy, conservation of
Mayer, Julius Mayer, 171
media studies, 13
Mendeleev, Dmitri, 201
Mendeleyev, 203

Merton, Thomas, 196
message
  in information theory, 10
meta-language, 127–8
meta-theater, 127
Metropolitan Museum of Art, 189
middle measure, 2, 3, 6, 27
  and healthy body, 170
  in play, 166
  and practical reason, 19–21, 161–207
moire pattern, and sentences, 145–6
money, exchange of, 176
Moore, Henry
  "Nuclear Energy," 194
morpheme, 123
Morrison, Philip, 62
Morse, Samuel F. B
  Morse code, 143
Myron, his discus thrower, 183

N
narrative, prospective view of, 150–4
nature, 192
  oppositional forces in, 4, 30n5
neo-cortex, balance between action and restraint, 167
Neolithic era, 85
nervous system, autonomic (ANS), 173
nervous system, central (CNS), 173
Newton, Isaac, 74
  laws of motion, 74
  second law of motion, 141
  third law of motion, 164
Next Generation Science
  balanced and unbalanced forces, 39
  gravitational force, 43
Next Generation Science Standards, 10, 12, 26, 31n14
  energy, 38
  modeling, 56, 89
North Star, 94

O
oar, rowboat, 51
Ogden, C. K., 198
Old Testament, Bible, 140
opposites, eternal conflict of, 162

P
Paleolithic peoples
  and origin of language, 119
"para-," Greek for "beside," 150
parallel patterns in sentences, 150
parsimony, law of. *See* von Baeyer, Hans Christian, scientific brevity of expression
Patience, card game, 201
Peirce, Charles Saunders
  icon as visual likeness, 107
  semiotics, 22
pendulum, 16, 42–3, 169
  harmonic motion, 43
period, development of, in composition, 151
Perkins, David N., 12, 31n16, 33n37, 203
  and combinatory play, 203
Pettigrew, J. Bell, 67
phonemes, 123
  sound patterns of, 146
photosynthesis, 173
phyllotaxis
pinecone, 67
Piaget, Jean
  children's learning as topological, 22
  development of language in children, 127
Picasso, Pablo
  "Little Girl Skipping Rope," 193
Pinker, Steven, 135
  and rhythms of speech, 145
Pinocchio, Walt Disney, 181
plane, inclined, 61
Plato
  on non and verb together, 131

on schooling as serious play, 165
thinking as an inward
    dialogue, 152
play. *See also* magic circle
    competitive, seen as strife, 165
    creative, 21
    serious (*see* Plato)
playgrounds, as magic circle, 165
plumb line, 16, 42–3
    ancient, 42
Poe, Edgar Allen
    "The Gold Bug," 143
    "The Pit and the Pendulum," 43
Polanyi, Michael, 3, 30n4
    "equilibration of forces," 109
Pope Alexander
    on antithesis, 148
    "Windsor Forest," 184
Pound, Ezra, 197
Power
    atomic, 194
    balance of, 169, 170
    practical reason, 2, 167
predicate
    from Latin "to proclaim," 137
    usually a general conceptual
        word, 132
proof, in algebra, 103
proportion
    inverse, 49, 74, 115
    studied in middle school, 114
prostheses, 37
Pythagorean theorem, 16, 90–2, 97

R
ratio(s)
    equality of, 28, 114–15
    inverse, 49
    inverse, and inverse proportion,
        compared, 114
    as mathematical expression, 49

Read, Herbert, 237
    two kinds of narrative, 150
rhyme, 149
Richards, I. A., 198
right angle
    as fundamental principle of
        measure, 88
right, inalienable, 178
robotics, 37
roller coaster, 61
Rope, knotted
    and right angle rope stretchers, 89
rotation
    and symmetry, 48
Russell, Bertand
    importance of Pythagorean
        theorem, 90

S
Sachs, Oliver, 188
Sartre, Jean-Paul, 192
Schlink, Bernard, 20
Schmandt-Besserat, Denise
    theory of accounting, 86
science course
    begin with a lever, 35
Scout Finch, 180
screw
    seen as inclined plane, 65
    and spiral form, 67
screw propeller
    fins, wings and flippers, 67
sculpture, mobile, 191
seesaw, 4, 7, 12, 15, 16
    and balance scale, 40
Seesaw, Margery Daw, 40
self-assessment. *See* Perkins, David N.
self-possession. *See also* Stein, Gertrude
    and skill, 191
Sender-Receiver diagrams, 8, 9, 23
sensorimotor coordination, 2

sentence
  as assertion, 18, 131, 134, 138
  balanced, and opposing ideas, 77
  as basic unit of discourse, 129
  composition of, 128
  diagrams, 134–6
  as fundamental assertions, 137
  and information hovering, 144
  is basic unit of discourse, 17
  Shakespeare's, 139
sentence points forward
  hovering, 130
serious play, 164–6, 167, 175, 186,
  196, 200, 201
Shannon, Claude, 7–8, 31n12
skill, 35, 36
smart board, 7
Smith, Adam
  "the invisible hand" and balancing
  feedback, 174
sound and sense, among children
  seen as equivalent, 123
sound and sense, relation of
  seen as arbitrary convention, 123
"is," Spanish version of, 137
Spielberg, Steven
  Lincoln, 101
Star Lore in Egypt, 93
star measurement, ancient, 96
Stein, Gertrude, 134, 154
Stevenson, Robert Lewis
  Treasure Island, 143
Stewart, Ian
  mathematical proof, 104
"Stone Soup," 182–3
storytellers Majorcan, 137
Stout, Rex, 166
Strunk, William, 133
submarine and buoyancy, 73
substantives, 133
Sumerians
  divisions of number, 110
Suzuki, David, 172
swing, interval of, 184

symbol
  as 1-D sign, 23
symmetry theory
  in arts and sciences (*see* Weyl,
  Herman)
sympathy, 181
synaesthesis, 199
synecdoche, 156
syntax, definition of, 125
systems theory, 12

T
Table of Elements, Periodic, 201
tally, abstract sign
  Paleolithic peoples, 120
Taoism, 197
Teresi, Dick
  on Galileo, 100
Thales
  measurement of Great Pyramid, 99
thinking
  multi-dimensional, 64
  one-dimensional, 6, 185, 201
  three-dimensional, 6, 38, 39, 54,
  63, 64, 66, 68, 70, 201
  two-dimensional, 6, 86, 89, 90, 103
Thucydides, 170
time, lives governed by, 120
Tolkien, J. R.R., 182
  The Hobbit, 182
tongs, 53
torque, 68
trade, and history of arithmetic, 87
trivium
  Latin for "three-way," 1
truth, 137
  Aristotle, 177
truth and beauty, 196

U
United Nations, 170
U.S. Department of Agriculture, 172

V

van Rijn, Rembrandt, 2, 4, 22, 30n2
Vermeer, Jan
   Woman Holding a Balance, 187
verse, shaped, 185
vertigo, imbalance, 186
vertigo, in amusement park, 61
via media, Latin
   middle way, 21
video games, speed stick of, 69
Vitruvius
   on water screw, 71
von Baeyer, Hans Christian, 27
   Morse code, 143
   scientific brevity of expression, 63–4

W

Wallace, Alfred Russell
   governor, fly-ball (*see* evolution)
water, as leverage
   water screw, 71
water level
   'spirit level', 42
Watt, James. *See* governor, fly-ball

wedge, 62
Weyl, Herman, 19
wheel and axle, 58
wheelbarrow, second-class lever, 52
Whitehead, Alfred North
   on humpty Dumpty, 128
   patterns in algebra and
     English, 103
Wiener, Norbert. *See* cybernetics
wisdom, practical. *See* practical reason
words, as forward-looking
   symbols, 131
Wordsworth, William
   "There was a boy," 492
work, and energy exchange, 174
writing
   origin of, and counting, 85

Y

Yutang, Lin, 198

Z

zero, invention of, 111

The manufacturer's authorised representative in the EU is Springer Nature Customer Service Centre GmbH, Europaplatz 3, 69115 Heidelberg, Germany. If you have any concerns regarding our products, please contact ProductSafety@springernature.com

Printed and bound by CPI Group (UK) Ltd, Croydon, CR0 4YY

23/03/2026

02076739-0003